LEADERSHIP
TRAINING

A Sourcebook of
Activities

ELIZABETH M CHRISTOPHER
& LARRY E SMITH

Kogan Page Ltd, London
Nichols Publishing Company,
New Jersey

First published in 1993

Kogan Page Limited
120 Pentonville Road
London N1 9JN

Published in the United States of America by Nichols Publishing, PO Box 331, East Brunswick, New Jersey 08816.

(Sections of this book first appeared in *Leadership Training through Gaming*, published by Kogan Page and Nichols Publishing in 1987.)

British Library Cataloguing in Publication Data

A CIP record for this book is available from the British Library.

ISBN 0 7494 0988 6

Library of Congress Cataloging-in-Publication Data
Christopher, Elizabeth M.
    Leadership training : a source book of activities / Elizabeth M.
  Christopher and Larry E. Smith. — 2nd ed.
        p.   cm.
    Rev. ed. of: Leadership training through gaming. 1987.
    Includes bibliographical references and index.
    ISBN 0-89397-390-4 : $79.00
    1. Leadership—Simulation methods. I. Smith, Larry E.
  II. Christopher, Elizabeth M. Leadership training through gaming.
  III. Title.
    HD57.7.C53   1993   93-34128
    658.4'07353—dc20   CIP

Typeset by Koinonia Ltd, Bury, Lancashire.
Printed and bound in Great Britain by
Biddles Ltd, Guildford and King's Lynn

Contents

List of activities

Chapter 11: Negotiation Activities

Chapter 12: Activities for cross-cultural communication

Chapter 13: Activities for the management of conflict

Chapter 14: Activities for management training

Acknowledgements

We would like to thank the following people and organizations for the help they gave us, directly or indirectly, in writing this book:

In Australia:
B W Neville and R S Hubbard from whose game 'The Multi-Purpose Multi-Phasic Tower Building Blocks Game' we adapted 'Infernal Towers';

Eileen Quigley and Narelle Isaacs from whose original idea we developed 'New Year's Eve Hat'.

In the USA:
The East–West Center, Honolulu, Hawaii;

The Japan–America Institute of Management Science, Honolulu.

In Japan:
Language Institute of Japan, Odawarra.

Introduction

This book has a circular theme: it is about leadership, and about your leadership of groups of people who are learning about leadership.

Leaders come in all shapes and sizes. They are army officers, fashion designers, managers, parents, politicians, sports coaches – and people like you, who take formal responsibility for others' learning.

As in all other forms of leadership, your control of the classroom consists of influencing people to achieve your goals. In exchange your followers should acquire new skills and become able to accept responsibility for setting their own goals. Constantly you work to put yourself out of business by delegating more and more to your followers until they can look after themselves and you are free to walk away in search of new challenges to your leadership skills.

This book contains a variety of activities to demonstrate how to influence people. Every activity is designed to illustrate in some way the cause-and-effect relationship between leader behaviour, follower response and task accomplishment. Most would-be leaders need to learn how this relationship works. No doubt some charismatic leaders are born and not made, but if you are not one of them don't despair: virtually everybody can become competent in leadership by acquiring a basic set of relevant skills.

The argument that leadership can be taught like accountancy or welding is particularly relevant in the management of organizations. In developed or developing countries today employees arrive at leadership by relatively narrow and specialized paths. They start out as accountants, computer programmers, nurses, social workers, systems analysts, teachers, technical sales staff or whatever; they do well in their chosen fields and get promoted to management level, which involves leadership. Then they have to employ a range of interpersonal skills that maybe they haven't needed before, that previously they may even have avoided, such as delegation, negotiation of conflict, and appraisal of others' performance.

Moreover, in today's global village many organizational leaders now operate in multicultural contexts where English is an international language and leader behaviour has to accommodate itself to many cultural differences.

Who the book is for

The book has been written for anybody who wants to use interactive learning methods (directed discussions, structured experiences, roleplays, games and simulations) in settings where they are formally responsible for leadership training with groups of people. This applies not only to professionals such as teachers, social workers, youth leaders, cross-cultural communication experts, human resources development consultants and health professionals, but also to those not formally trained but equally professional, such as community leaders. What follows was written with this very wide diversity of potential group leaders in mind. We apologize if certain statements seem obvious to some readers.

What is in the book

The book is a collection of activities designed to illustrate in various ways the kinds of behaviour that leaders have to learn: situational uses of power; matching people to tasks; setting and achieving goals.

The activities range from relatively objective small-group discussion starters through more involved exercises such as roleplays to simulations of real life that may rouse participants to vehement responses of agreement or contest.

How to use the book

The teaching profession is full of dire warnings about the so-called dangers of using games and simulations as learning strategies because of their capacity to arouse strong emotions in the players. It is true that games evoke delight and anger, as anybody knows who has played snakes and ladders with children or watched a football match with adults. There is no denying that teachers who use games, roleplays and simulations in the classroom are taking emotional risks: but they take a calculated gamble because the payoff is the active involvement of students in the process of their own learning.

The argument that interactive learning methods can be dangerous is often both overstated and one-sided. Simulation exercises are harmless enough in themselves; the explosive elements, constructive and destructive, are created through class leaders' behaviour during presentation, direction and debrief. Teachers are well aware of this, which is why some of them prefer to avoid the whole experience.

We describe in this book where we think you, the classroom leader, may encounter problems, how to sidestep them if possible, and how to solve them if they do occur. We hope you will enjoy the book as well as find it useful. We welcome you and wish every success to you if you are a new recruit to interactive learning methods, and we salute you if, like ourselves, you are an old hand at playing games.

PART 1
LEADERSHIP SKILLS

Chapter 1

Assuming leadership for interactive learning

This chapter discusses the following aspects of teachers as supporters, enhancers and monitors of interactive learning:
- How to deal with misunderstandings about the value of interactive learning.
- How adults learn through experiential activities.
- How adults are motivated to learn.
- The responsibilities of the class leader in interactive learning.

How to deal with misunderstandings about the value of interactive learning

If you have used interactive training methods to any extent in organizational settings you will probably not be surprised by the following story, which is about the different perceptions people have of experiential learning.

A colleague of ours was newly appointed as training officer of a large corporation. Keen to impress, she suggested to the managing director that she use a simulation game to demonstrate leadership skills in a seminar for senior managers. From behind his big desk, the MD looked at her coldly over his spectacies and replied: 'My managers aren't here to play games!' He was expressing a commonly held belief that games are a waste of time and money in training programmes. Companies pay for their staff to attend seminars and conferences that are designed to improve their productivity, not entertain them.

What the MD was not taking into account was the fact that professional productivity depends on more than a trained capacity to absorb information, facts and figures. Learning and problem-solving are part of a continual and lifelong process of change in attitudes, values and beliefs which occurs through a never-ending negotiation between new information and what they already 'know'. Games, roleplays, simulations and other interactive exercises provide a kind of 'base camp' from which to make forays into new worlds. Such activities are known territory; their parameters are set. They have roles and rules, beginnings, endings, and limited consequences. They are comfortable learning grounds and good to have in training programmes because – as the great educator John Dewey (1974) argued — the process of exploration into a new world is not without pain. Nobody discovers a new world without having to forsake the old.

How adults learn through experiential activities

Arguably, motivation to change (which includes motivation to learn) can be grouped under three major headings:

- The desire to keep some kind of control – to maintain power – over situations, self and people as they shift and change through the vicissitudes of life.
- The need continually to adjust personal relationships to keep pace with change.
- The intellectual challenge of solving problems as they occur along the way.

In other words, learning – which we equate with problem-solving and define as relevant change within the learner – can be said to be about power, people and problem-solving: and so are interactive learning methods. Everybody who has played interactive games –

tag or tennis, cards or charades, snakes and ladders or snooker, football, basketball or backgammon – will recognize the same motivations in all of them. All involve solving some kind of problem and supporting one's team-mates to beat one's opponents and win the game.

People experience these motivations in different degrees and proportions: some enjoy the sociability of a game more than winning it, others will cheat their best friends to win. Some people play games to keep fit, others develop logical thinking through pondering over a chessboard: but most games evoke the whole range of power, people and problem-solving feelings; which is why virtually everybody likes games in some form or other.

Games are a form of interactive learning; they support and foster the motivational component that all learning contains – even something as abstract as mathematics. Many factors impinge on students' learning of mathematics: the personality of the teacher, the teaching method (with its respective emphasis on cognitive, emotional or skills learning) and the individual student's own learning style. For example, some people respond well to a 'chalk-and-talk' exposition of mathematical principles because they like facts to be presented in linear and orderly arguments whose logic they approve and understand. Others – like a friend of ours – may not be so happy with this kind of teaching strategy because they need to be able to relate abstractions to experience. Our friend used to bewail the fact that she was 'no good at maths' until we pointed out she had no problem with balancing her cheque book, working out the interest rate on her mortgage, comparing two unequally sized jars of coffee in the supermarket to find the cheaper or calculating how long a journey would take if she stopped for afternoon tea with Aunt Jessica on the way.

'But none of that is mathematics!' cried our friend. 'That's just *life!*' So it is, and so some people will learn more about mathematics through experience-based teaching methods like games and simulations rather than hearing lectures or reading books. Admittedly there are published taxonomies which argue that some types of learning are not emotional, but our experience over two lifetimes of teaching is that it is impossible even to begin to control the learning processes of ourselves and others unless there is prior recognition of the emotional or feelings component, ie the motivation to learn.

How adults are motivated to learn

Over the years we have been asked to design and evaluate many educational games for younger players as well as adults, and we have come to the conclusion that while most youngsters enjoy these activities, they do not always appear to learn as much from them as do more mature adults. However, this result may be due more to the behaviour of the session leader than the interactive learning material itself: for example, many primary school teachers and youth workers find experiential learning methods extremely effective. This may mean that those of us who are accustomed to working with adults need to acquire slightly different presentational skills for younger students rather than changing our teaching methods. The argument goes as follows.

People learn indirectly from interactive methods. First they experience the interaction with other group members and with the session leader, then they are encouraged to relate this experience – and their observations of others' experiences – cognitively to wider, more general and theoretical contexts. Some educators argue that children are not as capable in this process as are adults. For example, Malcolm Knowles (1977) suggests that experience-based learning methods are more appropriate for adults than for children because the former have a much wider framework of knowledge and experience within which to locate their responses.

We have some doubts about this line of argument because from earliest infancy (and even earlier, according to some theorists), children begin the experiential learning cycle. Long before they can talk they are capable of reflecting on their experiences and generalizing from them to experiment actively with new behaviour. A simple example is the way very young children learn before they can talk to recognize that a bottle-shaped or cup-shaped object means 'drink': and so they start to yell every time they see such a thing – only to learn that they do not always get a drink in return. Then they modify their behaviour accordingly. By the time children start school, they have built up reserves of life experience that in some respects may be deeper than those of their teachers; and they may have already learned survival tactics in a harder school than anything the Department for Education can provide.

Nevertheless, children and young teenagers do seem to experience some difficulty in thinking in metaphors: that is, in relating class-room experiences to real life. Perhaps this is partly because they are socialized under most educational systems to think that games are fun and learning is not. Also many young people may not be able to realize the learning potential of interactive material like games and simulations if they suffer from a short concentration span, a high level of free-floating aggression or low motivation.

Acting on these assumptions, we have included in the book some activities we designed or adapted for groups of youngsters of vari-ous ages from about 12 to 18 years. Built into these activities are features that seem to increase players' concentration, release their aggression in constructive ways, and motivate them at least to see some advantages and possibilities in trying to take more control of their own lives.

The responsibilities of the class leader in interactive learning

As session leader you have to maintain an effective balance between authority, task and people; but often leadership styles become unbalanced because of conflict between leaders' personali-ties and other psychological or logistical factors. For example action-oriented leaders may want to be involved with a problem rather than turn it over to qualified helpers – even when delegation would probably encourage more maturity and motivation in the helpers. Some session leaders find it difficult or impossible to leave players free to get on with the game even when this would be in participants' best interests: or they become so personally involved with the group that they overlook lack of relevant skills and push players into emotional experiences they are not equipped to handle.

On the other hand task-minded game leaders may issue instructions and expect performances without regard for players' morale or motivation: and power-hungry game leaders will dominate a debrief-ing session even when players know more than they do about the real-life context of the game. Use of authority is a critical variable in the total learning process. Directors can subvert or reinforce the structure of the activity, and can use their personalities to influence players' perceptions of what the activity is 'really about' – as the following example illustrates.

The activity was **Digicon** (Activity 40, Chapter 11). Its setting is that of a prison in which teams of players impersonate groups of prisoners locked in separate cells. Their only hope of getting the key and escaping is to give commands in an invented language to human 'robots'.

Digicon's scenario is established by a narrative device: the director verbally sets the scene by telling a story about imprisonment and escape, robots and their controllers. Thus the game leader gives players assumptions about the nature of the activity before it begins: which establishes a degree of consensus and predisposes people to receive the same kinds of learning messages from the activity. Moreover the nature of players' roles is defined in advance and therefore the kind of behaviour appropriate to each role; thus roletakers tend to restrict their interpretations to these preset parameters.

Digicon requires participants to work in small teams and the action includes rules that can be strictly enforced. These factors increase the director's control over the group. There is a logical and regular sequence of events, also under the director's control. The activity is competitive and task-oriented. Players' actions and reactions become concentrated within an ever-narrowing focus as the robots near completion of the task. They are more interested in who wins than in exploring their own possibly conflicting feelings about the nature of the activity.

The entertainment factor of Digicon disposes players to be relatively uncritical of it as a learning method; they are likely to respond positively to suggestions the director might make afterwards about what 'is' and 'is not' effective leadership and team behaviour. All these characteristics of the structure of Digicon work towards convergence, ie closure and feelings that right answers have been found to real-life problems.

Learning activities with this closed structure are especially suitable for conveying relatively unambiguous and concrete information such as the content of a particular theory, say Fiedler's theory of leader/task/followers interaction (Fiedler and Chemers, 1974). Closed structures are not so effective if the intention is to promote critical discussion of widely differing viewpoints.

However, the composition of the participating group is another critical factor in learning from interactive material. A structural leaning towards convergence will be corrected by individual players who hold opposing views about the relevant subject matter, and who are motivated to question the apparent messages of the activity. If they are highly pragmatic or empirically minded people (such as statisticians) they may be unaccustomed to learning through metaphors such as simulations and roleplays and may respond more critically than they would to a lecture or demonstration.

A teacher trainer called Peter directed Digicon at a staff development conference attended by teachers from all over the state. Peter wanted to demonstrate the advantages of small-group discussion as an attractive alternative to the traditional 'chalk-and-talk' classroom lesson. However, many participants came from conservative teaching backgrounds and he wanted to make his task easier by getting these diehards 'on his side' from the beginning.

He therefore made some changes to the original design of Digicon which effectively enhanced its convergent structure – though when later we asked him why, he was unable to say more than that these changes 'felt right' to him. He was aware from professional experience that the structure of an interactive learning activity influences the messages it conveys. This is what he did:

(1) He allowed no talking at all except for the robots' non-English command words, which had to be conveyed to their memory lists by mime. This heightened the communication barriers between prisoners and robots. Their efforts to overcome these barriers turned them into a very cohesive group – which worked to Peter's advantage in debriefing, when he wanted participants to agree that small-group work can be very productive.

(2) He allowed each robot to stay with its original cell of prisoners, instead of changing over the respective vocabulary lists. This had the effect of 'bonding' robots more closely to their commanders and further enhancing team spirit.

(3) He created some extra roles, those of jailers, to enforce the rules. He privately briefed these actors to wander round the room during the play, ensuring that nobody left their cells and the robots did not cheat. Effectively he increased his control over the group by employing agents.

(4) He presented the activity as a problem-solving exercise in which collaboration between team members was the key to winning.

The result of Peter's strategy was that, though the players became very excited and involved in the game with a great deal of noisy activity, particularly towards the end, his control over the activity was strong enough to direct their spontaneity to serve his ends. In debriefing he was quick to follow up any comments the players made that furthered his purpose. He began by asking: 'Did you enjoy the game?' – the first of many consensus-making questions. Immediately players began to comment on what fun it had been, praising it for generating a good group dynamic and 'getting [the conference] off to a flying start'.

Peter asked for examples and one of the robots replied that the cooperation between her and her team to create her memory-list had caused her to feel that she 'belonged' to her team-members. It became very important to her 'not to let them down' when the game was underway but this had made her feel 'anxious and frustrated' because their planning had been inadequate, though not for want of trying.

A player from another group reported he had observed with sympathy the communication problems in this woman's 'programme' and how hard she and her 'commanders' had worked to overcome them. He said that his sympathy was the deciding factor in his determination to release these prisoners when he himself became free. Peter suggested that in effect these teachers were saying that in a classroom, however highly individual students may be motivated, they need effective support from their peer group. This suggestion met with general agreement, and another player was prompted to add: 'Our goodwill as teachers is not enough by itself; the students have got to know what to do and how to do it!'

Peter then left this topic and went on to ask about communication barriers. Some participants replied that they had become very inhibited when first aware that they were not allowed to speak, nor to use actual words, but added that eventually they had worked 'almost intuitively' through body language with their robots to compose a word-list. Peter pursued this line until the discussion turned into a series of statements by players about the importance of trust and openness in communication, the need to work hard at understanding others and the importance of developing good communication skills to achieve these ends.

Then Peter suggested that the most effective communication skills had been demonstrated by the winning team 'because they won'. He encouraged the members of this team to describe a process of division of labour: how one of them had emerged as a leader and organized the others so that one person was responsible for inventing and miming the command words, another had written them down, another had supervised the robot's memory list, and he himself had directed the robot during play. Having established to everybody's satisfaction that appropriate division of labour had been a winning strategy under a trusted and competent leader, Peter asked if this also applied to the classroom; the general response was, 'yes'.

Peter asked the winning team to comment on their 'planning', making the unquestioned assumption that effective planning had been another key factor in winning the game. He might equally well have argued to the contrary: that the successful strategy had been creative improvisation and spontaneous flexibility. For example, the winning team had decided to assume they were in a cell with bars like a cage, not a locked room. This eliminated the need to instruct the robot with a command meaning 'unlock the door'. She had only to hand the key to the team leader 'through the bars'. This simplified both her vocabulary and her task, which made her easier to operate than the other robots. Furthermore the team that planned the most complex vocabulary was the slowest. However this line of reasoning was not part of Peter's debriefing. He wanted to make the point that effective teamwork by students requires a careful lesson plan. Therefore when one of the teachers drew attention to the breakdown of the slow team's plan, Peter responded with the suggestion that though overplanning can be self-defeating, improvisation is a risky tactic unless one knows one's group really well. Players were more inclined to agree with this because he had introduced the game from the beginning as a planning exercise and *took this for granted* when he debriefed it.

During this discussion, which lasted about three-quarters of an hour, Peter was able to extend players' learning from the game to the real-life activity of the classroom in a number of different ways. He had no problems in reaching agreement with the group. The discussion was animated and enthusiastic and the teachers plainly felt they had derived new and valuable insights on how to work cooperatively with their students.

Summary

While the value of traditional learning methods (such as lectures and demonstrations) remains high, adult learners in particular may be more motivated sometimes to learn through interactive learning methods that continually refer them back to their life experience. Some behaviours, like leadership, may be more effectively studied through activities such as small-group discussions, roleplays, games and simulations. However, the presenters of these activities have a responsibility to recognize their power as leaders; and to modify their leadership styles to serve the learning needs of the group.

Chapter 2

Active and passive roles in interactive learning

This chapter discusses the following:
- Does everybody have to take an active role in experiential learning processes?
- How to make 'passive' roles more active.
- Who sets the scene for interactive learning?

Does everybody have to take an active role in experiential learning processes?

Some people seem to become more motivated to learn if they are allowed to take observer rather than participant roles; yet much of the literature of interactive learning suggests that all learners need to participate – which implies that observers are not participants. We take the position that they are, and that people will learn a great deal about the assumptions, dynamics and hidden meanings within a given activity by watching it. In a simulation game, for example, observers see the game as a whole, and therefore may derive more objective meanings than individual players because the players are likely to interpret the activity according to a narrower, more personal experience.

Unfortunately, learning games are usually directed so that the only observers, as such, are those leading the game. Thus the session leader is frequently the only person to see participants' actions in overview and therefore the only one in a strong position to perceive how the pattern of conflict or consensus has evolved. The group is dependent on this one person's views, unmodified by perhaps completely different impressions that others may have received.

How to make 'passive' roles more active

Leadership is about increasing the motivation and maturity of followers. Therefore classroom leadership should work towards overcoming learners' passivity and developing their ability to take responsibility for their own learning. Two effective strategies are (1) to introduce activities in which only a few people are active players while the rest function as audience; (2) to videotape the game and play it back afterwards so that the 'actors' become the 'audience' and everyone can see the pattern of behaviour without being totally dependent on their leader to tell them what happened.

The concept that experiential activities create a pattern, or structure, of action is essential to understanding how they function as learning strategies. It is your business to provide a number of means by which players can examine this structure for themselves. They will recognize how the process of cause and effect evolves out of the relationship between you and themselves, and between each other. Players cannot always stand back, so to speak, and watch this process in overview while it is happening, even though some people by temperament are more objective than others. Nor can classroom leaders themselves always be aware of the nature, extent and effect of their behaviour on the group unless they constantly seek feedback from the group.

Let us suppose, for example, that you want an activity (perhaps as part of a management training course) to illustrate themes of leadership and power. The game Digicon was used in the preceding chapter to demonstrate a directional leadership style; but there is no reason why you should direct and debrief Digicon like this if you want to overcome any passivity in your learners and to encourage them to think for themselves.You may believe the object of interactive learning activities is to give participants multiple perspectives on a given issue, rather than to persuade them to reach conclusions predetermined by yourself. It is perfectly possible to use Digicon any way you want, provided you know how to juggle the three golden variables of any learning activity: goal, structure and group.

If you want to open up Digicon to these considerations, this is how you might do it:

(1) Introduce it with only the briefest of explanations. Keep the scenario simple – and therefore ambiguous. The element of the unknown will please some players and alarm or annoy others, which is all to the good because it fosters differences in people's perception of the game.

(2) Organize the players into mixed teams of different sizes. Put people together from different departments or organizations. Overrule any protests.

(3) Allow prisoners plenty of free discussion in each cell before instructing them to 'programme' their robots. Set no limit to players' inventions of command words.

(4) Monitor this process carefully, while appearing to be *laissez-faire*, and note the kinds of disagreements that come up. Identify any emergent leaders and any people who appear unusually passive or aggressive. When debriefing begins after the game, single out these people and direct some questions to them, to give them plenty of opportunity to express mutually divergent views. Remember that while Peter (in the previous example) needed a homogeneous group to serve his purpose, yours will be furthered by encouraging heterogeneity. You want multiple perspectives, not consensus.

(5) Make the obstacle course difficult and change over the robots' memory lists before they are 'activated'. They will suffer from mixed loyalties between their original team and their new commanders. These feelings will create ambivalences that later will hinder consensus in debriefing.

(6) Ignore all cheating, however flagrant, and permit robots to push and shove each other. Say and do as little as you can while the play is on. Let the players restructure the rules. They will become absorbed in the process of the contest as much as the outcome. The game should be a journey of discovery for them, not a race in which they have eyes only for the finish.

(7) In debriefing, concentrate on asking 'Why did you do such-and-such?' and 'What did you do?' rather than 'How did you solve the problem?' Identify different kinds of reaction, accept them all as valid and relate them to themes of leadership and power. Remain objective, uninvolved. Some players are likely to resent this behaviour because they were expecting you to tell them what the game 'meant'. They want to know what the right answers are, instead of having to think things through for themselves; but the aim of a non-convergent – or divergent – activity is to create conflicting views, not consensus. For example, on one occasion when we directed the game the way we have just described, two of three robots complained afterwards of having felt like the mindless puppets of incompetent manipulators who sought power (the key) through the robots' efforts, for which they received no reward. The third robot had worked happily with his commanders and felt satisfied with the relationship. These mutually conflicting responses made for a really useful discussion about the ways in which leadership is perceived by followers. Everybody had an opportunity to unload the frustrations and satisfactions they experienced in the game and were able to relate these feelings to the leadership behaviour – the uses of power – that the prisoners employed.

Who sets the scene for interactive learning?

As a trainer, you set up an experiential learning activity with specific objectives in mind. It is you, not the group, who first sets the scene and then monitors the action: and this behaviour, in itself, is likely to affect participants' responses to a critical extent. This is another way of saying that the kind of learning derived from interactive behaviour in the classroom will be critically affected by the leadership style of the class presenter. This statement will appear simplistic if it is taken to mean no more than that classroom interaction differs with every trainer and every group of players, but the implications are more profound.

It may be that Carl Rogers' (1969) word 'facilitator' for team leader is misleading to describe those who direct classroom activities, simulations, role-plays, and games. The term 'facilitator' is intended to convey the notion that the classroom leader is a non-participant in the sense of refraining from influencing the outcome. The opposite, however, is more likely to be true because, where experiential learning activities are concerned, the non-participating organizer is perceived by the players to be in the position of final authority. This suggests that classroom leaders must not abrogate but interpret the leader roles that players have ascribed to them by consenting to play the game.

The following is another example of a teacher who was well aware of both her authority and how to use it with a group of students very familiar to her. The activity was **New Year's Eve Hat** (NYEH) which you will find under Activity 28 in Chapter 10. It is much less convergent in structure than Digicon, and requires participants to impersonate characters who are handicapped and those who are not. They all have to make paper hats to wear in a fancy hat parade. Some players are physically handicapped by having their thumbs or wrists tied together, by being tied to their chairs, by being blindfolded, and so on.

The activity basically is open-ended because it has virtually no rules and permits a wide variety of interpretations. There is no big story build-up as in Digicon, no given crisis to overcome, no preset problem to be solved, no shared assumptions about the nature of the task because the criteria for success are arbitrarily decided by the players themselves each time the game is played.

The story and the action begin simultaneously with the players facing a situation rather than a problem. So what do they do? They make hats and wear them in a parade, and judges award prizes to the winners. In theatrical terms, all the action takes place 'on stage' whereas in Digicon much of the action has already taken place before the game begins. This makes NYEH an inherently more existential experience because participants assume their roles as the activity begins. They have no past, only the present, whereas Digicon provided them with a history that they had to 'live up to'.

Theoretically this makes a divergent activity like NYEH an ideal structure within which to explore alternatives rather than come to conclusions. However, notwithstanding this open framework, an experienced director can close players' options off to a remarkable extent and, by changing the structure of the activity, alter the content of its communication.

Flora is a high school teacher of English literature, who wanted her students to derive unambiguous messages from the activity.

Her class consisted of 23 15-year-old girls and her aim was that they should study the theme of prejudice as it related to a play they were reading – called *The Shifting Heart* – about immigrant settlers and the discrimination they faced.

Flora directed NYEH with this class in order to ask them afterwards: 'Were any of the characters in *The Shifting Heart* "handicapped"?' and she wanted an affirmative answer. Throughout the activity she adopted a highly authoritarian leadership style, including instructions to the judges about the criteria they should use to assess the hats; and she gave some of the players much more effective materials than the others. This is part of her report on the results.

> They were seated at long trestle tables, ten players, five at each table, facing about 17 judges . . . and then I began the scenario, and you could have heard a pin drop as I told them this exciting business of the hats . . . And then I went round with string and tied their hands together and tied one hand to a chair. I blindfolded one girl. She was terribly upset about being blind, she really was distressed. . . and another, I tied string right across her two arms, like a thalidomide baby. They were quite horrified by the handicaps . . . I had to say really firmly to the girl with the blindfold: 'You are blind!'. . . She had a tiny little scrap of paper to make her hat with, and she said to me, sort of tragically: 'Could I have another piece, please?' And I said: 'No! Sit down!'

This is how she described the reactions of the students:

> [When I asked them after the game how they had felt] immediately people said, 'frustrated', 'annoyed', 'irritated', 'horrible'. And I said, *'Good!* Do you think that people who are handicapped all the time might experience those kinds of feelings?' And then we started to talk about the people in *The Shifting Heart* and whether any of them were handicapped. And that was how I related the game to the play. They were a good class and they came up with: 'Yes, they were handicapped because the central family were migrants and this was a handicap for them in the context of the play.'

Flora asked the students to write an essay relating their experiences in NYEH to those of the characters in the play. She awarded the best grade to the essay from which this quotation comes, though she said that all the essays were of a high standard and expressed similar ideas: 'Handicapped people are always discriminated against, whether they have lost an arm, as in the game, or, as in *The Shifting Heart*, they are migrants'. It is hardly surprising that Flora's girls were 'a good class' and 'came up with the right answers'. She used her authority as director to impose constraints on the players that evoked frustration and anger. ('It was a screaming match and some of them felt quite cross at the end of it.') She then channelled these emotions into consensus about the sufferings of the protagonists in the play-text.

Flora was satisfied that her form of evaluation – the students' essays – gave her the feedback she needed about the learning potential of NYEH, which she assessed as high. We think her direction and debriefing of the game, in the context of her teaching aims for that particular group, rank even higher.

Remember the following seven sources of power she – and you – have at your disposal, to be used sparingly or laid on with a trowel, before the game, during it, and at any time you may need them during its debriefing.

(1) Your *expertise* should have preceded you. Flora was generally recognized to be one of the most effective teachers in the school. Players should know in advance that you will be in charge of their group for this session. If the group is obstreperous, do not hesitate to remind them of your expertise. Tell anecdotes about your previous experiences of playing games, for example, and show by your manner and bearing that you are an authority.

(2) You may need the power of *important connections*. Flora had all the authority of the school behind her. Depending on the circumstances and the group, it may ease your path if the most senior member of the firm has introduced you – or if you can mention having run a training session in which their chief exectuive officer was a participant.

(3) You, like Flora, have *information* power. You can tell people where they can learn more about whatever it is they want to know; you can answer their questions and share your insights borne of experience.

(4) You have, like Flora, the power of your *personality*, which you have spent years practising to make your most powerful teaching skill. For example, you may have acquired a kind of calm authority which conveys the message: 'I know what I'm talking about; you will learn something of value by listening to me!' Some personalities have this attribute to such an extent that they become 'gurus' to thousands, perhaps millions, of people. Or you may be an older teacher whose authority is derived from the vulnerable and gentle wisdom of the years. Or perhaps you command respect by the power of your mind to grasp and retain a wide range of detailed information. On the other hand, you may rely on your ability to charm and delight your students: by the way you wear your clothes, dress your hair, and gesture with your hands, you may offer yourself as a model and your students may find themselves thinking 'I want to be like that!' Or you may be able to build a rapport with students through your sensitivity to their feedback, verbal and non-verbal; and may have developed a highly flexible teaching style that can accommodate itself to many kinds of learning. Or you may be so knowledgeable, have such a powerful recall of facts and figures, that you command respect.

(5) You have the power of your *position*. You have been specially invited here to lead this group. The whole situation is set up to communicate the message that you are in charge. Never be afraid of silence during interactive learning. It can be one of your most effective tools to emphasize something, to initiate discussion (by putting psychological pressure on the group to break the silence), or to draw attention to something that has happened or been said. You can use silence as a punishment, as we noted earlier, or as a reward. Respectful silence can be a tribute paid by you to a participant who has just said something particularly insightful, before you draw the group's attention to it.

(6) You have the power to *reward*. Rewards come in many shapes and sizes: a friendly smile, a word of congratulation; above all, you have the power to make the activity a rewarding experience for at least most of the players.

(7) You have the power to *punish*. This power may be very limited. If your players are powerful people themselves, they are not going to burst into tears at your frown; nevertheless, punishment is at your disposal to some extent. A calculated silence, a vigor-

ous shake of the head, a thoughtful stare – one or all of these things can demonstrate this power if you need to use it.

Summary

This chapter has discussed the idea that observer roles are critical, rather than peripheral, during interactive learning. The linked concepts of passive and active learning will always overlap; and it is often the case that the observer sees the best of the game. The presenter should not be the only person in the room to see the activity in overview; at least a few group members should be in a position objectively to confirm or deny the perceptions of the presenter. This is an important part of the evaluation of interactive learning; and observers' roles will become even more useful if they are somehow built into the structure of the whole activity. It is the presenters who set the scene for interactive learning. The effectiveness of the whole exercise stands or falls, in the last resort, on the relationship presenters create between themselves and the group, and between the group and the activity.

Chapter 3

Dealing with emotion

This chapter discusses the following:
- The emotional content of interactive learning.
- The classroom leader as drama director.

The emotional content of interactive learning

Emotions are always liable to run high during active learning sessions. One participant told us, three years after playing a simulation game with a group of sales executives:

'I was angry, and *I'm still angry* at what happened to me in the game!'

Fortunately, her anger was a constructive emotion that fuelled her energy to work for the rehabilitation of handicapped people—which was what the game was about (NYEH; Chapter 10, Activity 28).

Failure on the part of session leaders to recognize the nature of players' responses can lead to resentment, hostility and rejection of both the leader and the activity. Activity directors will become confused and distressed, especially if they have been told by other session leaders that the activity in question is 'fail-safe'! This hazard, which educators acknowledge about the use of interactive learning methods, deters some trainers and teachers: but effective debriefing can save most situations.

A teacher called Brenda directed NYEH but carried out no debriefing. She recorded the activity and her account illustrates that an essential part of directing a learning activity begins when it ends: debriefing is the director's final and most powerful method of organizing players' perceptions of the action. If players are left to themselves to interpret the experience, it may not occur to them to make the cognitive connections that the activity was designed to promote.

Brenda teaches in a training college for elementary school teachers and directed NYEH with a group of 32 students whose average age was 23. She wanted to introduce them to non-traditional and dramatic teaching methods; and she created an activity in which the players became actors and audience for a comedy in which clowns derided the antics of victims and fools. She established five players as hat-makers, and handicapped four of them, set up a panel of three judges as caricatures of the public personae of Margaret Thatcher, Nancy Reagan and Princess Diana; and directed the majority of the group (24 people) to be their audience. The judges performed their parts with such zest that the audience literally shrieked with laughter. Mrs Thatcher introduced the panel by assuming an upper-class accent and a manner of great refinement:

> May I say what a very great pleasure it is to be invited to judge this competition. As a former Prime Minister of Great Britain I am delighted to welcome Her Royal Highness the Princess of Wales, and also the distinguished wife of the former President of the United States, Mrs Ronald Reagan. Rest assured that our criteria for judging your hats will include not only your personal difficulties but their suitability for this very elite function . . .

'Diana' and 'Nancy' then proceeded to patronize the handicapped hat-makers and devalue their work, and the audience loved them for it. At one point Mrs Thatcher said to a severely handicapped contestant: 'Now your hat has a certain impact but we feel that as Princess Diana is here as one of our guests, it is perhaps just a leetle bit pretentious. We can't have a crown-like effect. . .' (Here her voice on the tape was lost in the gales of laughter from the audience.) The hat-makers evolved into inferior characters and the judges into absurd but powerful figureheads. Not surprisingly, some of the handicapped players afterwards expressed feelings of resentment ('I was upset when she said my hat was tacky; I expected them to say, "Oh, well, she had a hard time making it . . .."').

Brenda was satisfied that the exercise promoted the kind of learning she wanted her players to acquire but the results of its evaluation by questionnaire were not as satisfactory as she would have liked. She found herself faced with a problem that frequently occurs with interactive learning methods: her subjective feelings about the success of the activity were at odds with the empirical evidence.

She had designed a questionnaire for assessment and she administered it to the players about a week after the game, but found that only 4 out of 22 responses included any reference to the activity as a learning method. The only connection that most students made between the activity and real life was that they reported they now appreciated better the plight of the disabled. Though this response is commendable, it was disappointing from Brenda's point of view because it was largely irrelevant to her teaching aims for the activity.

Why had the students limited their comments to the content of the activity without also considering it as a teaching method? One answer might be that NYEH had provided its young and inexperienced players with such an entertaining experience *per se* that they were not able to generalize from it to a different theoretical framework without assistance, and this had not been provided since there was no debriefing.

Nineteen out of 32 players replied at considerable length that what they had learned from the game was greater awareness of the difficulties faced by the handicapped in real life, not only because of their physical handicaps but also because of the attitudes of some members of society. Seven out of 32 respondents wrote to the effect that though handicapped people are not often openly laughed at in real life (as they were in the game), they may nevertheless be treated as inferior by people who think of themselves, without justification, as being superior.

Thus the players looked beyond the entertainment value of the game to find a serious meaning in the audience's hilarity and the judges' derision; but these ascribed meanings did not extend to a consideration of the activity as a teaching tool. However, Brenda was satisfied. Her conclusion was that:

> It was enthusiastically received and was a great success – I would run this session again with another group. It was most suitable. They needed to enjoy it themselves to be inspired to

try something like it when they are teachers with their own students. The main judge was exceptionally good and provided great entertainment. . .

Her focus was on the entertainment value of the activity rather than its real-world implications; and though we can't presume to criticize this, we think she could have taken it further. Her direction of NYEH was so powerful that it appears to have generated learning potential on a much more profound level than the message that 'games can be fun'; and a debriefing session would most probably have realized this potential.

This example perhaps helps to explain why some teachers and trainers find experiential learning activities work successfully for them, and some do not. It is arguable that they work most effectively when the aims of the activity are reinforced by discussion; and when the character of the learning group is taken into account. In the long term Brenda achieved this harmony. She was able to introduce her students to the advantages of games as a teaching method through regular contact with them throughout the length of their studies, which extended over several years. She used interactive learning methods on a regular basis and there was plenty of opportunity for general reflection about their structure and effects.

Though debriefing is important, it is also important that directors of learning activities do not feel they have to cram as many conclusions as they can into one debriefing session immediately after the activity. It may be more effective to titillate players' curiosity by limiting the debrief to asking a few critical questions. The activity may then linger in their minds as an intriguing and stimulating experience to which they will refer real-life events as they occur.

The classroom leader as drama director

Interactive learning methods such as 'structured experiences', games, roleplays and simulations can be compared in some respects to drama. The role of the session leader can be compared to that of a theatre director, who guides actors to interpret their roles.

This does not mean you should coach players how to behave in experiential activities, but that you can encourage them to call on their own natural emotions to behave as they feel they would if the situation were real life. In effect you suggest that participants find out how they behave in the given situation and then ask themselves and each other if their response was as effective in the circumstances as they would wish. If so, why? If not, what are some of the ways they might consider changing it in real life?

Moreover, through interaction, a collection of individual learners becomes a working team or ensemble whose united effort is greater than the sum of its parts. The business of the class leader is to recognize how much responsibility each group member is capable of assuming at any given point and what that person's greatest contribution to the team is likely to be.

Theatre directors, when they have selected a play or a theme for improvisation, impose more or less direction on the actors depending on who they are. For example, with a cast of professionals who have worked together frequently, there may be no need to be authoritarian, unless there are in-group dissensions. On the other hand, with a group of amateurs, or with professionals who have never worked together before, the director may need to oversee closely the allocation of roles, and may have to provide a great deal of explanation.

This is leadership behaviour which Hersey and Blanchard (1977) call 'high in task and low in relationship', but the proportion will vary depending on the mix of actors. The director continues to give explanations or lead discussions until the actors gain a sufficiently clear understanding of what they need and want to do. The director then initiates the dramatic action and the individual actors engage in the process of becoming an ensemble or a team. The director is still task-oriented but now there is more room for human feelings and for relationships to develop as the actors explore the dimensions of their roles.

As participants become more confident in their roles the director focuses less on the task as a whole and more on encouragement and support for individual actors. Finally, the director delegates the entire task of interpreting the drama to the cast and – if there is to be a public performance – sits in the back row on the first night, applauds loudly, and rushes backstage afterwards to tell everybody how wonderful they are.

Let us now compare this sequence of behaviour with your own, assuming that you intend to use experiential learning methods, such as a structured roleplay, for example:

(1) You have selected a 'text' – an appropriate activity.

(2) You explain the 'scenario' and 'script' to the players and ask questions to ensure rules and roles are understood.

(3) Your behaviour as group leader conveys authority and credibility. The only relationship that you *must* have with your players to start with is that these busy and often self-important people should perceive you as somebody from whom they are likely to learn something to their advantage. It would be nice if you could present yourself as being likeable as well, but don't worry too much about that at this stage: it is more important that they respect you.

(4) Be task-minded and reasonably power-oriented in this early stage of the activity. If you appear tentative or unsure of your goals, the participants may keep you talking forever rather than getting on with the activity. They may even try to avoid it altogether. Give them essential information in a confident manner to keep them with you until they get involved in the game. Your wisest assumption – unless you know definitely to the contrary – is that your team is low in motivation, unsure of what is going to happen next, and very likely suffering from feelings of inadequacy. Therefore, you need to project a strong, confident image – which does not mean an aggressive one – and convey the reassuring impression that you have directed this activity many times and it's a sure-fire winner.

(5) Players and observers now know what the roles are and understand the rules. With any luck and/or skill on your part they are becoming interested (if only mildly) in the action. As the motivation level of the group rises, and as they become more capable of taking responsibility themselves for the game, allow yourself proportionately more human interaction. Supply added information and listen to individual problems that may arise as the game gets underway: generally become more encouraging. However, keep the task firmly in mind, for you cannot yet rely on the situation to take care of itself.

(6) Interaction is now in full swing and you are now an enthusiastic and sympathetic observer. Your only intervention might be to throw a problem back to the players when they try to dump it on

you – though there may be other occasions when you *have* to interfere: for instance, if a fight breaks out! Effectively you are now in the position of the theatre director who watches the final dress rehearsal from the back row of the gallery. The players are deeply engaged in building and/or observing a structure of action that is theirs, not yours. Your behaviour is neither interactive nor focused on task. You are functioning as a discerning observer of the problem-solving process.

(7) Afterwards, in debriefing, you remain in this delegatory posture, allowing the group to take responsibility for its own conclusions, based on direct and indirect experience of the activity.

(8) Your final task is to help group members relate their conclusions, ideas, concerns, etc to their pre-existing knowledge and life experience. Monitor this discussion carefully, alert to correct any mistakes of fact, to add more information, to offer examples and suggestions, and to ask constructive questions in order to enlarge debate and encourage creative problem-solving. However, do only what you think is required of you. You are now almost completely out of the power-phase and well into a people-oriented, problem-solving mode – but prepared to pick up power again if the group seems to lack the maturity and responsibility to take control of their own learning.

Throughout the whole game experience, you have moved continually between power, people, and the problem to be solved.

An example of debriefing an activity – by a method which is relatively impersonal – is to comment on each group's 'performance' as if they were a cast of actors. We all play roles in real life, in an attempt to present ourselves to others in various 'characters'. The great Russian director Stanislavsky (1962) suggested that a character is built in physical terms: body, voice, manner of speaking, walking, and moving. These actions convey meaning to others – they are what he called 'the inner pattern' of an actor's part. Following Stanislavsky, the British director Tyrone Guthrie (1971) laid down a number or rules for beginner actors; and you may find these useful also for helping participants in an activity such as **Walk-on** (Chapter 9, Activity 6) to perceive how their verbal and non-verbal language influence those around them.

For example, in a group discussion, committee meeting or social conversation, it can be observed that people often signal in advance when they are about to speak, by some small sound, gesture, or movement while someone else is still talking. Guthrie advises actors, before they say or do anything on stage, to take a breath. He argues that the more deeply actors have to feel, the more deeply they must breathe. This breath must be taken not when they hear their cue, because then they will be late and create a meaningless pause, but 'when, probably from the previous speech of your partner, you get the idea that governs your own speech or reaction'.

If you video an activity such as Walk-on ask participants, as they watch the replay, whether they think that the more effective speakers appear to signal their entry into the discussion, for instance by an intake of breath or some slight movement just before they begin. Does this appear to catch the attention of the group, and give the would-be speaker a chance to talk?

On one occasion when we pointed this out after playing Walk-on some observers protested that one of the most effective speakers, who had moved in and out of his group's conversation with apparently effortless ease, had not physically moved at all. We replayed the tape and it did seem at first that this man had adopted a posture of great repose, sitting in a calm and relaxed way throughout his time 'on stage'. We played the tape one more time, with everyone crowding around the monitor and watching as closely as possible. We saw at last that he had the knack of taking a breath in exactly the way Guthrie describes. His speech flowed from an initial 'signalling' inhalation and thus followed the words of the previous speaker in smooth continuity. We asked this man (a youth leader) if he was aware that this was his communication style. He replied that he had no idea of it and would try to forget it, in case he became self-conscious: but however self-conscious people may feel when they first begin deliberately to study their body language, the increase in self-knowledge that they achieve should ultimately give them greater leadership power.

Several discussion questions emerge from all this. Imagine you are talking to someone and recognize those signals that indicate they want to say something, though they are too polite to interrupt you openly. Is there any point in your continuing to talk, even if you want to? Is it not likely that the other person has stopped listening to you because they are merely waiting for their chance to speak? If so, when eventually you take over the conversation again, you might do well to repeat the important points you made earlier, on the probability that the other person or people stopped listening for at least a few seconds before you stopped speaking.

People's non-verbal behaviour can also be recognized as a sequence of impressions. Observers can learn to anticipate and change the sequence of others' behaviour patterns. Guthrie argues that it is exactly this sequence of impressions that an actor must build up in order to achieve credibility in the role.

We remember an occasion during Walk-on when a woman positioned her chair so that she did not have to sit full face to the others but sideways, her hands tightly clasped in her lap and her body more than half turned away. She did not look at anyone even when directly addressed. Though she turned her head over her shoulder towards the speaker, she kept her body turned away: but after a few moments' general conversation she felt confident enough to volunteer a comment, and as she did so, she automatically made several slight gestures with her hands to loosen the tension. Her whole body began to look more relaxed and soon afterwards she turned directly to face the others, adjusting the position of her chair to move it closer to them.

Another woman in the same class (though not in the same group) began by placing herself almost out of camera range but ended by picking up her chair quite unselfconsciously and moving it right into the circle. When she watched herself doing this on the tape replay, she was astonished. She had been aware of moving the chair but had no idea how conspicuously she had signalled, first her reluctance, and then her willingness to be part of the group.

Finally, power relationships can be studied in body language not only by noticing where people place themselves in relation to others but also how men and women behave towards each other; and again our example is taken from Walk-on. On one occasion we all watched while a man walked on stage in front of his two female group members and placed his chair directly facing the camera so the other 'actors' were virtually forced to sit with their backs to it. He was thus both upstage and centre stage of the camera, which in the theatre is the best position from which to command the attention of the audience. His verbal behaviour added to his success at 'upstaging' the others because he spoke clearly, even loudly, and sounded confident. The other two players were both young women and he appeared to take it for granted that they would defer to him, which they did. (We talked later about how women are conditioned to defer to men in leadership roles.)

When he had seen himself on the monitor in playback, we asked him if he had been aware of all this. He replied that he had been aware of how he was behaving: he had never seen himself on television before and was determined to make the most of the opportunity, even at the expense of his colleagues. This led to a discussion about people's motives for doing things. If they want something badly enough, they will behave forcefully in order to get it, which indicates the importance of personal motivation and goal-setting for leaders. It is often the case that some people will achieve their objective merely because they feel more strongly about it than their potential opponents and therefore their influence on followers is more effective.

If this behaviour is recognized as a sequence of impressions, then it can be interrupted at a point most likely to throw the person exhibiting the behaviour off balance. For example, if one of the women had asked the camera-hogging man to move his chair, she could more easily have prevented him later from stealing the show. If she had recognized his initial behaviour as the beginning of a pattern, she might have been more concerned about cutting it short.

However, in this case, the self-image of both women was so low that they could only feel grateful for not having to face the camera, even though doing so was the object of the exercise. One of them had sat miserably hunched on her chair, with both arms tightly crossed over her chest – a signal from many women in Western cultures of reluctance and anxiety. (Westernized males, when they are feeling insecure, tend to put their knees close together and place their hands together in their laps. When they feel more comfortable, they often spread their legs and let their open hands rest lightly on their knees.)

Summary

This discussion has concerned the emotional content of interactive learning, the need to create a group dynamic in which everybody is contributing their special knowledge, skills and attitudes towards the common goal. In this respect (though not in others) interactive learning as a classroom activity can be compared to actors rehearsing a play. The classroom presenter behaves somewhat like a theatre director who is by turn authoritarian, consultative, democratic and *laissez-faire*. Debriefing an activity can sometimes be done in terms of actors playing roles.

Chapter 4

Directing interactive learning activities

The aims of Chapter 4 are:
- To discuss session leaders' motivations.
- To identify three different kinds of motivation that inspire session leaders in sequence and combination.
- To distinguish between formal and emergent leadership behaviour.

Leaders' motivations

As a session leader of interactive learning methods you probably involve yourself with your students in response to three motivators, in sequence and in combination.

(1) You have been accorded the degree of **power** you need to accomplish your task without intruding too much on your students' own sense of power.

(2) The participants may be highly skilled specialists, timid novices, or assertive teenagers; but whoever they are, you need **people-skills** to persuade them to trust you to guide them safely and competently through the exercise; and to help them benefit from the stimulus of interaction.

(3) You and they have also been challenged by **the problem** of interpreting the activity in ways you can all usefully relate to real worlds.

The motivations that inspire session leaders

Relevant theory argues that virtually all human motivation can be grouped into these three categories – the need to achieve power, to influence people, and to solve problems – which makes experiential activities remarkably appropriate for learning about leadership. Since you are the person ultimately responsible for choosing and directing a classroom activity, your behaviour is the key variable which will determine what kind of learning participants derive from the whole exercise. To some extent the personality of the teacher is critical to all teaching methods and no two teachers are interchangeable, no matter how similar their fields: but when interactive learning material is the medium, the director's *leadership style* is the vital ingredient.

As session director you are the designated leader: you do not need the common consent of the group, as you would do if you were an emergent leader: and you maintain power by the same rules that put you in a leadership position in the first place. Nevertheless you risk at least an attempt at rebellion by an emergent leader if you have no other power tools at your disposal. There has to be an exchange between yourself and your group, in which you get the satisfactions of leadership (including emotional and psychic rewards such as a sense of success) and in return they gain a sense of security through accomplishment. They have learned something new or achieved some goal in 'knowing' more at the end of the activity than they did at the beginning.

This result occurs only when group leaders are concerned with more than their own status; which is why some session presenters, though they are designated leaders, are not effective managers of learning activities.

Emergent versus formal leaders

When you direct Activity 31 **Making Money** (Chapter 10), you will probably notice a difference in behaviour between *emergent* and *formal* leaders. Leaders in Making Money have to emerge out of the group, with its tacit consent. They rely on personal power such as personality, knowledge and information: but later they may formalize their position by imposing rules, sometimes successfully, sometimes not; and by preventing their followers from questioning the assumption of their formal status.

Participants who become leaders in interactive learning processes demonstrate certain behaviour which can usefully be interpreted by session leaders to help them become more effective. For example leaders emerge out of experiential activities because:

(1) They find that leadership gives them a personal reward, not necessarily financial. Some people are more interested in the experience of power than in any other aspect of the activity.
(2) They are motivated by a feeling that they can succeed.
(3) They receive acceptance from and support by the group.
(4) They maintain leadership through:
   - Group acceptance;
   - Group satisfaction, which may or may not include tangible profit, though it does so in some of the money games you will find in the book;
   - Their ability to satisfy the needs of both their group members and of their superiors (ie the session leader). It is worth noting that this means activity leaders must take cognizance of the needs of the session director, who always retains the final power arbitrarily to deprive any player of leadership status.

This is another reason why we do not like the word 'facilitator' to describe a session leader's behaviour. Players are always aware, at some level, that this person is the final authority. However, session leaders also are answerable to higher authorities. If they cannot satisfy their clients, they do not get to play games any more.

Leaders are not necessarily the people who are most visible. They don't have to sit at the head of the table – though this does give them an initial 'edge', of which they may or may not choose to take advantage. There are other physical, psychological and even geographical circumstances favourable to leadership, such as being bigger, quicker off the mark, or louder than other people. But these advantages will not help emergent leaders if they don't suit their leadership style to the temperament of the group.

Authoritarian leaders are likely to be rejected by democratically minded groups unless they also have persuasive skills. Leadership style theory focuses on what leaders do, not what they are; it focuses in particular on three categories of behaviour: group goal facilitation (problem-solving); individual prominence (power); and group sociability (people).

An example of near-rejection of group leader by group, in spite of the leader's power, is that of Elaine, a professor in a university school of health administration and an extremely skilful director of learning activities. Elaine wanted to use NYEH (as did Flora and Brenda), but in this case to argue the case for affirmative action in employment. She wanted players to accept the argument that employment applications from traditionally underprivileged members of the workforce (women, migrants and the handicapped) should receive special consideration. Therefore, like Peter with Digicon, Elaine's objective in directing NYEH was judgemental; but NYEH's open structure, without alteration, makes it hard for players to arrive at consensus. The action is more likely to induce divergent and inductive thinking than convergent deductions. Elaine, like Peter, interfered with the structure of the game. However, unlike Peter, her manipulations were not altogether successful. We think this is because the composition of her group was more mixed than Peter's and it contained some members who were ideologically opposed to the concepts she wanted to convey via the game.

She introduced NYEH by reminding her players: 'Some of you are going to have to work in personnel departments and you're going to be faced with this issue of discrimination in employment, including the question of whether you give special advantages to people solely on the grounds that they have been discriminated against in the past.' Thus she informed her students in advance that the activity would be about discrimination in employment; which gave it a history to indicate its future – a sense of direction that structurally NYEH does not have.

She described the scenario in a fairly authoritarian way, was democratic about handicaps and role allocations, and *laissez-faire* during the play. When debriefing began she made sure the judges' criteria for assessment of the hats were debated, by asking as her first question: 'What comments would you like to make on the judging?'

Having started her players on a discussion of the judges' behaviour, Elaine said very little until a player commented: 'I think the judges should have taken into account the disabilities of the hat-makers.'

'Let's talk about that now,' said Elaine. She then took a moment to organize the class so that she could command everybody's attention ('If you'll just move around so we can see each other . . .') before asking the judges to give their reasons for not taking handicaps into account.

One of the judges argued that this would have been to judge handicaps, not hats: 'It would be like giving them a prize for their disability instead of rewarding the best hat. So we decided that judging would be on the best hat and how well it fitted, and originality and use of resources . . .'

Elaine called for general comments on this, stressing several times that the issue was important and asking again whether women and other underprivileged members of the workforce should receive special treatment to compensate them for past discrimination. She met with some opposition. One player replied that the object of job selection is to advantage the employer, not to disadvantage the employee: 'Because, you know, a female, after working a year or so, may fall pregnant. It's a risk to employ her and in any operation we try to minimize the risk.'

Elaine gave this answer short shrift. She said: 'Do you realize that what you're saying is against the present law? You could be taken to court for it.' She appealed to the judges: 'You two are both women and you made the decision not to compensate the handicapped players for their disability. Do you see the analogy, that in real life you will be professionally discriminated against – you will be "marked down" – because of the disability that you might have a child?'

The judges were reluctant at first to accept this argument, but Elaine persisted with it until one woman said: 'I'd want to be assessed the same as a male applicant. I'd want to be equal.'

One player was firm in his refusal to accept the concept of affirmative action. He persisted in his argument that women are poorer employment risks than men and to compensate them for being so would be to invite economic disaster. Finally Elaine told him: 'I can guarantee that your attitude will have no effect on the assessment that I shall make of your studies in this course, but it will have an effect on your future, and it's important for you to realize that. What you should be thinking about is how to make your organization flexible enough to take account of women's lifestyles, because you're going to be stuck with them whether you like it or not.'

Thus Elaine worked hard to present her viewpoint via NYEH, including what might seem to be unscrupulous behaviour on her part, since it consisted of a veiled reminder to one student that she had the power to 'fail' him if he disagreed with her. Nevertheless, given that particular activity, Elaine's personal objective for using it, and the nature of the group of health care professionals she was working with, it is difficult to see how she could have done better. The participants were mostly very conservative and held traditional views about the employment of women. Affirmative action was a new concept to them and they had difficulty with it. As it was, Elaine's introduction to and debriefing of NYEH succeeded in changing the attitudes of at least some of them from outright rejection to thoughtfulness and even a degree of acceptance.

She might have interfered more with the game itself, as Flora did, by giving the judges the criteria they should use. Or perhaps she could have cast some of the handicapped characters as women, and given them an egg to hold while they made their hats. This could have simulated the problems that working mothers have with pregnancy and child care.

Emergent leaders

These three kinds of behaviour can be clearly identified by watching the way people play games. For example, leaders will be more or less heedful of the game's objectives, of their own individual prominence, and of the feelings of the rest of the players, depending on whether they are more concerned to achieve a task or form a group relationship.

If there is a considerable amount of group consensus about the game's objectives, then an emergent and task-oriented leader will have a relatively easy time because the group will perceive clearly that it is being led towards the accomplishment of a common task. In these circumstances it is not difficult for a would-be leader to achieve and retain individual prominence; the group will see the leader's goals as its own and there will be a good balance between task and group relationships.

However, sometimes the task is either relatively unstructured or ambiguous. Therefore, if emergent leaders want to become powerful they cannot afford to appear too task-oriented. They have to be on such good terms with the group that they can convince all the other players that it *is in their interests* that their leader become more powerful than the rest of them. Otherwise the players will reject the leader. This was illustrated very well by the man who started the'Two-up' school in Making Money (see the account of this in Chapter 10, p. 161). The players had so much fun that they did not begrudge him his profit.

On the other hand, if leaders become too concerned about the feelings of their followers, they may achieve a very good relationship with the group but fail to complete the given task. The managers in **Get Smart!** for example (Activity 36, Chapter 10) will not achieve the high productivity that was the stated objective unless they find some compromise between the safety of their workers and their own management aims – maybe by redefining the nature of the task, as did one group of teacher-players who made hats to sell instead of the Smarties.

Summary

Directors of interactive learning sessions need a fair degree of self-knowledge, including awareness of their own motivations. There appear to be three major motivational forces that drive leaders' behaviour: a sense of power; the satisfaction they derive from group acceptance and acclaim; and task accomplishment. Classroom leaders in interactive learning may sometimes surrender their motivational needs to serve the needs of the group. Moreover their formal leadership status may be challenged by emergent leaders from within the group; then they have to decide whether or not to resist the challenge. Their decision will be made on the basis of the kind of behaviour that will most effectively promote group learning.

Chapter 5

Debriefing the activities

The aims of Chapter 5 are:
- To identify the basic goals of an interactive exercise on leadership skills.
- To discuss group acceptance, task structure and personal power as critical factors in leader success.
- To provide some examples of the effects of skilful debriefing.

The basic goals of an interactive exercise on leadership skills

As summarized in the previous chapter, there are three essential factors in leadership: the degree of *acceptance* of the group, the *structure* of the task, and the individual *power* of the leader. These are three areas to which you can direct the group's attention when you discuss, wise in hindsight, what happened during the activity.

Group acceptance, task structure and personal power as critical factors in leader success

How did group leaders project the power of their personalities in order to be accepted by the group? How did they inspire their followers to 'go along with them', not necessarily because they liked them (though that would help), but because the followers felt the situation, whatever it was, was in safe hands?

How did group leaders organize their teams and tasks so they worked with the strengths of their group members? How did they buttress areas where the group was not so strong, thus ensuring a well-motivated team?

Who gained power through their interpersonal communication skills?

The Photocopy Machine (Activity 38, Chapter 11) provides a useful example for identifying whether individuals are primarily power-motivated, people-motivated, or task-motivated and how they will behave as leaders in each of these modes. One player reported that though she is now a manager she used to operate the machine constantly before she was promoted so she said that in the situation of the structured experience (the photocopy machine had broken down) she would put aside essential work on next year's budget, go to the photocopy room and fix the machine.

While this was a valid option in the context of the exercise, her action may not have been the most effective in terms of leadership because it obscured the need to ask many questions about how the office was run:

- Why was nobody but her trained to repair minor malfunctions in the copier?
- Why did the copier keep breaking down?
- Why did everybody keep running to her to solve the simplest problem without taking any responsibility themselves?

Answers to the above questions can be found by reference to seven kinds of power that leaders are said to have at their disposal (Hersey and Blanchard, 1977) – including, of course, classroom leaders:

(1) *Expertise.* In the above illustration the manager could have delegated her expertise, rather than using it herself, by showing the office workers how to fix small breakdowns.
(2) *Information.* She should have information about a local printer who could be relied on in emergencies.

(3) *Connective power*. The manager might have useful connections with senior management (or the machine's supplier) to provide the office with a brand new copier.

(4) *Legitimate authority*. She could lock the copyroom door and allow only a few selected people to use the equipment.

(5) *Personality*. Because of her personality, the office manager in our example postponed her own important work to fix an office problem. If her action encouraged the team to think of her as a democratic and supportive leader, this could have been a powerful strategy.

(6) *Rewards*. This officer manager has a range of rewards at her disposal, from ordering a new copier to smiling sweetly at the people who helped her fix the old one and reassuring them it would be OK from now on.

(7) *Punishments*. Maybe the manager might demand that the person who last used the machine should be responsible for its repair in the future.

Effective leaders acquire knowledge and self-knowledge to use these seven sources of power appropriately depending on the capabilities, receptivity and responsiveness of their followers and the nature of the task. But how are inexperienced leaders to know what is appropriate behaviour for them, and when and why such behaviour should occur? This is where interactive learning methods like structured discussions, roleplays, games and simulations are so useful. They make leadership behaviour visible and audible in constructed contexts that are both magnifications and simplifications of real-life situations and events. They serve to illustrate individuals' relationships to organizational, social, natural and mechanical structures in terms of power, human relationships and task accomplishment.

A good example is **You Choose** (Activity 1, Chapter 7). Because the game is designed to be played at the beginning of a new course, the results can provide you with useful information about participants with whom you are going to work for the next hour, day, week, etc. After the activity it is likely that you can pick out one or two obvious leaders, and you will probably have a fair idea of the amount of motivating you are going to have to do with the group as a whole before you can get on with your real task. You will know whether you have on your hands a bright-eyed, bushy-tailed mob of power-hungry executives who will challenge you every step of the way; or a group of potential followers who will hang on your slightest word; or – more likely – some of both or something in between.

For instance, did all of the groups come up with a game? Or did none of them? Exceptionally high, or unusually low, productivity are two extremes of behaviour by small working parties with designated leaders. Large accomplishment by a group is argued to result from a combination of effective leadership and motivated followers (Fiedler and Chemers, 1974). Therefore, if none of your groups could invent a game in the allotted time (ie if their productivity was unusually low), you are going to need all your motivation skills to inspire these participants to work effectively as a team under your leadership.

Hersey and Blanchard (1977) imply that in these circumstances the class leader should begin by behaving like a benign autocrat, keeping a large measure of control over learners' learning before adopting a more democratic, and finally a hands-off, attitude. On the other hand, if every group in You Choose generated several game suggestions and everybody appeared to be willing, eager and able to participate, then for the rest of the session you can probably afford from the beginning to take less personal involvement in participants' learning and to delegate a relatively large amount of goal-setting and decision-making.

Remember also that the extent to which the total exercise was experienced as more or less rewarding will have been dependent on the temperament of the participants. For example, you might want to make the point that one cannot generalize about leader behaviour because it depends so much on circumstances. People will accept this happily if their personalities are relatively non-judgemental and they feel comfortable in ambiguous situations. If they are inclined to be judgemental, look for certainty and require rules to govern behaviour in all circumstances, be prepared for controversy even with a highly motivated group of participants.

If you are relatively new to gaming, you may want to make You Choose a little easier for yourself by building more structure to give you greater control over outcomes. For example, you could provide each group with a length of rope or a ball and ask them to devise a game with it, including a set of rules. This takes some of the pressure off the players because you have supplied more input to their thinking and therefore gained more influence over their decisions.

You may like to refer back to these notes when you consider playing You Choose; but it is only one example. We have used interactive learning material for leadership training in Australia, Britain, Japan and the USA. Virtually all the participants – including people from many cultural backgrounds – reported that they gained insights not only into leadership but also into the behaviour of colleagues and foreigners. Unfortunately, however, an activity that stimulates the creativity of one group may leave another cold; and there is no solid theory to explain why.

We think the key lies in the behaviour of the classroom leader and the relationship that develops (or fails to develop) between leader and learners. Structuring this relationship is an art in itself, that needs to be practised from the very first moment you meet your group. For example, here are a few general guidelines for introducing new subject matter:

- You need to sound sufficiently authoritative to impress those participants whose primary motivation is power. They want to acquire knowledge, therefore they need to believe you can help them to do so; but they like to maintain control over situations, so they will upstage you if they think they can get away with it.
- You need to temper authority with personal warmth to avoid alienating those learners whose primary motivation to learn comes from group involvement in task accomplishment and personal feedback on performance.
- You need to arouse the intellectual curiosity of those who are most strongly motivated by the recognition that here is an interesting problem to be solved.

So far, the examples we have used have been longer simulation games; but in Chapter 7 you will find a number of short games that we have discovered to be consistently useful for motivating participants and introducing major concepts and assumptions on which the rest of the session is to be based. Each one of these exercises could be adapted appropriately for the beginning of almost any conference or seminar. Furthermore, it is not mandatory to use them as warm-ups at all; they can be played as games in their own right at any time as 'triggers' to start a new section of your material or to illustrate some point you want to make as you go along.

All of these games can be played with groups of about five people upwards to almost any number. The largest group with whom we have played them was approximately 150. More than one exercise can be used with the same group, but we find that the most effective technique with games in general is to use them *sparingly*. Therefore, if we begin a session with a warm-up game, we then revert to another teaching method entirely for a while, such as giving a mini-lecture, asking the group to complete a questionnaire, or initiating some kind of discussion.

Introducing one experiential activity after another can be counterproductive. You will find you get better results, and students' interest is more sustained, if you vary your teaching methods.

Summary

This chapter has identified the basic goals of interactive exercises for leadership skills: to achieve participant acceptance and support; to structure them effectively and to harness the power of the director effectively, in terms of learning objectives. Thus group acceptance, task structure and personal power are critical factors in successful learning interactions

Chapter 6

Designing, selecting and evaluating experiential learning activities

The aims of Chapter 6 are:
- To discuss where to get ideas for interactive learning exercises.
- To identify design criteria.
- To discuss the provision of game materials.
- To provide practical examples of designing interactive exercises.
- To demonstrate how to design activities over which the session leader can maintain control of outcomes.
- To discuss the evaluation of interactive learning methods.
- To discuss the advantages of recording an activity on video.

Where to get ideas for interactive learning exercises

Always be on the alert for ideas you can shape into an interactive learning exercise. Such activities can be inspired by almost anything – reading a novel, seeing a film or listening to an anecdote at a party.

In our experience, the most productive ideas come from stories, films, plays and television, that is, from fiction. Fiction writers, dramatists and storytellers have to shape their living material in order to give it structure and meaning – which is what you have to do when you create a structured experience. If you adapt a fictional (or narrated) idea, situation or event into a game, some of your work will have already been done for you by the author. With experience, you can also adapt virtually any existing longer game that you hear about or get out of a book. You can simplify it, rearrange it, and generally cut up its organization, thus tailoring it to your specific needs. The criteria that you should keep in mind are discussed below.

Design criteria

First, the activity must be – or you must be able to make it – relevant to the rest of your material. Thus, for science students you can take a basic activity such as **Human Pyramid** (Activity 27, Chapter 9) and turn it into a strategy for learning about the process of digestion in the human body (as we did for **Down It Goes!** Activity 22, Chapter 9).

Second, the game should aim specifically to illustrate one basic theme. Of course, it will provide examples of a range of human emotions and behaviour, because the actions of human beings are the raw material from which the game is made, but your debriefing, of necessity, has to be selective. It has to focus only on comparisons and contrasts in players' behaviour that relate directly to your subject matter – which means you have to be very observant of players' responses. Therefore, you do not want to create a great deal of general and irrelevant activity because you will not be able to take it all in.

Third, the game should be product-oriented, and involve people in conflict. These are the ingredients for ensuring dramatic content. The players need to become involved in some visible problem-solving activity, preferably where there is a *product*, like the answer to a puzzle or any sort of outcome that can be evaluated and used as a criterion by which to examine the action. You may find it useful to remember that one definition of drama is 'people in conflict'. This does not mean that the players have to start fighting each other, or that there need be any kind of aggression. The conflict may be a dialectic between one idea and another that creates something new: thesis – antithesis – synthesis. The more dramatic the game is, within reason, the more likely it is to evoke highly visible results. This is one of the reasons why we suggest you should sometimes videotape the activity, so you can watch how people have reacted to it, in order to help you make it more effective in the future.

To compare experiential activities to drama is to suggest that they contain the potential to surprise, even shock, the participants. To use another metaphor, in a sense they are explosive devices, though their detonations usually stimulate players' amusement, curiosity, interest and surprise rather than deeper emotions. However, it is important to remember that you are playing with dynamite. Surprise can quickly turn to outrage, amusement to derision and hostility, and curiosity to rejection.

Do not make the mistake of thinking that players cannot become upset by short and simple games. People's responses to experiential material are always complex and, however elementary the game, you have to be quick on your feet to control the results. The message of this book is that it's not only what you do, but also how you do it, that makes for failure or success with experiential learning material. We think there are three factors involved in choosing a learning activity: your learning objectives; the structure of the activity (ie its rules and procedures); and the character and temperament of the group of people who will experience the activity.

Our final case-study is of a beautifully relaxed debriefing of **Gerontology** (Activity 41, Chapter 11) in which the shape of the activity, the director's objectives and the temperament of the group came together in a most harmonious way. In Gerontology (which has a more open structure than Digicon or New Year's Eve Hat) the participants sit on chairs, which represent their homes. They are tied to the chairs with lengths of rope to represent the limit of their mobility. They are given paperclips to represent money and a paper and pencil as their 'memory'. They are told that they are in the role of old people in society and that there is a 'bank' and a 'welfare agency' to which they can go if they need help. Periodically the 'Grim Reaper' plagues them with illness, poverty, or death. Apart from these constraints, they can do whatever they please and create whatever kind of community they want.

A friend of ours, Erica, directed Gerontology with a group of health professionals: doctors, senior nurses and administrators from Asia and the Pacific. When the game was over she introduced the debriefing with: 'All of you are going to be working as health professionals with old people. What is there in this game that you can learn about dealing with the aged in our society? Given a society that says you shouldn't let people commit suicide, or that you shouldn't kill them off, do you think we ought to do anything different about old age, as people and as administrators?'

Note that she said this *after* the game, not before it. Thus she did not interfere with its structure. She pointed out that there had been a marked difference in role behaviour between two people, Sandra and Alastair, who had played the parts of welfare officers. The other participants agreed with her. One player complained that Sandra had been so authoritarian that 'I couldn't be bothered hassling with her', while another praised the 'compassion' of Alastair, who was generous with public funds. Erica asked: 'Does that mean that people can't be bothered dealing with bureaucrats if there are alternatives available in society? Is that one of the reasons the compassionate agencies are always short of money?'

She was also quick to enlarge on other points that she wanted the players to discuss. For example, when a man said that in the game he had refused to help 'poor Alan' because he was suffering from a 'terminal disease' and was 'too far gone', Erica asked, 'Does that mean there's no point in us trying to help someone who has no hope?'

This prompted an Asian player to comment: 'I found the meaning of life when I got hospitalized. It wasn't the security that really mattered. I realized that I wanted to live. I was struggling all the time to live.' His statement stimulated a discussion about the quality of life for old people in different cultures.

An American participant said he thought that in middle-class white American culture, 'a lot of old people are quite glad to be rid of the burden' (ie to die). Someone else challenged him on this by saying: 'Just because we think old people have no purpose doesn't mean they think like that.' Another player added: 'I was feeling like that (when I was in role as an old person). I didn't have any friends and I was ready to die. But the next minute, friends came to my aid and I suddenly felt rejuvenated and exhilarated.'

The discussion proceeded along these lines until some group members spontaneously began to suggest some possible real-life alternatives for old people, such as: 'What's wrong with people over 65 forming their own cooperatives?' The discussion focused throughout on what had happened in the game rather than on how players had solved a predetermined problem – which gave Erica a great deal of freedom to range outwards from the game experiences to encourage a kind of brainstorm for creative thinking about old people's place in society, the contributions they can make, and the special needs they may have.

This example, the others we have referred to, and many more, led us to create the following table. It summarizes what we believe about the ways in which you can organize an activity, including its debriefing, so that its content conveys to players the meanings that you intend.

Closed Games	*Open Games*
'This is the problem: how will we solve it?'	'This is the situation: what will you do?'
(1) Players are encouraged by leader's preliminary remarks or warm-up to make the same general assumptions about the game and to create a feeling of 'togetherness'.	Preliminary discussion or warm-up is aimed to reveal heterogeneity of group and disparity between members and their views.
(2) The leader is perceived as a benevolent authority figure.	Players are not encouraged to look to the director for a lead (which may cause feelings of resentment).
(3) Differences between players are shown to be functional by encouraging division of labour.	Differences between players not assumed to be functional. Therefore conflict is more likely to arise.
(4) Leader forms teams, gives instructions, sets the scene, answers questions; is seen to be in control.	Leader says and does as little as possible.
(5) The setting of the game and the characters have a 'past'. Players are asked to imagine events that happened prior to the action of the game. They begin at a point of *crisis*.	The game setting has *no 'past'* and the action takes place 'on stage'. Players are offered a *situation*, not presented with a crisis.
(6) The characters are constrained by detailed information and specific role instructions.	There are few rules, little detail is provided, therefore there is opportunity for chance happenings, or the whims of the players.

(7) Players are organized into teams or sub-groups. They all play by the same rules.

Number and arrangement of players are comparatively unimportant. Groups may have uneven numbers, or individuals may work alone. Some interpret the rules differently from others.

(8) The players' point of attack is a moment of crisis.

The players embark on a journey rather than grapple with a crisis. Thus there are multiple plots and diffuse action.

(9) There are distinct steps or stages in the game, directed by the leader and occurring at fairly regular intervals with the aim and effect of progressing the action along specific lines. There is a sense of order and regular pace.

Stages in the game are not clearly marked. Some seem more important than others. Changes occur because of the activities of the players and are due to general causes. Pace and rhythm vary. There is no sense of order and balance.

(10) Each step proceeds logically from the one before. The action is goal-oriented and forward-looking.

Minor actions spin off from major ones in an apparently illogical manner. The characters are process-minded and present-oriented.

(11) There is a single line of mounting pressure, with stimulus towards cooperative problem-solving and emphasis on outcome.

Emphasis is on players' reactions, the situation as it develops; less compression of events, more chance happenings. Events are diverse, emphasis is on behaviour, not outcome.

(12) Players' choices become increasingly limited as events close in to constrain them.

There are multiple lines of action, a need for individual decisions. Events do not accumulate to confine the players.

(13) Observers' interest focuses on how the players will solve the problem rather than what they are doing, which tends to predetermine the nature of the outcomes; there is a sense of inevitability.

Players act autonomously, constrained only by their real-life restraints. There is room for 'deviant' (minority) opinion and behaviour.

(14) Players derive pleasure from shared experience. Conflict is seen as reconciliatory. There are problems and answers.

Players find themselves more thoughtful than pleased. There is a lack of certainty and an awareness of new possibilities.

The provision of game materials

There is another aspect of designing games that we should discuss, and that is the provision of game materials. We have already advised you to 'keep it simple' when you set out to create a game, and this advice applies also to its materials. One of our activities, **Who's the Leader?** (Activity 9, Chapter 7), has the requirement option of costume props but otherwise, for the most part, you will not find they demand materials that are complicated or difficult to provide.

We find ourselves almost automatically rejecting games that we read about or hear about if they require a long list of supplies. If games can be compared to drama and described as 'people in conflict', they can also borrow a metaphor from the theatre: 'two planks and passion'. In other words, a game, like a play, need be no more than an empty room across which some people move while others watch them.

Metaphors can be carried too far, but this one may serve to illustrate that the players' actions and feelings are paramount in experiential activities. Therefore, as a general rule, it is best to use what you have at hand when you design games and use your imagination to make them appropriate to your needs. Virtually anything can become game material, as illustrated in **Ponsonby** (Activity 29, Chapter 10) which we designed during a conference for educators, on simulation games, in Melbourne some years ago. It is the most complicated design we have to offer in this chapter but it was truly a 'trigger' in the context of the conference and it confirms our point about using what you have got.

Practical examples of designing interactive exercises

To illustrate these points, we want to take you in some detail through an experience of a game we invented as a warm-up for a management training session on leader legitimacy. It later was formalized as Who's the Leader? (see above). The players found their own and each other's responses so thought-provoking that the game became a sort of touchstone against which to test the rest of the session for 'truth'. But in spite of its effectiveness, and although it was designed to meet all of the criteria listed above, the response of one player made us aware that the game can be explosive.

The seminar was about acquiring confidence – self-legitimacy – in leadership roles. Somebody raised the point that most people at one time or another are worried about what to wear because they are anxious to 'give the right impression'. This started us thinking about the clothes people choose to wear to create an aura of power. The group dispersed temporarily to collect some props – a suede jacket, a fur coat, a few scarves, hats, gloves, bangles, baubles, beads, etc. When the group reconvened several players got right into the spirit of the thing and dressed up to the nines; and the observers were supportive and asked constructive questions. One 'actor' wore the fur coat and then announced that he was a union representative (which in fact he was in real life). When his audience commented that he looked more like a capitalist, he said he wanted to demonstrate his egalitarian principles. Why should not workers be dressed as luxuriously as their bosses?

However, most of the other players – who, remember, were all managers in real life – disdained to wear any articles of costume and insisted their own suits were appropriate for the status of a leader. (Note for inexperienced session leaders: there's no need to panic if players do not do what you ask them. Work with them, not against them. If the game is supposed to be about dressing up, like this one, and people won't dress up, don't worry; ask them why they don't think the costume articles are appropriate. Keep the questions respectful, impersonal, non-threatening, and pertinent to the exercise.)

One man had real problems in dealing with another male player who dressed up very fetchingly as a female. He kept making suggestive remarks about this player's sexual preferences, which were taken in very good part by the victim but which annoyed the rest of the group. Moreover his tasteless behaviour continued into the session. He frequently made the relevant player the target of innuendoes and other verbal abuse – always with a smile and the pretence of joking. Since his behaviour was damaging people's concentration and creating an uncomfortable atmosphere, finally we had to introduce the topic of sexuality in the workplace (via Activity 69, Chapter 14). After some initial embarrassment everybody was willing to talk about their feelings regarding this one man's behaviour; and after that he kept quiet. We cite this example of having to fight fire with fire, so to speak, by using one activity to debrief another.

Keeping control of the activity

The tighter the structure of the activity the more control you will maintain over outcomes. This can be a critical factor, even for experienced classroom directors, if they are faced, for example, with unruly or potentially explosive groups.

We remember quite well the experience of running a warm-up session for about 18 drop-out adolescents at a youth and community centre in a disadvantaged suburb of a disadvantaged city. They were too peer-oriented to form sub-groups, and when we asked them to think of a game, they came up with something they called 'Treasure Hunt'. They asked us to give them half an hour, disappeared out of the building, and came back not much later with the strangest assortment of items – including a hairbrush, a packet of cigarettes, a can of soup, a scarf, a screwdriver, and a large potted plant. They solemnly asked us to evaluate these goods, the winning item to be the one we thought had been the hardest to steal. They made no attempt to disguise the fact that the whole lot had been shoplifted and, while we appreciated the trust these young people reposed in us, we learned to keep a tighter check on group members whose imagination was not limited by mundane matters of law and order.

Classroom leaders who use interactive learning material often like to begin with a 'warm-up' exercise – also known as an ice-breaker. This is argued to 'set the scene' and make it easier for the session leader to introduce and process the material that follows. Unfortunately this tactic sometimes results in participants being asked to do quite straightforward things – like introducing themselves – in complicated, time-consuming and even embarrassing ways. People may be told to interview each other in pairs, for example, and then introduce their partners to the whole group. Or they may be asked to play guessing games about each other, draw self-portraits, or write some personal information on a label to pin on themselves, then go round the room trying to match their likes/dislikes/personality traits with those of other people, and so on.

The arguments for warm-ups are that they create an atmosphere of relaxed informality, so that people get to know each other while simultaneously gaining individual self-confidence and mutual trust; and that because such games are fun, they provide stimulus for learning. We agree that these are desirable aims at some point during a training session – though not necessarily at the very beginning – but we find many warm-ups to be a virtual waste of time at any stage. When we have only a few days or even hours in which to introduce busy people to a whole range of new material, everything that happens in the classroom has to be part of a sequence of learning and every exercise needs to perform a number of linked and related functions. Warm-ups must act as triggers for this process, rather like a starter's gun at a race-track, to overcome that initial inertia familiar to us all when faced with the prospect of having to think.

An essential time-management skill for class directors is the ability to recognize when experiential activities are likely to be the most effective strategy and when some other learning method will probably be better. For example, new group members are always interested in who everybody is and what they do; therefore the quickest method of providing this information is to label everybody and hand out some essential information about them all, one copy per person. It seems unnecessary to spend half an hour playing games to get people to learn something which they may very likely forget, when instead they can be supplied with a written record they can read in a few minutes and retain for reference.

This suggestion is particularly relevant when the group possesses good social skills and members start moving around of their own accord, shaking hands and chatting briefly with each other. It is only when people seem tense and ill at ease that a game is likely to be the most economical strategy in terms of getting them group-minded as quickly as possible.

However there are times when even the most experienced session leaders are in danger of losing control of the situation. We used to run sessions regularly for the Australian Institute of Management in Sydney, for mixed groups of business people from different organizations all over Australia, including public and private-sector managers. Many of them had not volunteered for the course but had been advised by their superiors to attend, because they were deemed either to lack assertion or to be too aggressive. No matter how carefully we designed the material, the results were always unpredictable because we had to deal continually with two very ill-matched kinds of people. One kind would glare at us and say loudly: 'I can't understand why I'm on this course. I never thought I lacked assertiveness!' The other kind would avoid our eyes and mutter in embarrassed tones that, yes, probably, er, well, they weren't always very good at speaking up for themselves at meetings and things. (One man had actually been on the first day of his vacation, skiing in the Snowy Mountains, when he was summoned 450 miles back to Sydney by his head office to attend our seminar. He didn't utter a single word the whole of the first day – and at that stage we did not know why, which was rather unnerving.)

To put it bluntly, when you have a collection of potential bullies on the one hand and victims on the other, the business of building a workable group dynamic becomes problematic. On these occasions we often begin with a game like You Choose to give people a chance to settle down a bit. Also it gives us the opportunity to identify those players who are likely to try and dominate the group and us, and those who are going to need a lot of encouragement to open their mouths at all.

The advantages of video

If you do decide to play one or more warm-up games, you can do more than teach participants each other's names and get them to feel a bit more friendly towards each other, and you can also video-tape the activity. It surprises us that few training manuals recommend videotaping, yet there is almost no formal classroom where recording facilities are unobtainable. Alternatively, a portable audio-cassette recorder can provide participants with a means of hearing themselves as others hear them. Neither video nor audiotape has to be replayed immediately – they can be kept for a more appropriate time, or not used at all – but at least these resources are there if you want them. You have something tangible to help participants improve their presentation skills: and during a residential course, for example, participants are often very pleased to have something to look at and discuss in the evenings.

We think that training manuals do not normally suggest using a video recording system because of trainers' complaints that it takes too long to set up, replay, and analyse a video recording, and that videotaping defeats the purpose of a warm-up, which is to produce an atmosphere that is relaxed and informal, yet conducive to learning. However, we do not agree with this line of thought. Our experience has been that many teachers do not understand and are nervous of educational hardware such as video; they think that such hardware is more complicated than it really is – for instance a camera can be set up and left running. Not only will the camera record a surprising amount of the action, but the players, after the first few minutes, seem to forget its presence.

Evaluating interactive learning methods

It is difficult – some would say impossible – to assess the learning components of any exercise in isolation. There are many books available which make the attempt, but when it comes to evaluating games, we think the best is still the one written by Campbell and Stanley in 1963, called *Experimental and Quasi-Experimental Designs for Research*. It is nothing to do with games as such, but it describes clearly a number of research designs that can be adapted by game leaders with relative ease.

We have also invented or adapted some methods of our own. One is to offer young respondents a number of line drawings of faces, all with different expressions. One face is smiling happily, another has question marks coming out of it in all directions, another is frowning and angry-looking, and so on. We ask the students to pick the face that best reflects their own feelings, and then encourage them to tell us why. Another method is to ask the students to write an essay describing their experiences in the game. In Chapter 2 we described how a teacher, Flora, asked her class to do this after playing 'New Year's Eve Hat' (Activity 28).

Because we have been playing learning games internationally for a number of years, we quite often meet up again with educators and business people who remind us they once participated in a particular game with us. They often say: 'I'll never forget. . .' and then go on to describe what it was they found so memorable about the experience. Sometimes we ask them: 'What do you think you learned from that?' and we usually get a reply that satisfies us. For example, one man, referring to Get Smart!, said: 'I think it taught me a lot about negotiation. I know that ever since playing that game I've looked for people's "hidden agendas" when I'm dealing with them.'

Of course, one cannot legitimately extrapolate from so little data, but it is arguable that feedback like this, over a long period of time, is perhaps the most cogent reason for teachers to continue using games as learning strategies. Teaching can, in some ways, be compared to marketing. It is a relatively easy matter to sell anything once, but when customers keep coming back for more, retailers become aware that they must be doing something right. Perhaps the fact that we are still 'in business' is the best reference we can offer for the effectiveness of the activities in this book.

We hope that by this time it has become apparent that we believe that the content of an experiential activity – ie the meanings ascribed to it by the players – is dependent partly on the form in which it is presented to them. In other words, with interactive learning material as with any other form of communication, the medium is a critical factor in how the messages are received and understood.

Moreover, we think this explains why interactive learning is often such a risky business and why evidence for its effectiveness is so hard to come by. Anybody who has researched the literature of experiential education will be aware of the controversy that bedevils games, simulations, roleplays and other learning activities even after decades of their use in all kinds of environments. Enthusiasts are convinced that in some circumstances, and for some forms of learning, simulations and other game-like activities can be a more powerful and economic teaching strategy than any other. On the other hand critics argue such activities are of doubtful value because they are impossible to evaluate, sometimes counter-productive to learning because many people 'hate playing games', and in any case, unnecessarily time-consuming.

Between these extremes fall many teachers and trainers who would like to use interactive learning methods but are unable to find suitable material and lack adequate briefing. We finish this chapter with a brief discussion of evaluation methods for experiential learning activities. One of the problems with most standard techniques such as feedback questionnaires is that they are not really designed for games, being intended for students to assess more traditional teaching methods such as lectures or demonstrations. Therefore many such questionnaires contain questions like: 'How do you rate the lecturer's presentation on a scale of one to five?' Answers to questions like these may actually mislead evaluators rather than give reliable feedback. For example it often happens after an experiential learning activity that participants retain either an exaggerated respect or a residual anger for the director who has provided them with a powerful experience (possibly one with which they may not have been entirely comfortable). These heightened feelings usually gain their proper perspective with time and are a natural part of the change process called learning. But while they last they can play havoc with empirical assessment if made too soon after the event. On the other hand, as indicated by Brenda's use of open-ended questionnaires (page 33), surveys can be extremely useful in spotting weaknesses in the director's presentation of the activity, or in its structure.

Another problem in evaluating interactive learning material is that it often forms part of a course, seminar, or workshop and it is difficult to sort out which learning came from what input. For example, if an activity is directed at the beginning of a seminar and then assessed, this is likely to devalue its effects – say if participants have not had time to develop a team spirit. Alternatively the activity may receive too much credit for getting the course off to a good start because other variables have been ignored – participants' motivation, perhaps.

We have already mentioned two evaluation methods of interactive learning material – essay and open-ended questionnaire. Each was considered effective by Flora and Brenda, respectively. Essay writing by players after a game has the advantage that it effectively reinforces learning by being in itself another kind of learning method; and open-ended questionnaires can become mini-essays if the respondents feel strongly about their replies, as Brenda's students did. However, in our experience, such lengthy replies are the exception rather than the rule. Most respondents reply very briefly to questionnaires, which is not usually satisfactory where games are concerned because more detailed feedback is required. We like to use an activity to assess activities. We call it **Contract** and reckon it is as good a way as any, and better than some, to get honest feedback from participants about what they think they have learned.

CONTRACT

Time required About half an hour.

Aim Contract is designed to evaluate the learning from an activity which is part of a course in which other teaching methods have been used, but it can be adapted fairly easily to evaluate a game as a single experience on its own. Its 'closed' structure leads participants towards some kind of consensus.

Group size Groups of 3 – 7 people.

Environment Classroom or seminar room arranged café-style, so each group can sit at its own table. Prepare the questions, one copy for each participant.

Procedure

(1) To guard against bias on your part, ask 1 – 3 players to act as leader (or panel of leaders) in place of yourself.
(2) Ask the leader to form groups of 3 – 7 people, each group to choose a representative who will summarize the feelings of the group after discussing the questions below.
(3) Give the questionnaires to the leader for distribution; and ask the leader to request that group members discuss their replies in private (some groups may prefer to go to another room, if one is available).
(4) After 15–20 minutes, the leader calls everybody together in a plenary session. Each group representative in turn is asked to summarize their team's response to each question and the leader posts the replies.
(5) The leader now throws the game open to general discussion. Any group member can ask anybody any question.

Evaluation Participants are asked to discuss the questions listed below.

Closing You can now take over and summarize the whole exercise by drawing up a verbal contract between yourself and the participants, each of you agreeing to contribute to the aims of the group as a whole, in the ways that have been previously discussed.

If you are not going to take part in the rest of the course or seminar (because other presenters will be in charge of the remaining material), the contract will be in three parts:

(1) An undertaking by you to bear in mind the directives of the group and act on them when directing activities in future.
(2) An undertaking by you to distribute copies of the contract to all the other presenters who will be in charge of the course, for their information, to act on as they think best.
(3) An undertaking by the group to apply what they have learned about themselves to the rest of the course.

Questions

(1) What did you DISLIKE about the activity in which you took part?
(2) What did you DISLIKE about the way the class director handled the activity?
(3) What did you LIKE about the activity?
(4) What did you LIKE about the way the class director handled the activity?
(5) What did you find LEAST helpful personally?
(6) What did you find MOST helpful?
(7) What are your goals for this course/seminar/workshop? For example:
   • More theory?
   • New behaviour?
   • New contracts?
   • Peer interaction?
   • What else?
(8) What learning methods do you think help you most? Lectures? Discussions? Reading? Activities such as the one you are discussing now? What else?
(9) What attributes, experience and special skills do you think you have, as a member of this group, to contribute to the group's learning?

Summary

This chapter has argued the need always to be on the alert for ideas that may lead to designs for interactive learning exercises – from books, films, TV and the everyday stories people tell about problems they have encountered and how they responded. The suggestion has also been offered that you can learn to adapt existing games and activities to meet your specific needs. Design criteria are: relevance to learning needs; the illustration of one basic theme; the involvement of people in conflict (with themselves, each other, ideas, problems, whatever); and a specific 'product' to emerge from the activity, such as the solution to a problem. Presenters will remain in control of outcomes through consciousness of their learning objectives, adherence to rules and procedures, and awareness of the nature of the learning group. Evaluation of interactive learning is based on the subjective responses of participants (what they liked and did not like about the activity and the behaviour of the presenter), the parts of the activity they found most and least helpful respectively, in achieving their own objectives for the exercise; and objective measures such as tests, essay writing, videotape and the like.

PART 2
LEADERSHIP TRAINING ACTIVITIES

Chapter 7

Warm-ups and other introductory activities

1 YOU CHOOSE

Time required This activity will last a minimum of about one hour and considerably longer if the group is large. With more than, say, 50 people, you can expect it to take the whole morning. After reading about it, we hope you will decide the activity will be worth the time.

Aims

- To remove barriers to the free exchange between group members of ideas and opinions.
- To demonstrate leadership behaviour.
- To practise group management of conflict and cooperation.

Group size Any number from about 5–150 people

Environment We usually offer this activity on the morning of the first day of a new course or seminar. It takes us comfortably to the first coffee break at least. You can direct it in virtually any class-room, however rigid the seating plan.

Procedure

(1) Provide a short explanation of the aims and objectives of the exercise (see 'AIMS' above).
(2) Put everyone into small groups of about 3 – 5 people, maybe as many as 7 if the class is very large. If there is only one group,

that's OK, but this activity works best with larger numbers.

In our experience the most difficult circumstance under which to put people into groups is when there is a large number of people (more than 50) and they are sitting in rows in fixed seats. If you are faced with this set-up and would like to play You Choose, this is how you do it:

Ask every third person in the front row, and in every alternate row after that, to raise their hands (this sounds complicated but isn't, as the class has to work it out, not you – which is a game in itself and part of the whole warm-up process). Wait patiently until everyone has stopped counting rows and looking at each other to find out who is the third person. You can offer a helpful remark from time to time if you think the process is getting bogged down. Eventually the designated people will identify themselves and raise their hands.

Ask them to call out their names, and post these on a blackboard or flipchart where everyone can see them.

Announce that these people are group leaders. Ask them to introduce themselves to the person on either side of them, and to the two people directly behind them in the next row, in order to form their groups. There will be some twisting and turning round on chairs, but that doesn't matter. Thus a number of groups are formed, each of 5 people. There will probably be one or two people left over on the ends of rows and so on, so you could suggest that any 'spares' can introduce themselves to their nearest leader and join up with that leader's group.

(3) Explain to everybody that the task for all groups is to think of *one* warm-up game for *the whole class* to play in 5 minutes' time. It must be a game that everyone can play easily in the present circumstances, that stimulates everyone's *creative thinking*, and that lasts no more than 5 minutes. Post the following criteria somewhere:
- think of/invent a game;
- duration of game: 5 minutes;
- to be played by everyone present in the room;
- to begin at (5 minutes from time of writing);
- to stimulate creative thinking.

(4) Ask if anyone has any questions, and answer them, but don't allow yourself to get dragged into tedious debate (power-oriented

people on the one hand, and people who are low in motivation on the other, often choose to argue rather than cooperate.)

(5) After 5 minutes call out the name of each leader in turn and ask for their group's suggestion. If they do not have one, put a dash against their name and move on. Keep the whole thing moving briskly. You may end up with half a dozen suggestions against every name, or with no suggestions at all, or with something in between – it doesn't matter which. This is a fail-safe game providing you keep your head.

(6) Ask each leader in turn to tell everyone what happened in their group. If the room is large and the acoustics bad you may have to repeat or paraphrase loudly. Try to post up a few good quotations in any case, just to ensure that everyone has a similar understanding of what has been said, and you have something to refer back to later. Be sure to obtain the speaker's agreement, in every case, that your paraphrase is what the speaker really intended to say. If numbers are large you may want to ask for a couple of volunteers to be scribes at the blackboard. Accept without comment (except for encouragement) anything the leaders tell you, and allow any interruptions from their group members, provided each group does not take more than its fair share of time, depending on the total number of groups.

Evaluation When everyone has finished, ask them to contemplate the following leadership themes, which you are now posting or have prepared in advance. (If the group includes members from different cultures, you should emphasize that there may be cultural differences in the ways people answer these questions – and of course you will substitute your questions for ours if you are dealing with a subject other than leadership skills.)

Power. Ask everybody to think about how their group leader used the authority of this designated role. Were they authoritarian? Democratic? Hands-off? What effect did leadership style have on task accomplishment?

Motivation. Did leaders do or say anything that helped to motivate, support or encourage the group?

Task. Was it important to all leaders and groups to accomplish the given task, ie to think of or invent a game? Or did some of the discussions turn into get-to-know-you sessions? If this happened, how did the relevant leaders feel about it?

Challenge. Were there any emergent leaders in any of the groups who appeared to challenge the designated leader's authority? How did the followers perceive their leaders? Did they perceive them as being capable? Or did they think they could have done better themselves?

If you have the time, and want to turn You Choose into a larger and more complex game, at this point ask all group members to rate their respective leaders on a scale of 1 to 5, on the four criteria of power, motivation, task and challenge. Then ask the leaders to average out the scores of all their group members and call out the results, which you post. You can solicit further feedback by asking the group members with the highest-scoring leader to provide actual examples of their leader's effective leadership.

If your participants are statistics-minded they may start making a fuss at this point about the exercise being statistically invalid because the samples were so small. 'What do you expect to prove with only three groups?' we remember a man asking contemptuously. We answered that by referring to a number of other occasions where the game had indicated – as on this occasion – that effective leadership occurs through a combination of the style of the leader, the temperaments of the followers, and the nature of the task. (Remember what we wrote in a previous chapter about sometimes having to use information and expertise as power tools? This is an example of when we had to do just that.)

The first time you direct You Choose, you might want to remember this incident and avoid the problem yourself by stating in advance that you are using the results merely as illustrations of a number of different leadership styles, without trying to draw hard conclusions. On the other hand, if you should decide to play the game on a number of different occasions – particularly if the groups are varied – you can collate the results, write them up for transferral to transparencies, and use an overhead projector to demonstrate to your next group, for example, that leadership appears to be *situation–specific*, which will take you comfortably to a discussion of Hersey's leadership curve (Hersey and Blanchard, 1977).

It is worth remembering that, for some reason we have never quite fathomed, game participants are often keen to know how their performance compares with that of other groups. Therefore this kind of feedback is always well received.

Closing Whether you play the short or the long version, you need to reserve 5 minutes of You Choose in case participants really do want to play one of the games that was devised or suggested during the exercise. After all, this was ostensibly the object of the activity and you have to be as good as your word. However by this time it may have dawned on them that the medium was the message – the activity itself was the game it was supposed to create.

2 BRAINSTORM

Time required This activity has to be timed carefully as below, or it will take hours:

- 5 minutes for explaining the exercise;
- 3 minutes for getting the players into groups, selecting reporters and volunteers;
- 5 minutes for general discussion about topics that the volunteer would like brainstormed;
- 5–10 minutes for brainstorming;
- 5 minutes for refining the ideas;
- 10–15 minutes for the plenary session.

Perhaps three-quarters of an hour altogether unless you have a really large class.

Aims

- To encourage people to begin thinking creatively by generating a lot of ideas quickly – especially if group members are low in motivation and self-esteem in general, and have short concentration spans.
- To convey the message that novel and unusual ideas are to be encouraged.
- With cross-cultural groups who are sharing English as an international language, and where some people have a greater command of the language than others: to assist in integrating and developing language skills.
- With groups of young people: for career planning, to expand their job horizons.

Group size From about 5–25 people.

Environment A classroom or seminar room arranged café-style so that small groups can sit at their own tables. Alternatively, groups can sit in circles on the floor. Provide coloured felt-tipped pens and newsprint paper.

Procedure

(1) Initiate a general discussion about the problems participants encounter in whatever context the group has come together. For example if the session is with school-leavers on career planning,

what difficulties have group members experienced in choosing a career or finding a job?

(2) Allow the discussion to continue until you become aware of a few individuals with specific problems who might benefit from brainstorming. For instance, if the session is concerned with managing change, examples might be: 'I can't see the need for change: our present system is working very well as it is'; or: 'My problem is that we're not initiating enough change'.

(3) Form groups of 5–7 people round each individual you have selected who is willing to be 'brainstormed'. Ask each group to form itself into a circle.

(4) Ask each team to choose a reporter, and then announce the rule that nobody shall criticize anybody else's ideas. For instance, if the topic is 'Why change?' the group is encouraged to think of as many reasons for change as they can in the given time, no matter how apparently silly the reasons may sound. If the selected people are school-leavers maybe the brainstorms will be about what kind of career they might pursue. If the participants are there to learn English, volunteers might like to be brainstormed with ways to improve their pronunciation, gain a larger vocabulary, increase their ability to negotiate in English, and generally gain more confidence in speaking the language.

(5) Announce that all ideas will be recorded by each group's reporter for discussion later.

(6) The various reporters write down all the ideas in coloured felt-tipped pens. (If practical, give each reporter a different coloured pen.) The reporters can write on the floor, in the middle of the circle, or their team can huddle with them round a table.

(7) Give everybody about 5–7 minutes to brainstorm before announcing that the inventive phase of the game is over and the evaluation about to begin.

(8) Each group now goes back over all their ideas, narrowing down to one or two that really appeal to their volunteer, and elaborating on these as they see fit.

Evaluation Initiate a final, plenary, phase in which each group takes it in turns to describe to the whole class what happened in their group.

Closing Brainstorm can have some surprising results. On one occasion, one of the volunteers was a teacher who elected to be brainstormed on other careers he might follow apart from teaching. Afterwards he reported: 'I didn't realize until now just how miserable I am as a teacher. This exercise hasn't taught me what it is I want to do next, but it has shown me what I definitely *don't* want to do!'

On another occasion, also a career planning seminar, a teenager reported that nobody had been able to come up with any career she really felt she wanted to pursue. Her group members (her school colleagues) were clearly frustrated by the whole experience – until she added: 'Of course . . . what I'd *really* like to do . . .'

'Yes, yes, what is it?' her team–mates urged her.

'What I'd really like to do is. . . be a cook!'

This was just about the only job the brainstormers hadn't thought of; but apparently the whole activity had triggered her own creative thinking. We are happy to report that eventually she went to technical college and trained as a cook, and that we were invited to her graduation – which included a magnificent lunch cooked by the graduates.

3 THUMBS UP

Time required About 20–30 minutes.

Aim To provide clues to individuals' problem-solving styles.

Group size From about 8 people to virtually any number. We have directed this activity at conferences with literally hundreds of participants. The essential requirements are that you can be seen and heard clearly by everybody; and that you can hear people's comments from the floor.

Environment A classroom, seminar or conference room.

Procedure

(1) Ask everyone to put both hands out in front at arm's length. The easiest way to explain this is for you to demonstrate it physically.

(2) Ask them to clasp their hands together and to note which thumb is on top (wriggle your own thumb in illustration).

(3) Ask them to put their hands down by their sides, and then, as quickly as they can, to re-clasp their hands out in front of them with the *other* thumb on top (demonstrate this). Wait a moment for the experience to sink in.

(4) Ask people now to fold their arms across their chests, and then, very quickly, to re-fold them *the other way*.

(5) Ask everyone to turn to their neighbour and tell that person *how they felt* during the whole exercise. Give everyone a few minutes to do this. You may have to help them at the start, for instance, by indicating to someone who their 'neighbour' is, putting the occasional threesome together if one person does not seem to have a partner, and so on.

(6) Listen to the noise level. It will probably build as people get into their stride, peak, and begin to descend. Wait until most people seem to have stopped talking and are obviously expecting you to do something. In strongly people-oriented groups the buzz of talk will go on for ages. If the chatter gives no sign of abating by itself, give it, say, 5 minutes at the most and then get everyone's attention.

People high on problem-solving tend to be quieter than people-oriented players but even if there is almost no discussion do not become unnerved – wait for at least 2 or 3 minutes without saying anything more, even if by now there is complete silence in the room (though take courage, we have never known this to happen).

Evaluation Ask the class as a whole for feedback. Ask them to repeat aloud some of the remarks they were making to each other, for you to post on the board. There may be some hesitation, but if you stand there, waiting, with the chalk in your hand, sooner or later someone will call out something like 'Awkward', which will start the ball rolling.

It is most important that you do not prompt anyone at this stage, though if the group is exceptionally quiet you could ask one or two leading questions, like: 'Did anyone dislike it?' Someone will probably either agree, or give some form of qualified 'yes', and then you can ask: 'In what way?' and so on, until people give you *their* noun or adjective to describe what they felt ('Well, I felt such a fool!' or 'I didn't like it because I didn't understand the point of the exercise!').

If the group is large and mixed, you will get some wide variations in responses, such as 'It shows the power of habit'; 'It was fun, I love doing things like that!'; 'I wondered what was the point of the whole thing.' Post them all, in summary (but get the speakers to agree to the summary and do not replace their words with yours unless *they* think your words are better).

When everyone has had time to contemplate this feedback introduce them to the idea that nobody sees the same task or problem in quite the same way. For instance, some people will be more inclined to interpret a situation in terms of human feelings and relationships because those are the things that interest them most; others tend to see problems as challenges to their ingenuity; still others are more inclined to solve the problem or accomplish the task by use of power (over themselves or other people). If they cannot adapt the problem or task to their particular problem-solving orientation, they are likely to lack motivation to solve or accomplish it.

Ask participants to comment on the statements you have recorded. For example:

- 'I felt funny.' Is this a subjective and personal statement about the individual's feelings, without much or any attempt to question those feelings?

- 'I was afraid I wasn't doing it right.' Does this comment imply that the speaker was aware of ambiguity and found the activity mildly stressful as a result?
- 'What's the point?' Does this question suggest a need to be told the usefulness of the activity? Is the question a challenge to the authority or credibility of the class leader?
- 'What are we supposed to learn from this activity?' Is this a more abstract response, indicating a deductive attempt at convergence; to pull the whole experience together into a meaningful whole?

Everyone is capable of being motivated by combinations of needs for power and people and problem-solving, and, no doubt, the need that is uppermost in any one individual at any one time will depend on a great many complexities and circumstances, some of which the person can control and some of which are part of the larger environment. Nevertheless, people do appear to develop (or to possess from birth) a *propensity* towards one kind of motivation rather than another. Some people seem to like playing power games more than others, for example. Why they feel the need to do so is another matter, and not within the scope of this book.

The point is that your participants should understand that these patterns exist and begin to recognize inside themselves the kinds of problems and situations that most motivate them – if they are to develop effective leadership styles.

Closing One of your responsibilities is to help participants learn to work as a group rather than as a collection of isolated individuals. Groups generate their own learning. On the law of averages, if nothing else, the group knows more than you do about almost everything. Your job as leader is to release the learning power of the group, which should go far beyond your input to levels and dimensions you could never bring them to by yourself.

You can encourage this group dynamic by helping members to perceive their unique problem-solving strengths, and by suggesting ways they can apply these to the service of the group as a whole. When this begins to happen the line between 'teacher' and 'learner' disappears altogether. The roles become interchangeable and you and the group continually negotiate meanings in a dynamic of mental energy that is often called synergy.

This process occurs when any teaching method has been effectively used, but with interactive learning methods it seems to be enhanced. Experiential activities can generate an intellectual 'high', and however exhausted you are by the end of the session you are wiser than when you began because you have shared the learning of the group.

4 TO BE OR NOT

Time required About 20 minutes.

Aim This is another short activity to illustrate the need for team members to put group needs before their own, for effective problem-solving.

Group size Minimum of 6–10 people.

Environment Indoors or outdoors, space enough for at least 6 people to stand or sit in circles or squares.

Procedure

(1) Ask everyone to form groups of 6–10 people and then to stand or sit in a circle or a square. If there are lots of people, form two or more circles.

(2) Give any one individual in each of the circles the word 'to'; then give the word 'be' to the person beside them, and so on until the six people respectively have been given the words 'To-be-or-not-to-be', one word at a time. With the larger circle you add the words 'That-is-the-question', again as single words, one to each player. If you are short of players, you can allocate more than one word to each.

(3) Ask the players to say their words out loud, in turn. The first person will start off tentatively or boldly, as the case may be, saying 'To.' Note that we have written a full stop after the word to give a sense of how the player is likely to say it – as if it were a complete sentence in itself. The next speaker, realizing it is his or her turn, will say: 'Be!' This process continues until everybody has had their turn. The result almost invariably is a spoken series of apparently disconnected words uttered at random.

Evaluation Rehearse the group several times until they learn to listen empathetically to each other, to pick up the previous speaker's word, add their own, and pass the combination on to the next in line so that the whole sentence assumes rhythm and meaning.

Closing This is also a very good exercise for improving people's concentration. You do not have to use Shakespeare – a prose passage from a book or newspaper will do just as well. You can write your own – perhaps with subtleties, as in: 'Look out! Oh, dear; I *did* warn you about the puddle! Are you very wet?' which requires the speakers to decide on the ordering of information and to adopt a number of different intonations, depending on different meanings and the intentions of the speaker.

5 SIMULTANEOUS INTERPRETATION

Time required About 20 minutes.

Aims

- To improve participants' concentration.
- To increase empathy.

Group size Groups of 5–7 people.

Environment Classroom or seminar room with space for players to sit in circles. Provide a book, newspaper or journal: anything suitable for reading aloud.

Procedure

(1) With 5–7 players sitting in a circle, ask one player to read aloud continuously from a book or newspaper.

(2) Ask the person on the reader's right to repeat every word, the second they hear it, to the next listener and so on round the circle until it all gets back to the reader. With practice, teams can become so skilful that their readers will hear their own words repeated in their ears like echoes of their own voices.

Evaluation Foreign language interpreters can become so fast with their translations that they are known as 'simultaneous interpreters', which is where we got the name for this activity. These translators appear to develop almost intuitive rapport with a speaker, even somebody with whom they have not worked before, so that it really seems as if they know what will be said before the words leave the speaker's mouth. Participants in Simultaneous Interpretation are not being asked to translate what they hear into another language (though that might be another useful game), merely to repeat what they hear.

Closing This exercise can easily be adapted to increase fluency in speaking and understanding a foreign language, and players will not find it very difficult to develop the concentration and empathy that make this such an effective game.

6 ROGER'S GAME

We call this activity 'Roger's Game' because a man named Roger first described it to us.

Time required About 20 minutes

Aim To illustrate the power of leaders to persuade people to behave in ways they might not otherwise choose.

Group size Minimum 8–10 people; preferably about 15 – 20, maximum probably about 30. Roger's Game is suitable for classroom environments where there are not too many people and where there is space for each individual in turn to come up to the blackboard.

Environment The classroom, with blackboard or whiteboard and various coloured pens or chalks. This activity requires a money pool. Ideally it should be filled from participants' individual contributions. If for any reason this is unlikely to happen, bring enough small change with you to *give* (not lend) each participant a minimal sum to make up the pool.

Procedure

(1) Announce that this is a game about winning and losing.
(2) Take 5, 10 or 20 pence from each player to put into a common fund for prize money. If warranted by the socio-economic status of the players, you may be able to squeeze them for 50 pence or a pound each. Usually the more money there is in the fund, the better motivated are the players. If you are working with a cross-cultural group, some members may have conservative views about gambling. In these circumstances it might be better to substitute, say, wrapped sweets for money.
(3) Draw on the board a matrix of 6 squares by 6, ie 36 squares.
(4) Pick two people in the class to be team leaders. You will get the most visible results from the activity as a whole if you select participants whom you have already decided are competitive in temperament, which is why Roger's Game is best played when you know your players reasonably well. Use words such as 'team-member' and 'leader' to encourage a spirit of competition.
(5) Ask the leaders to pick their teams by taking turns to select one person from the group until everyone has been chosen.

(6) Toss a coin to decide who chooses first. If there is one person left over at the end, that person becomes umpire. If numbers are even, then you are the umpire. Appear to be taking all these preliminaries very seriously.

(7) When the teams are made up, give one leader a stick of coloured chalk and the other leader a piece of chalk of a different colour.

(8) Tell everyone that the game is a version of 'Noughts and Crosses', or 'Tic–Tac–Toe'. In Roger's version, team-members take turns to make either a zero or a cross on the board. There will be 18 turns and the object of the game is for each team to get as many complete rows as they can, horizontally or vertically, of zeros or crosses as the case may be. Repeat this information as often as you need but do not say any more about the objectives of the game.

(9) Tell everyone that each completed row will win 20 pence for the successful team (or 50 pence or 10 sweets or whatever is in the pot). Suggest that leaders brief their teams and give them a few minutes to discuss strategies, which you may find they do in whispers so the rival team cannot hear them.

(10) Line the two teams up in front of the board, leaders in front of their respective teams. Make sure each leader has a piece of chalk. Start the game on the second hand of your wristwatch: 'Ready...Steady...GO!'

Starting with the leaders, each team-member has 15 seconds to approach the board, make the relevant cross or zero, hand on the chalk to their next-in-line team-mate, and go to the end of the line themselves; and so on, each team marking the board alternately until all the turns have been completed.

(11) Start counting the seconds out loud if anyone is slow to move. Keep up the pace and pressure, to increase the suspense.

Evaluation We have played this game dozens of times, with a great variety of learning groups, and it is almost always played competitively. That is, at least one member of each team will deliberately prevent the other team from completing a row. Usually the saboteurs are given verbal encouragement by their team-mates. The usual result is either that no one wins a prize or that someone makes a mistake in the excitement of the moment and allows one line to be completed. If this happens, we duly hand over a prize.

Then we point out that theoretically the maximum number of lines that can be completed up and down the board is three by one team and three by another, which would yield a reasonable prize for both teams; however, this can happen only if both teams cooperate. So what do the words 'to win' and 'to lose' mean? Is winning a zero-sum affair in which winning means inevitably that someone else has to lose? Be prepared for this argument at first. It will come as a surprise – even a shock – to some players that there should be any doubt about the matter: '*Of course!*', they will say: 'You have to beat your competitors!'

You may care to suggest that winning is easier with somebody else's help; or that others will help you win if they can see something in it for themselves.

You may want to reveal the strategies you used to 'set them up' for Roger's Game by disclosing that you:

- chose the more competitive participants to be team leaders;
- made verbal assumptions that the game was competitive, which directed players to see it that way themselves;
- managed the timing of the activity so that players were given no opportunity to stop and think of alternative ways to play the game;
- motivated players to feel competitive by offering prizes to the winners;
- processed the whole activity in a linear, logical, step-by-step way that concealed its built-in assumptions.

Under all these influences, participants' game tactics were not based solely on objective criteria. Their perceptions were critically affected by the ways in which the activity was presented.

Closing If you should come across a group that refuses to 'play your game', and the teams decide to cooperate instead of working against each other (though we have seldom had this experience), discuss with them why your leadership was not effective. You can learn a lot about your leadership style from their answers.

7 EITHER...OR

Time required About 20 minutes

Aim To help people increase their awareness of how they make choices by recognizing some of the influences that make them decide to do one thing and not another. This recognition is an essential component in understanding how leaders lead and why followers follow.

Group size Ideally about 15 people; but you can play Either...Or with as few as 5 or 6, and as many as 50 or more. If numbers are large then either the furniture must be moveable or there must be some other empty space available, like a hall, foyer, lounge, or even the school playground.

Environment This exercise follows appropriately any static activity in which participants have been sitting at their desks or tables for some time.

Procedure

(1) Ask everyone to stand in a line down the middle of the room.
(2) Tell them that you are going to ask them some questions which they are to answer by moving three paces to the left or to the right, or by staying where they are. The first set of questions is:
   • 'Are you Yesterday? (If so, move to the left.)';
   • 'Are you Today? (Stay where you are.)'; and
   • 'Are you Tomorrow? (Move to the right.)'
   Repeat the questions several times if needed. Note that you are asking the players to identify themselves with all of the accrued meanings that they personally attach to each of the words.
(3) There may be some initial puzzlement, after which a few people, more or less, will step to the left or right. Wait until the shuffling stops, then ask those who have visibly made a decision why they chose to move one way or the other. For example, maybe they are Yesterday because of their love of the past – old customs, buildings, etc; or Tomorrow because they are young and the future belongs to them. When other players hear these statements, some may leave the centre and move to either the left or the right, as they realize what is expected of them. Others will choose to remain in Today. Again, ask why people voted with

their feet the way they did. You can think of any number of 'either...ors' for yourself, but here are a few suggestions:

- Are you: – a wordprocessor? – a gold fountain pen? – or a simple lead pencil?
- Are you a sign that says:– 'Open to visitors'? – 'No trespassers'? – or 'Back soon'?
- Are you: – a mountain? – a valley? – or a plain?
- Are you: – the earth? – the sea? – or the sky?
- Are you: – the city? – the country? – a dormitory suburb?
- Are you: – Yes? – No? – Maybe?

Evaluation Our favourite 'either...or' is: 'Are you a Volkswagen? a Rolls Royce? or some other kind of car?' The reasons that people give for being one of these, or another kind of car altogether like a four–wheel drive or a convertible, reveal a lot about themselves. They say things like: 'I'm a VW because I'm reliable, economical and safe'; or: 'I just like the whole concept of being a Rolls Royce – the power, the luxury; it's being a cut above the rest'; or: 'I'm a Jeep because it reminds me of camping in the mountains'.

Closing Encourage the participants to ask one another questions about their choices. The explanations are always interesting, the listeners find them informative, and the whole process is likely to increase self-awareness and understanding of one's own and others' motivations.

8 STATUS

Time required About 20 minutes.

Aim To illustrate how assumptions about authority and power affect behaviour.

Group size From about 5 people to virtually any number, providing you have the space for them all to stand in line (the line can snake about the room if necessary).

Environment This is another exercise in which players have to move about the room, this time in order to create a kind of living opinion poll. Therefore the environment should be relatively uncluttered with furniture. You will need a supply of sticky labels, suitable for affixing to participants' foreheads.

Procedure

(1) Give the sticky labels and a felt-tipped pen to one or more volunteers (depending on numbers of players).
(2) Ask participants to brainstorm occupations they might consider working in, all things being equal. The volunteers write each occupation on a separate label.
(3) Label all the players at random with one of these stickers and ask them to move around and read each other's occupations.
(4) Ask everybody to form a line down the centre of the room in order of status, with the person whose occupation is highest in status at the head. How they decide this order of status is up to them.
(5) Tell them that they have 10 minutes (or 15, or even longer if the group is large and vocal). After that, do not get involved at all; pass all questions back to the group. Stress that it does not matter by what criteria they choose to define 'status'. It is up to them to form the line any way they want. You may have to urge them along a bit by emphasizing the deadline or suggesting at which end of the room the head of the line should stand, but eventually you will probably see an uneven straggle of people, some of them still arguing about who stands in front of whom.
(6) Tidy them up a bit ('You're a nurse. Do you think your status is higher than that of this sales clerk? Well, then, you stand in front of him like this!').

Evaluation Initiate discussion about the order of rank. How and why did it come about? The kind of information that you want to reveal without asking for it directly is whether people's attitudes towards a particular occupation create a self-fulfilling prophecy about the position of the owner of that occupation in the line. Did players' occupations affect their own behaviour and the behaviour of others towards them?

For example, the occupation of paediatrician is high-income and high-status. Did the player labelled 'Paediatrician' have any problems getting to the head of the line or near it? Did that player *expect* to have any problems? On the other hand, if a player was labelled 'Refuse Collector', did that person end up near the end of the line? If so, did the player dispute it, or accept it as appropriate? What about professions such as 'Teacher' and 'Social Worker'? Where did they end up in the line?

Did anybody offer any criteria for status that were not based on money?

Closing In our experience, 'Status' is most effectively played with cross-cultural groups, groups of political activists, groups of players who in real life belong to disadvantaged minorities, and groups of very senior executives (though trying to stick labels on senior executives' foreheads is a status game in itself). Different groups come up with very different lists, and the game always seems to cause interested – sometimes heated – debate about personal values versus the opinions of society; and about status, money and power.

9 WHO'S THE LEADER?

Time required About 20 minutes; longer if participant numbers are large.

Aim To evoke discussion about the ways in which people's appearance affects their behaviour and the behaviour of others towards them.

Group size From about 3 people to as many as you have time for.

Environment Classroom, seminar or conference room. There are two ways you can run this activity:

(1) Provide a variety of 'dressing-up' accessories: an assortment of hats, jewellery, scarves, ties, walking sticks, umbrellas, and any items of clothing you can beg or borrow.
(2) If you can't or don't want to assemble these things, then cut coloured pictures out of old magazines, of men and women in as wide a variety of faces, bodies, clothes accessories and settings as you can find. Cut out dozens of these pictures.

Procedure

(1) Divide the class into groups of 3 – 5 people.
(2) If you have dressing-up items, give each group in turn the whole lot and send them out of the room for a few minutes to create images of power or weakness, riches or poverty, authority or ridicule, credibility or scorn: anything they like.
(3) While one group is dressing up, initiate a discussion on the theme of 'clothes make the man or woman' with particular reference to symbols of authority and power; and the reverse.
(4) Call the costumed group back after about 5 minutes. Ask them to make a fashion parade for the rest of the participants.
(5) Initiate a discussion about the effect of these created images on viewers. For example a woman participant in one of our sessions wore a bowler hat, a string of pearls round her neck and a sash at her waist; and carried a rolled umbrella. Older members of her audience called out: 'Charlie Chaplin', 'Judy Garland' and 'Marlene Dietrich'. Younger people said: 'Career woman'. Thus we were given a historial perspective on society's view of androgynous costume on a woman: at one time indicative of her role as entertainer; and more recently her aspiring role as manager.

(6) If you don't have dressing-up clothes, give each group an assortment of coloured pictures and ask them to find faces, costumes, accessories, settings to illustrate themes such as power, leadership, stress, conflict and so on. Then ask group members to explain their selections.

Evaluation How do outward appearances affect our perceptions of people's class, status, wealth and power, or their opposites? We remember one group that talked for nearly an hour about clothes as devices to legitimize and demonstrate the power of the wearer. Participants showed each other some of the articles they habitually wore (like a very expensive and elaborate wristwatch) as status symbols.

The men in particular talked about other possessions as symbols of power, including cars, houses and beautiful women. We were able later to extend this line of thought to explore some of the power symbols that women have traditionally adopted, like expensive jewellery, furs and perfume; and what kind of power these symbols suggested compared, say, to women in 'buttons and bows': and what dress tactics today's women managers might adopt to demonstrate their legitimacy as leaders.

Closing A word of warning: people sometimes respond in unexpected, even alarming ways to this activity. See our comments in Chapter 6, p. 63.

Chapter 8

Brain-teasing activities to promote creative problem-solving

10 MY CAR WON'T START

Time required About 20 minutes.

Aims

- To provide participants with useful clues to their personal problem-solving styles.
- To demonstrate the unique strengths of each style.

Group size From about 5 people to virtually any number, provided everybody can see the board or screen.

Environment The classroom, a seminar room or conference hall. You need to be able to post people's comments, ie a large blackboard or whiteboard and chalk or pens; or an overhead projector and screen, and transparencies you can write on under the lamp of the projector.

Procedure Ask participants to imagine that they are already late for an important appointment some distance away. They get into their car, but it won't start. What is the *first thing they would do*? (Depending on the composition of the group, you may want to substitute moped or bicycle for car. If you are working with students from China, for example, the vehicle would probably be a bicycle.)

Evaluation Players solve this problem verbally in a variety of ways and there is no 'right' or 'wrong' solution – as always in these activities. However, the answers provide useful clues to the problem-solving styles of the respondents. For example some people reply immediately that *first* they would try to fix their means of transport. In other words they would use their theoretical knowledge to solve a practical problem. This behaviour contrasts with that of other people, who say they would *first* seek to telephone to change or cancel the appointment. Answers along these lines imply a sense of future, a desire to impose control over events by making plans. Still others turn first to the resources of their present environment, including the people in it. Their solutions include begging, borrowing, or stealing some alternative form of transport. They would 'hitch a lift'; 'call a friend'; or 'borrow my spouse's car' (whether the spouse needs it or not).

This problem-solving style requires good powers of persuasion in individualistic cultures where you are supposed to solve your problems by yourself – like those of Britain and America, for example – but less so in countries like Japan. A Japanese businessman on a management training course once told us that in this situation in real life he would stand in the middle of the street and stop any car, asking the driver to take him to his destination. This reply was culture-specific; we could not imagine him getting away with it in Sydney or New York or London, and we were very much impressed that he took it for granted he could do so in Tokyo. Other frequent solutions to the problem are:

- 'I'd look at my watch to see how much time I had.'
- 'I would just sit and think about it for a few moments.'
- 'I wouldn't have a problem; I always allow extra time for emergencies.'
- 'I don't know exactly what I'd do, but I know I'd keep that appointment somehow, if it was really important (to me).'
- 'I would think, "Oh God, this isn't my day", and go back to bed.'

Closing Most people, in such a dilemma in real life, would probably combine a number of linked and related strategies. They would check how much time they had, check the car quickly for small, easily repairable faults, make a telephone call about the appointment, find other forms of transport, get the car towed away, and so on. Most of us are reasonably competent at solving everyday problems: what is of particular interest to team leaders is the problem-solving *style* of individual team members. Is one member quick to fix things? Is another a 'natural' for finding alternative resources? Is a third an effective planner? Does a fourth demonstrate exceptional people-skills? And so on.

11 A to B

Time required 20–30 minutes.

Aims

- To present a problem whose solution requires abstract, logical thinking.
- To demonstrate experientially some differences between people's perceptions of a problem and the resulting differences in the method of solving it.

Group size From about 5 people upwards.

Environment Classroom, seminar room, conference room.

Procedure Give the class the following problem and let them work it out individually and/or in groups, any way they prefer. Give them about 10 minutes to do so.

Problem I travel from A to B at an average speed of 20 miles per hour. Without stopping or deviating from my route in any way I return to A. At what speed will I have to complete the return journey in order to average 40 miles per hour for the *round trip?'*

Evaluation Most people average the speeds and calculate that the return journey must be made at 70 miles per hour (20 + 40 = 60 divided by 2 = 30). In fact the answer is infinity (in other words, it can't be done) because nothing can alter the fact that the travellers are being asked to complete a distance in the same time they have *already taken* to cover only half of it.

Generally speaking, people who are temperamentally well suited to abstract problem-solving – ie who enjoy puzzles for their own sake – are likely to arrive first at the right answer because they have worked it out logically, one bit at a time, and deductively, ie by a process of convergent reasoning, and therefore they will also be able to explain why.

Sometimes participants will respond apparently intuitively with the correct answer without knowing why. Problem-solvers like these appear to take a holistic view of a given situation. It is as if they become sensitive to the 'feel' of it and then respond with an answer that 'seems right' or 'sounds right'. Instead of breaking up the problem into a logical sequence their reasoning is non-logical and inductive; they make the problem bigger, and allow a number of possible solutions to converge on to it.

Both deductive and inductive problem-solvers are unlikely to be particularly worried if they get the answer wrong; they don't have a great deal of emotional capital invested in the outcome. On the face of it this seems a ridiculous thing to say, because why should anybody be upset if they do not get the right answer to a silly little guessing game? Nevertheless, 'A to B' make a lot of people cross – which is one of the things that makes it a good game – because they have based their answer on their own life experience. They know from experience that in real life if they are running late they can run faster and catch up: and they can't understand why this behaviour can't work under the given circumstances.

Closing You can explain until you are blue in the face that nobody can drive 40 miles in one hour if they have already driven for an hour and covered only half the distance. You can prove it by assuming the same average speeds over any distance; but experiential, pragmatic problem-solvers won't believe you.

One woman became so angry that we were thankful to call a temporary halt for lunch, with the promise to clear the matter up afterwards. She was the only person in the class who had continued to reject the right answer and we could not get on with the course until she was satisfied. We were dreading the afternoon session, but when it began the woman nobly asked if she could stand up in front of the whole class. This is what she said: 'I didn't eat any lunch. I've spent the past hour with a pencil and paper, working out this wretched problem by assuming a number of different distances for the journey; and I can't do it. I realize now that no matter what the distance, the journey can't be done. I still don't know why, but I want to tell everybody that I'm sorry I was so rude, and that I accept their answer.'

She became much happier when one of the group members offered the comment that the answer to 'A to B' lies in the relationship between the two average speeds; and that if the travellers were allowed a lower overall average speed, say 30 instead of 40 mph, they could indeed do – at least in theory – what the woman suggested, ie drive faster on the return journey and increase the overall average speed from 20 to 30 mph. Thus the woman was able to say: 'I knew it was a trick!', which left her self-esteem relatively undamaged. People who are fundamentally more concerned with human experience than facts and figures tend to put a low value on numeracy. Hence, their self-respect is undamaged if the solution to a problem is shown to be 'only a matter of figures'.

12 SHIPS OF THE LINE

Time required About 20 minutes.

Aims

- To practise logical thinking
- To practise rhetoric – ie persuasive argument.

Group size From about 5 people to virtually any number.

Environment Classroom, seminar room, conference hall.

Procedure Give the class this problem, to solve any way they like:

Many years ago, at 12.00 noon daily, a ship from the P&O line used to leave Honolulu for Sydney. The journey used to take seven days. Also in those days, at 12.00 noon daily, a P&O ship used to leave Sydney for Honolulu. The course was the same, the journey also took seven days, and all times were GMT. Once I boarded one of these ships at Honolulu, bound for Sydney. How many P&O ships did I see on my journey?

Evaluation It really doesn't matter what the 'right' answer is to this problem, because in attempting to solve it the discussion will range far and wide, to cover the International Date Line; whether the traveller is standing on the port or starboard side of the ship, and so on.

Closing We have found it an advantage sometimes not to know the answer to a puzzle. It puts all the onus of responsibility on the students. After a moment or two of outrage that they have been offered a puzzle without a short-cut to the answer (ie by waiting passively for the 'teacher' to tell them), a few people will start tackling the problem in real earnest and come up with a solution that everybody can usually be persuaded to accept – which is a good example of leadership style.

13 HARRY'S DOG

(Based on a less-detailed version of this game, called 'John's Dog', in Pfeiffer and Jones, 1975.)

Time required About 20-30 minutes.

Aims

- To demonstrate how the perception of a problem will prestructure people's attempts at a solution.
- To serve as a motivating warm-up for young learners studying mathematics or budgeting and finance.

Group size From about 5 people to virtually any number, in small groups.

Environment A classroom set up café-style so small groups can work together; or any setting where people can be grouped into small work teams.

Procedure

(1) Recount the following story to the whole class: Harry had a small fluffy dog of which he was very fond. His girlfriend liked the dog too. When she offered to buy it from Harry for £10, which was all she could afford, he felt that she had to have it. However, he missed the animal so badly that he gave his girlfriend £20 the next day and took the dog home. His friend, whose name was Mary, still wanted the dog, so she saved up another £10 and offered Harry £30. Poor Harry did not like to refuse so he let her have the dog and took the £30. But by this time he was feeling fed up with the whole business, so after a couple of days he went to see Mary, gave her £40, and asked for his dog; which is the end of the story.

(2) If requested, recapitulate the main points of the story. Then ask these questions:
- Did anybody finally make a profit out of these transactions?
- If so, who and how much?

(3) Ask everybody to write down their answers without revealing them to each other.

(4) When they have had a few moments to think about it, ask people at random to read out what they have written. You will find that others volunteer their answers as soon as they realize how differently they have perceived the problem.

Evaluation Some people will reply that Mary made a profit of £20, which is the right answer if the question is interpreted as a simple matter of economics, of profit and loss. They add up the total income and outgoings of one of the characters and subtract one from the other. Mary's income was £60 and her expenditure was £40. Therefore, since she made a profit of £20, Harry incurred a loss of the same amount. Some people have difficulty with this transition and you may have to post the income and expenditure of both characters.

It is quite likely that some people will say to each other: 'Here, you be Harry, I'll be Mary, and you be the dog!' Then the dog will trot meekly from one to the other, while they solemnly exchange torn-up pieces of paper for money; then when the play is over, they count the pieces to find out who has got more. Some people will get the answer wrong, but that is because they have made a mistake in their arithmetic, not because they have perceived the problem differently from those who got it right.

However, there are usually some others in the group who have been motivated to find answers that are different in kind. They will reply that Harry's profit was that he kept the dog; or that his loss was that he lost his girlfriend; or that the girlfriend was the greater loser because she lost both the dog and – they presume – Harry; or that everybody won because it could reasonably be assumed that Harry, Mary and the dog lived together; or that the dog was the ultimate loser because it had a nervous breakdown.

Closing Initiate a discussion about differences in perception of the problem. Those who 'heard' the story as one of profit and loss treated it as a zero-sum calculation. Those who reasoned like accountants thought in terms of profit and loss. But participants who experienced the emotional content of the story perceived the ending in terms of human relationships.

Point out to everybody that you deliberately told the story from the 'human angle' in order to provoke this range of response; and add that leadership in management consists partly of doing exactly that: of presenting facts and figures in terms of the kind of behaviour they expect of their followers.

Harry's Dog is an example of how you can take a very basic activity like a straightforward mathematical puzzle and dress it up dramatically to provide a real experience for the participants in learning how to learn.

14 THE SHOE SALESWOMAN

Time required About 20 minutes.

Aims to illustrate:

- a variety of problem-solving styles;
- that people solve problems according to their personalities;
- that there is no 'one right way' to solve a problem.

Group size Any number that you can cope with, from about 5 people.

Environment The classroom.

Procedure

(1) Recount the following story:

A customer goes into a shoe shop and buys a pair of shoes that have been marked down in a sale to £12. He pays for the shoes with a £20 note. The sales assistant does not have change at that early hour of the morning, so she asks him to wait, and runs next door to the Italian greengrocer, who changes the note for her. The assistant then returns to her customer and gives him £8 change; he leaves the store with the shoes. Later in the day, the greengrocer comes to see her, very upset. He has spotted the £20 is counterfeit, and has informed the police, who will visit her shortly. The poor woman feels very bad about this, apologizes to the greengrocer for all the trouble she has unwittingly caused, takes £20 out of her till to reimburse him, and prepares herself for the arrival of the police.

(2) Ask the question: how much actual cash is she out of pocket now? (You are not talking about the stock value of the shoes.)

(3) Ask everybody to write down the answer but to keep quiet about it. Alternatively you can form small groups to discuss the problem.

(4) After a few moments, call a plenary session to compare answers. Post all answers to facilitate discussion.

Evaluation Of course people work out the answer differently, some in their heads, some on paper, while others suspect some kind of a trick and waste their time looking for it. The simplest explanation is probably to point out that the answer is £8, because the counterfeit note was only a worthless piece of paper and does not count. The saleswoman received £20 from the greengrocer which she returned later, therefore all she has lost is the £8 change she gave the customer.

However, as with Harry's Dog, when you dramatize these puzzles in the telling you increase the likelihood that some players will act out the problem physically in order to 'see' the answer for themselves. With The Shoe Saleswoman some people will use 'real' money, in the form of paper, to work it out. In fact, we have known people to use their own money from their wallets, laying it out on the table in front of them and apportioning the various sums to designated players. You may not always evoke such a variety of responses, but it is fairly safe to predict that there will be a range of replies; and you can draw this to the attention of the class.

Closing As with Harry's Dog, this activity provides an illustration of some of the differences between experiential and abstract problem-solving styles, and you can point to the advantages and disadvantages of both: for example, that dramatization is slower, if you are looking for a particular kind of answer – ie mathematical – but richer if you are looking at human behaviour and personal interaction.

15 THE PRINCESS AND THE PEASANT

Time required About 20 minutes.

Aim To encourage people to start thinking creatively.

Group size From about 5 – 15 people.

Environment The classroom. You will need one copy of the story for all participants.

Procedure

(1) Tell the story of The Princess and the Peasant (see below).
(2) Give a copy of the story to each participant, and let everybody talk about the problem for as long as they want – which probably will be about 5 – 10 minutes.
(3) Offer your solution to the puzzle, but if anybody comes up with a different solution, so much the better.

Evaluation Your answer is that the peasant drew a card and without looking at it, tore it up, ate it, and said: 'Let the king draw the other card so that I may learn my fate at his hands. If he draws "marriage" I will know my card was "death" and I will accept my fate. But if the king's card reads "death" I will know my card was "marriage" and I will be free to wed the princess.'

Closing Participants often offer solutions that entail the kind of trickery the king demonstrated. For example they will say that the peasant bribed the person who put the cards in the basket; or that he told the princess to substitute 'marriage' for 'death' on the cards. One participant suggested to us that the story was an old French tale; and that the queen persuaded the king to write the letter 'm' on the cards for 'mort' (death); and the king was too stupid to remember that 'm' also stands for marriage.

It really doesn't matter what suggestions people make. The only object of the activity is to shake their brains up a little.

HANDOUT
The Princess and the Peasant

A peasant wanted to marry a princess. Her father, the king, was furious and ordered that the peasant should have his head cut off for impertinence.

But the peasant was handsome, and the queen was sentimental and wanted her daughter to be happy; so she persuaded the king to give the peasant a sporting chance.

It was agreed that he should draw one of two cards out of a box and accept what was written on it as his fate. One card would say 'marriage' and the other 'death'. If he refused to draw, he would die. However, the king cheated and marked both cards 'death', and put them in the box.

The queen saw this and rushed off to tell the princess, who was able to warn her lover of the impossible dilemma and the dreadful peril he faced. But when the time came, the peasant appeared unafraid. He drew a card – and married the princess and lived happily ever after. The king was so furious he died of a stroke and the queen inherited the realm.

How did the peasant manage to avoid the trap set by the wicked king?

16 THINK OF A CUBE

Time required About 15 minutes.

Aim To evoke creative thinking.

Group size About 5 – 15 people; but you can run this activity with virtually any number.

Environment The classroom.

Procedure

(1) Ask everybody to sit in a comfortable and relaxed position. You can do a short relaxation exercise first, if you think the group will benefit from it, such as deep breathing or bending and stretching.

(2) When everybody is quiet and still, you assume the mantle of a storyteller and say, with suitable emphases and pauses:
  - 'Imagine a cube …whatever comes into your mind that is in the shape of a cube …'
  - 'Now separate the cube into two …'
  - 'Now separate each of the two pieces of your cube into two …'
  - 'Now get rid of them and see what you're left with.'

(3) Ask these questions:
  - 'Did you picture a real or an abstract cube (eg a piece of sugar or a shape in the space)?'
  - 'Do you know what it looked like, felt like, tasted like?'
  - 'What colour was it?'
  - 'How big was it?'
  - 'Where was it? Was the setting clearly defined?'
  - 'Were you there with the cube, wherever it was?'
  - 'Was anybody else there?'

(4) Repeat the exercise. Ask everybody again to imagine a cube. Take them through the actions described in 2 above.

(5) The next set of questions relates to dividing the cube:
  - 'Did you divide it or did it divide itself?'
  - 'Did anybody help you?'
  - 'Did you use a tool?'
  - 'Did you hear anything?'
  - 'Did you get your hands dirty or sticky?'

- 'Did it divide cleanly or was there a mess?'
- 'Were the two pieces equal in size?'
- 'When there were four pieces, were they all cubes?'
- 'Were they all alike? Were they very small?'

(6) Repeat step 2.

(7) Ask how people made their cubes disappear: 'How did you get rid of it? Did it just disappear, like an animated cartoon? Did you eat it? Throw it away? Give it away? Wish it away?'

Evaluation As they repeat the exercise people's imaginations begin to stretch and they will improvise details. We remember a woman describing in minute detail how in her mind she was in her kitchen and there was a lump of sugar in front of her on the wooden chopping block. She went to cut it with a knife but she cut her finger and got distracted by the blood, a drop of which fell on to the sugar. She became fascinated by the contrast of red on white. When she had to cut the sugar again, she tried to cut it in such a way that there was a tiny speck of blood on each piece. There were too many for her to count – lots and lots of tiny cubes of sugar all over the block, all touched with one drop of blood. She did not know how to get rid of them all; the vision had become stressful. She found herself thinking, 'If I don't get rid of them, if I just walk out, I shall be frightened to go back into the kitchen'. So she shovelled them all up with her hands into a plastic bag and then tipped them out into the garden for the birds to eat.

Closing It seems odd at first, perhaps, that this woman should report she had enjoyed the experience. It may be that adults are not given enough opportunity in everday life to exercise their imagination and that a game like Think of a Cube fills a gap. However, when you get feedback as strong as this from a warm-up or trigger game, you know you have got at least one participant in your group whose imagination will run way ahead of you. That is great, but if her learning style is not balanced by the styles of other participants who are more theoretical or abstract in their responses, you will have to make those responses yourself.

With luck, you will find some players who have dreamed up cubes that are shapes in the air, that divide themselves like computer graphics, that vanish without fuss and without trace. Note also that some people are more visual than others, while others are more sound-oriented. (Some participants in Think of a Cube will tell you that they heard it break; others will express astonishment at this concept.)

These kinds of feedback will help you to structure group discussions so that the participants hear more than one viewpoint. This will enable students to develop a multidimensional view of a problem and its solution, rather than seek one right answer.

17 TEST WITH A MORAL

Time required About 15 minutes.

Aim To help participants look beyond the apparently obvious.

Group size Small groups, say of 5 – 7 participants.

Environment The classroom. Prepare one copy of Test with a Moral (on p. 116) for each participant.

Procedure Distribute a copy of Test with a Moral, one per participant. Ask them to complete it; and wait for their reactions.

Evaluation We are sorry to have to report that many adults and most of the young people to whom we have administered this test get at least halfway down the list, and usually further, before they become at all suspicious. The majority of players aged around 11 to 13 take it all quite seriously. They assume that the questions are designed to test their ability to follow instructions, to write and draw neatly, and to recognize simple geometric terms like 'triangle'. The test does not strike them, at first, as being very different from many 'class tests' they have had to endure in the past – which we think is an indictment of such tests. Some players complain that they have been tricked when they complete Test with a Moral without reading it first. On the other hand some people report they are glad they didn't read it because they enjoyed doing all the tasks, which they found relaxing in a pleasantly mindless way.

Closing This is an effective exercise for sharpening players' concentration and increasing their motivation for the next activity.

HANDOUT
Test with a moral

Can you follow directions? Try this timed test, allowing yourself three minutes only.

(1) Read everything carefully before doing anything.
(2) Print your name in the upper right-hand corner of this paper.
(3) Circle your name.
(4) Draw five small squares in the upper left-hand corner of this paper.
(5) Put an 'X' in each square.
(6) Sign your name at the top of this paper.
(7) Under your name in the upper right-hand corner, write your telephone number. If you do not have one, write the number 100.
(8) Call out loudly the number you have written, so that everybody can hear you.
(9) Circle this number.
(10) Put an 'X' in the lower left-hand corner of this paper.
(11) Draw a triangle round it.
(12) Count out loud in your normal speaking voice, from 10 to 1 backwards.
(13) Draw a rectangle around the word 'corner' in sentence number 4.
(14) Punch three small holes in the top of this paper, with your pencil or pen point.
(15) Call out loud: 'I am nearly finished'.
(16) Now that you have finished reading everything carefully, do only sentences 1 and 2.

18 GRAPEVINE

Time required About half an hour.

Aim

- To encourage creative thinking about communications systems in organizations.
- To demonstrate flow-patterns of communication, and where delays and bottlenecks can build up.
- To illustrate how people can increase their learning capacity, and their pleasure in learning, by exchanging information effectively.

Group size Grapevine is played in two rounds, with teams of 6 people. It is a competitive game, so you will need at least 12 players, and if there are any observers left over, so much the better. They can change places with team-members in Round 2.

Environment The classroom, with plenty of space for players to sit in circles of 6. Provide yourself with:

- stopwatch;
- pack of playing cards;
- pen or pencil for each player;
- adhesive labels to stick on players' foreheads, stating whether they are A, B, C, D, E or R (which stands for Runner);
- masses of paper for them to write on.

You can cut up sheets of paper into smaller squares to prevent waste.

Procedure
(1) For Round 1, put each team into a circle. All the circles should be as large as possible, so use the whole space of the room. Each circle consists of 5 team-members, preferably sitting on the floor, each person facing outwards from the circle. The sixth member of each team stands or sits in the middle of his or her circle.
(2) Label the foreheads of the people in each circle A, B, C, D and E, respectively.

(3) Give these 5 team members in each team a playing card per person and ask them not to let anybody else see what it is.

(4) The sixth person in each team's circle, the one in the middle, is labelled R. These players are the Runners who have to run messages for their respective teams.

(5) The object of the game is that every player must complete a list naming the card each person in the circle holds. The rules are:
- No talking is allowed.
- Information has to be shared by written notes, which are carried by the Runner.
- Everybody in any one circle can communicate with their Runner, and with the person on either side of them in the circle. Thus A can communicate with B and E; B with A and C; C with B and D; D with C and E; and E with D and A. For example, player A may write a note addressed to B, asking: 'What card is C holding?' A then raises his or her hand, the Runner comes over, checks that there is only one question on the note, then takes and delivers it to B.
- If any team-member talks, the whole team is penalized by having 30 seconds added to its time.
- If a team-member is caught cheating by showing his or her card to another player or players, the team is disqualified.
- As soon as team-members have received the replies that they need to complete their lists, they stand up (though they can continue to receive and send notes from and to their neighbours who have not yet finished).

(6) When all of the team members in a circle are standing, the Runner collects the five lists and brings them to you, who have been timing the round with a stopwatch.

(7) The winner is the team whose runner is the first to reach you with the five complete and correct lists.

(8) When Round 1 is over, Round 2 begins. The players are labelled and seated in circles as for Round 1. The objective is the same – ie all 5 team-members shall know what card each of them holds – but now team-members can communicate only with the Runner and one other player in the circle (we usually designate C to be this person, for no real reason). Again the players can send only one note and one question at a time, but now all their questions are directed to C. They raise their hands when they want the Runner, and stand up when they have received enough

information from C to inform them of the card each of their 4 team-mates holds.

Evaluation Theoretically, the time taken to complete Round 1 should be shorter than for Round 2, because in Round 1 more people can communicate with each other directly, and in practice this is usually the case.

However, several factors can complicate the issue and Round 2 is sometimes shorter – for example, if the sole information disseminator (player C) is quick and accurate, the Runner is fast, and the other 4 players have organized their questions effectively and have their notes ready for the runner. Also they have the advantage that they have already played Round 1, so if they are quick learners their working speed will have increased.

These are all observations that you can share with the players when the game is over; you can also help them to relate these observations to the basics of organizational (ie group) communication.

Closing Grapevine often has the effect of increasing group cohesiveness and individuals' sense of commitment to their team. Initiate a discussion about the unique quality of individual contributions to the group by drawing real-life parallels from the game – the ability of one person to collate information from a number of sources, for instance, or the speed and accuracy of another.

Chapter 9

Youth leadership activities (also effective with adults!)

19 THE EGG ADOPTION PROJECT

We adapted this game from an original by Dave Wheeler, who ran it as a student assignment for a course in Child Care General Studies in Australia. We have also heard of it being played in a guidance class with 16 to 17-year-olds in a private school in Honolulu, which makes it an international exercise.

Time required One week.

Aims

- For youth leadership training, to evoke discussion of the problems and commitments of single parenthood, or parenthood in general.
- To simulate some of the responsibilities in caring for people, children, pets, or any living thing that cannot take care of itself.

Group size Any number.

Environment The scenario is that each student in the group adopts one raw egg and keeps it safe and well for one whole week. The 'parents' have to keep a daily diary describing their experiences, itemize and account for any financial outgoings in connection with the adopted egg, and complete a questionnaire at the end of the experience.

Procedure Give each youngster a raw egg at the beginning of the week with the following instructions.

(1) The egg must be kept comfortable – neither too warm nor too cold.

(2) It must be kept safe and healthy by being given plenty of fresh air, sunshine, and exercise in safe surroundings where it cannot be damaged.

(3) It must be kept neat and clean with regular washing.

(4) It must not be deprived of human companionship. Either the 'parent' or a competent surrogate must be with it at all times during its waking hours.

(5) It must have access at reasonable intervals to a stimulating environment. It must be talked to, and taken on outings. It can be carried in a pocket, providing it has enough air and its comfort is checked regularly.

(6) While the 'parent' is sleeping, the egg should be kept close by, preferably within sight.

(7) If the responsibilities of 'parenthood' become too great, the 'parent' may hire an egg-sitter for 50 pence an hour and this expense must be noted in the diary. (Dave Wheeler's suggestion is that at the end of the week all such money should be collected and donated to charity.)

(8) If disaster should occur and an egg be lost or broken, the 'parent' must pay the funeral costs of £2 and observe a period of mourning of not less than two days. After this period another egg may be obtained.

Evaluation The questionnaire asks the name and age of the 'parent' and is to be completed at the end of the week. The respondent has to answer questions such as:

- Which period in the week was the most difficult and why?
- Which was the easiest and why?
- How did other people react to your becoming an egg parent?
- Why do you think they reacted this way?
- How many hours during the week did you spend with your egg in your physical possession?
- How many hours with your egg outdoors?
- How many hours without your egg in your care?
- What was the total cost incurred by you on behalf of your egg?
- Did your feelings about your egg change during the week?

- Describe any such change.
- Has this exercise altered your feelings about the responsibilities of parenthood?
- What similarities do you think there are between the demands made on you to care for your egg and the responsibilities of having a real child?
- What additional demands would a child make on you?
- What rewards did you find in caring for your egg?
- At what age do you think you would like to start your family?
- How many children do you think you would like to have?
- Are there any further comments you would like to add?

Closing Anecdotes about The Egg Adoption Project include those of 'parents' who painted faces on their eggs, gave them names, took them into the shower with them, made clothes for them, and bought them toys. There is the story of the parent who broke her egg and was too upset to go to school for two days; and the tale of the egg 'father' who made his real-life sister take care of his egg because he said it was more her job than his – even though his little sister had nothing to do with the project. Both boys and girls have reported that by about the fifth day of the experiment, they became really 'irritated' by the responsibility of caring for their eggs. It ceased to be fun and became a burden, even though the actual work was slight. On the other hand, egg 'mothers' sometimes report a real fear of becoming too attached to their eggs, so they make conscious decisions to view the whole experiment very pragmatically.

In this connection, it is interesting to note that a leading American paediatrician, Dr Berry Brazelton, suggests that when mothers know that they will have to separate early from their infants because they have to return to work, they deliberately withhold emotion from the child. Brazelton goes on to argue that therefore a necessary bonding process is not completed and the affected children may suffer permanent emotional damage which can affect all their relationships.

This is an idea to discuss with participants in The Egg Adoption Project because the position of married women in the workforce is constantly under threat in industrialized societies, particularly in times of economic recession. Arguments such as those of Brazelton should be evaluated within a socio-political context where there are vested interests in discouraging women with children from entering or re-entering the workforce. Making working mothers feel guilty for seeking child-care, rather than staying at home full time, can be a powerful and insidious form of social blackmail. The Egg Adoption Project can demonstrate how strong these pressures are.

20 GENE SCENE

Time required This activity should be run over two school periods, ie about 80 minutes, allowing for a break. It is not a good idea to play it in two separate class periods with other lessons in between.

Aims

- To illustrate some aspects of human genetic inheritance.
- To demonstrate the chance factor in genetic inheritance.
- To suggest the twin notions of dominant and recessive genes.
- To indicate possible results of combining dominant with recessive genes.
- To indicate some degree of inevitability in the inheritance of certain individual physical characteristics.
- To illustrate the discreteness of some genetic characteristics.
- To provide facility in working out some possible genetic combinations, which includes practice in elementary mathematical skills.
- To provide an example of a teaching method, particularly for school students who have problems with absorbing and retaining abstract information when it is presented via a traditional teaching method. Such students – who can become quite aggressive through sheer frustration if they cannot grasp the subject-matter – are often encouraged when they discover that a different teaching style can improve their motivation and concentration. This realization should relieve them of some pressure to 'perform' as model students by helping teachers to present material in ways students may find easier to relate to and learn from.

Group size About 8 – 40 participants: ideally about 16 – 24 students.

Environment

(1) This activity was designed for science teachers and teacher-trainers.
(2) The room must be large enough for the players to move around freely, preferably unimpeded by tables or desks, which should be either absent completely or pushed back against the walls.
(3) There should be a clear space in the middle to set up as many chairs as there are players, less two. The chairs are arranged as for the game of 'Musical Chairs', ie in a line down the middle of

the room, the chairs alternately facing one way and then the other.

(4) Prepare one copy per participant of the instructions described on page 127.

Mendel seems to have been somewhat discredited by modern geneticists, and we hope the content of these instructions will not outrage your views on genetic inheritance. The last time we played Gene Scene with a group of science teachers it was well received, but if you disagree with our suggestions below, you will of course prepare your own instructions. Any such changes should not affect the general objectives of the activity.

(5) Provide sticky labels that will adhere to players' clothing or foreheads.

(6) Provide a cassette player and a cassette of any music with a good, strong beat – but bear in mind that young people have strong likes and dislikes about music! If you are not *au fait* with the latest popular tunes, do some homework!

(7) The players will all need writing materials.

Procedure

(1) Divide the players into two groups, those with blue eyes and those with brown.

If most of the players have blue eyes, or brown, because of a shared ethnic background, divide them into groups of people who respectively can and cannot roll their tongues; or those who have curly hair and those whose hair is straight. Other possible genetic characteristics for Gene Scene players include the possession or not of earlobes; and the respective length of their toes. (Our examples refer to the possession of blue or brown eyes. If you want to use different examples, you will have to re-write the instructions.)

(2) Divide these groups into small working parties of about 3 – 5 people.

(3) Give each person a copy of the 'genetic instructions' on p. 127.

(4) When all participants have had time to read the instructions and you have answered their questions, give each person a sticky label and ask them to indicate their genetic inheritance by following the instructions.

(5) Set up a game of Musical Chairs, which you announce as Musical Genes. All participants move round the line of chairs in

time to the music and when you stop it they have to sit down on the nearest empty chair. There is always a certain amount of pushing and shoving at this point, which is all to the good. One reason why this game usually seems to be effective is that it alternates bursts of noisy physical group activity with short periods of concentration.

(6) Two people will be left without chairs; they stand in front of the line and become the focus of a brief general discussion about the eye colours of their parents. If these two people were man and woman and had a baby, what colour eyes might the baby have? Why?

(7) Remove two chairs from the line and restart the music for the next round of the game. Let the remaining players race around the chairs for a few moments before stopping the music to find another pair of blue or brown-eyed players. Initiate another short discussion, then remove two more chairs, restart the music and continue the game until there is one winner.

Evaluation Initiate a short discussion about the attributes and characteristics of people that they cannot change, like having blue or brown eyes; and those they have the power to develop or change as they will.

Closing When the game is over you may want to introduce the topic of racial prejudice based on the colour of people's eyes or skin or the shape of their noses.

HANDOUT
Gene Scene – Instructions

The eye colour **brown** is from a dominant gene.

The eye colour **blue** is from a **recessive** gene.

You have inherited 50 per cent of your genes (half of them) from your mother and 50 per cent from your father.

If you have **blue** eyes, this is because your inherited genes for eye colour **from both parents** are **blue**.

Therefore write 'bb' on your label (b=blue).

If you have **brown** eyes, **at least one** of your inherited genes for eye colour **from at least one of your parents** must be **brown**.

Your symbol, therefore, will be either 'BB' (B=brown) or 'bB'.

You do not know which it is, but for the purpose of the game you can choose to write either.

When you have written either 'bb' or 'BB' or 'bB' on your label in large letters, stick it on to your forehead so every-body can see it.

21 INTERSECTING CIRCLES

Time required One school period: about 40 minutes.

Aims

- To follow Activity 20.
- To enhance self-esteem in the players.
- To start players thinking about the relative importance of people around them to influence their lives.
- To start players thinking about the need for self-direction and leadership, to avoid the passive acceptance of other people's demands and influences.

Group size From 5 to 35 students.

Environment The classroom.

Procedure

(1) If the class is larger than about 7 students, divide them into groups of 5 – 7.

(2) Initiate a short discussion of the questions: 'Are you most like your mother? Or your father? Or are you just yourself?' Encourage students to debate whether they think their personalities are mostly derived from their genetic inheritance or more influenced by other factors, such as life experience, environment, the influence of friends and teachers, and so on.

(3) Ask all players to draw a circle which represents themselves.

(4) Now ask them to draw a circle which represents their mother, intersecting with their own circle in any way they like – or not at all.

(5) Then a third circle, to represent their father, which also intersects with their personal circle in any way they think appropriate, or not at all (and they may choose to intersect the circles representing their mother and father as well).

(6) Finally ask everybody to draw any other circles, in any relationship they please to the others. These circles should represent the influence of other people whom they feel have shaped their personalities – such as siblings or other relatives, friends and so on.

Evaluation Offer the suggestion that these intersecting circles represent what the artists feel about their own identity within these illustrated relationships. Ask any volunteers to share with the group their reasons for drawing their circles the way they did.

Closing Don't press for answers.

22 DOWN IT GOES!

Time required Construction will take about an hour, and then a couple of practice runs are needed until all the parts of the machine understand what they have to do. You should allow two classroom periods, back to back.

Aims This is another game (like Gene Scene) suitable for a biology or natural science class.

Its aims are:

- To illustrate the process of digestion in the human body.
- To promote teamwork.

Group size Any large groups of students, minimum about 20.

Environment The classroom. Prepare the following chart, to be posted at the beginning of the activity.

- *Food is chewed; passed down a long coil of gut; mixed with enzymes.*
- *Enzymes break up food.*
- *Food is moved along by muscle action.*
- *Soluble food is absorbed into walls of small intestine; is taken by blood to liver and stored; is taken by blood to other cells for energy.*
- *Insoluble food is passed through large intestine and out of the anus.*
- *Energy is released.*

Procedure

(1) (Optional) You may like to do a warm-up with the group before you start, since the 'body machine' the players are going to build will demand close cooperation between its living parts. For example, you could ask the players to stand in a close circle (or several circles if group numbers are large) and then ask a volunteer to stand in the middle, close his or her eyes, fall backwards and allow him or herself to be caught by members of the circle. Curiously enough, in view of the temperament of some of the young people we have worked with, we have never known anybody to get hurt during this warm-up. Nobody in our experience has ever been allowed by the circle to fall to the ground, though they have not always been handled very gently in the

process of being saved. If you have any doubts at all, remind yourself that if you were not a risk-taker you would not be a game leader, stand yourself in the middle of the circle, shut your eyes, and fall backwards.

(2) When you feel ready to begin Down it Goes! divide the players into groups of at least 20 people each.

(3) Tell everybody that they are going to build a body machine that will simulate the process of digestion in the human body, and assign the following roles to individual players:

- Fresh air (one or more roles, depending on numbers).
- Food (four roles).
- Jaws (two roles).
- Gut (at least five roles).
- Enzymes (two roles).
- Enzymes with villae, ie waving, whisker-like hairs (two roles).
- The division between the large and small intestine (one role).
- The liver (one role).
- If you have more players than you need, the remainder can form more 'gut' or they may prefer to stay outside the body machine, walking or running round it to represent the circulating fresh air.

(4) Two lines of players stand opposite each other to represent the two sides of the digestive tract. Each person in the line represents a part of the human body that is concerned in some way with the process of digestion, ie the jaws, the length of the gut (the alimentary canal), enzymes with and without villae, the division between the large and small intestine, the liver and the the anus. The passageway between the two parallel lines – the tract itself – is blocked in the middle by a player representing the division between the large and small intestine.

In diagram form, the body machine assembles itself as shown overleaf (remember each body part, body division and food state are represented by one person standing in the relevant position in the line).

(4 food mouthfuls enter here)

Jaw	Jaw
Gut	Gut
Gut	Gut
Enzyme	Enzyme

Division

(2 mouthfuls go to one side of the passageway, 2 the other)

Villae	Villae

(2 mouthfuls remain here, one standing each side of the passageway – they are digested food; the other two are pushed on down the
passage and out of the anus)

Liver	Gut
Anus	Anus

(2 mouthfuls, now waste products, exit here)

(5) The 4 'mouthfuls of food', one after the other, enter the passage
between the 'jaws', who push them (gently!) into two pairs, and
on into the 'alimentary canal'. The 4 players who line the canal
as part of the 'gut' continue this rhythmic pushing action until
the two pairs of 'food pieces' reach the 'enzymes', who separate
the pairs into single units. This brings the food pieces, one at a
time, to the 'division between the large and small intestine'. The
player who represents the 'division' pushes the 4 food pieces
into position as follows:

- Two of them are passed right down the passage and out through
'the anus', where they join the 'fresh air'.
- The other two merge into the 'gut wall' of the 'small intestine',
where the 'villae' extend their arms to receive them (one ends
up standing beside a 'gut' player in the line and the other beside
the 'liver' – see the above diagram).

In real life, when digested food and air meet in the bloodstream,
energy is released. Therefore, when all the food particles have
been assigned to their proper places, the whole body machine
should start to jump up and down and shout.

Evaluation The whole sequence of events is complicated; it has to be worked out first in slow motion with explanations and discussions at each stage of construction of the body machine.

Construction will take about an hour, and then a couple of practice runs are needed until all the parts of the machine understand what they have to do.

Closing

If the final performance is sufficiently synchronized, it can be performed to music, but we cannot guarantee you will get that far with your group. However, the activity is an effective learning exercise not only for its content but also for the encouragement it gives players to work together in harmony. They are able to see themselves as individuals, each of whom plays a unique and vital role in a problem-solving exercise that demands concentration but provides a stimulating activity that justifies the effort.

Players seem to find it informative and entertaining, though many are quite slow to 'catch on' to the concept of using people to make a living model. Down it Goes! is also a useful exercise for trainee teachers, both as an example of a learning game for young players, and an illustration of how to make factual, scientific information easily 'digestible'!

23 FIT OR FAT?

Time required One class period, about 40 minutes.

Aims

- To promote self-esteem.
- To encourage people to believe they can take control over many aspects of their own lives.
- To promote self-management.
- To demonstrate that different people use foods in different ways, depending on their bodies' specific needs.
- To emphasize that the various food elements are used by the human body in different ways for different needs.
- To encourage good general eating and keep-fit habits.

Group size Virtually any number, from about 8 players.

Environment The classroom. You will need to provide the following:

- a chair for each player;
- a pair of dice (with a cup to shake them in);
- a packet of balloons;
- a skipping rope;
- a glass of water;
- a stand-on weighing scale;
- a set of written forfeit cards, as detailed below.

Forfeits

- You are too thin; you need more fat in your diet. Miss a turn to blow up a balloon.
- You ate a take-away hamburger before dinner. Now you have indigestion. Miss a turn and drink a glass of water.
- You have been ill. Miss a turn and weigh yourself.
- Weigh yourself. If you are the right weight for your age and height, advance to the next vacant chair.
- You are too fat. Miss a turn while skipping.
- You feel the cold too much; you lack energy. Miss a turn and run right round the circle.
- You lack muscle. Miss a turn and jog round the circle.
- What is a calorie? Miss a turn if you cannot answer. (The answer is on the back of the card; a calorie is a measure of energy or heat.)

- What foods contain protein? Miss a turn if you cannot answer. (The answer is on the back of the card: meat, fish, eggs, cheese, grains and nuts.)
- Why do you need carbohydrate in your diet? Miss a turn if you cannot answer. (The answer is on the back of the card: for energy, body warmth, movement, growth, and cellulose for roughage.)
- How do you prepare food without using much fat? Miss a turn if you cannot answer. (The answer is on the back of the card: by boiling or steaming, cooking in a microwave or baking in an oven without fat.)
- Name two diseases associated with overweight. Miss a turn if you cannot answer. (The answer is on the back of the card: high blood pressure, diabetes, cancer, liver disease, gall bladder disease, clots in the blood vessels of the brain.)

Procedure Fit or Fat? is played on the same principle as snakes and ladders, in which players advance over a measured distance according to throws of the dice. If they land on a snake they lose ground and if they arrive at the foot of a ladder they move up.

(1) Set up as large a square of chairs as possible, all round the walls, one chair for every player, all facing inwards to the room. If you have a lot of players (and therefore a lot of chairs), you can line the chairs up in the shape of a 'Z', zig-zagging down the room. In fact, you can set up any arrangement of chairs you like, bearing in mind that players are going to have to move up and down the line.

(2) Divide the players into two groups of the same size. One group should seat themselves on every alternate chair. Each of these seated players is given one or more forfeit cards to hold (you can invent as many forfeits as you like). All of the chairs represent squares on a game board and the seated people are the 'snakes' and 'ladders'.

(3) The game players all start at the same point and take turns throwing the dice. The first player to throw a six begins the game by throwing again, then walking down the line of chairs, or round the circle as the case may be, counting chairs to the number shown on the dice. If this player lands on an empty chair, he or she sits on it. If they land on a seated player then this 'snake' or 'ladder' reads aloud his or her forfeit, which the

player who landed on this 'square' has to perform before the next player can throw the dice and take a turn. If the snake or ladder holds more than one forfeit card, the game player can choose one at random. The first game player to complete the line or circle is the winner of that round.

(4) In Round 2 the game players change places with the snakes and ladders. You can play as many rounds as you have time for, or the players have patience for.

Evaluation One way of evaluating the learning potential of Fit or Fat? is to distribute a questionnaire to all the participants, about a week afterwards, rewording the forfeits as questions and leaving a space at the end for any comments respondents may care to make about playing the game.

Closing Since you have not done any pre-testing, you will not really know how much new information was acquired by the players from the game but you will get some idea of the kind of learning they have absorbed if you study their replies qualitatively as well as quantitatively. For example, you could ask: 'How can you help your body to build more muscle? Give at least one example.' If the respondent replies: 'Jogging' it is probably reasonable to assume they learned that from the game, and you may be able to check on this personally with the individual student.

24 TEACHERS AND LEARNERS

Time required One class period, about 40 minutes, longer if numbers are large.

Aim To promote leadership skills

Group size Virtually any number of people from about 5 participants.

Environment The classroom.

Procedure
(1) Explain to everybody that Teachers and Learners is an activity to demonstrate what is, and what is not, good teaching. It offers students an opportunity to 'get their own back' on their teachers by giving them examples of how to teach. The participants are going to form small teams (or pairs as the case may be) and take it in turns to teach something to the rest of the group.
(2) Form small teams of 2 or 3 people. The exercise can be rather threatening for individuals on their own unless they have a lot of confidence and/or know each other really well.
(3) Give teams 5-10 minutes for their respective members to get into a huddle and decide what they want to teach.
(4) Get everybody together again, and invite the first team (the order of precedence is immaterial) to begin a 3-5 minute instruction to the rest of the group. It may be in the form of a lecture, a demonstration, or an enactment of some kind, depending on what learning method the 'teachers' choose. You may want to take notes for your own reference of each team's presentation.

Evaluation When all teams have finished, conduct an informal, oral 'examination'. Keep the pace brisk. Ask each team, in the order in which they made their presentation, to stand in turn in front of the class. Briefly recapitulate the names of the 'teachers' (unless all participants are well-known to each other), then ask the group what they remember about the subject of each lesson. Give each team a round of applause. Finally, ask everybody to vote in turn for the team they think was the most effective as a teaching unit. You will probably find that the group is very clear about which they think were the most easily remembered and popular subjects and/or teachers.

We have learned a lot from participants in Teachers and Learners: how to choose wine, the quickest way on foot from the university to the bus station, what to do if someone faints in the street, and many other useful things. We have also been the victim of some clever jokes – such as when we were informed most seriously of a secret code that dairy farmers put on milk cartons to identify the herd of cows the milk came from.

If you want to use this exercise with real-life teachers or trainee teachers you can initiate a general discussion (without getting too personal) about why some teaching behaviours appear to be more effective than others. Start participants thinking about the concept of 'teacher as leader'. You may find that some teachers already agree with this concept, some greet it as a new but welcome idea, and some dispute it on ideological grounds. If you do get the third type of reaction, offer instead the suggestion that teachers are managers – which may also come as a new idea to some, but which in general seems more acceptable to those of the 'teachers are facilitators' school of thought.

Whoever your participants are, give them examples from your observation of their respective performances of some critical factors which make for more- or less-effective management/leadership. For instance:

- *Personal presentation*: We remember one 'teacher' (in real life an analytical chemist) whose sheer charm and persuasiveness resulted in us all sampling a 'cocktail' before he told us how he had made it.
- *Quality of information*: This relates to the leaders' ability to impress people with the quality and amount of their knowledge and experience in a particular area. In Teachers and Learners you will find that there is always at least one 'teacher' who so obviously knows what he or she is talking about that everbody listens attentively, no matter what the subject.
- *Ability to motivate people to listen and learn*: We remember a 'teacher' who taught us all how to make a very complicated paper aeroplane. In real life, she was employed by a large bank as an instructor in the use of computers but she had been trained originally as a primary school teacher. The quality of her instruction and her ability to judge when an individual needed special attention were superb. She made the exercise not only

instructive (everybody could make the aeroplane after 5 minutes' practice) but thoroughly entertaining.

Closing If you want to play this game, don't forget to time each team of teachers carefully. You may have to interrupt them sometimes, though often they are so interesting that this is really frustrating. We are usually impressed by participants' ability to choose appropriate material and manage it within the tight time constraint. But if you find that some people have trouble with timing their lessons, you might want to mention the importance of time-management in your summing-up.

25 BEHAVE YOURSELF

Time required One class period, about 40 minutes.

Aims

- To study non-verbal behaviour and gain experience in interpreting it.
- To gain experience in negotiation, or persuasive behaviour, verbally and non-verbally.

Group size Any number from 2 people up.

Environment The classroom. Prepare in advance several sets of instructions. Here are some examples, but you can make up your own if you prefer to do so (eg, if you have some specific teaching purpose for the game):

Set one

Roleplayer A: Start talking to your partner about something that interests you and that you feel confident you can talk about for some time. After 3-4 minutes, or when you feel you have had enough, exchange roles/papers and start again.

Roleplayer B: Say nothing while waiting for your partner to start talking, but look encouraging. When your partner begins to talk, respond in an interested manner. Look at your partner, smile, nod, ask questions, etc, without trying to take over the conversation. After 3-4 minutes, or when you feel you have had enough, exchange roles/papers and start again.

Set two

Roleplayer A: (as for set one)

Roleplayer B: When your partner starts talking to you, look at her or him expressionlessly, as if challenging your partner to interest you. Continue to stare without saying anything. After 3-4 minutes, or when you feel you have had enough, exchange roles/papers with your partner and start again.

Set three

Roleplayer A: (as before)

Roleplayer B: When your partner starts talking, listen for a moment or two, then start fidgeting, crossing and re-crossing your legs, looking at your wristwatch, turning round to see who else is in the room, etc. If your partner stops talking, say, 'Yes, yes, go on!' but continue to appear inattentive. After 3-4 minutes, or when you feel you have had enough, exchange roles/papers and start again.

Set four

Roleplayer A: (as before)

Roleplayer B: Wait until your partner starts talking and then, without actually saying anything, indicate by your movements and expression that you disagree with what your partner is saying. If your partner stops, say something like 'Well, all right, go on!' but continue to appear to disagree. After 3-4 minutes, or when you feel you have had enough, exchange roles/papers and start again.

Set five

Roleplayer A: Talk to your partner about anything that interests you, but do not look directly at your partner at any time. You can look anywhere else you like – round the room, for example – or keep your eyes down. After 3-4 minutes, or when you feel you have had enough, exchange roles/papers and start again.

Roleplayer B: When your partner starts talking to you, respond as encouragingly as you can. Try to get a conversation going about your partner's topic. Ask questions, seek clarification, etc. After 3-4 minutes, or when you feel you have had enough, exchange roles/papers with your partner and start again.

Procedure

(1) Explain that this activity is a roleplay for people to play with each other in pairs and then to report back to the group.
(2) Give one role to each member of each pair of players, asking each one to read the instructions privately and then play their role accordingly. Explain that the instructions are self-explanatory.

(3) Follow the roleplays with a general discussion in which players share the contents of their instruction papers and describe what happened during their respective dialogues.

Evaluation You may find that some people are revealed as such self-absorbed talkers that their listeners virtually have to get up and walk away before the speakers become aware of their boredom and inattention. On the other hand, some people find it really difficult to give these signals because in real life their habit is to continue to present an appearance of interest even if they are bored out of their minds. Not surprisingly, these passive listeners are often women because more women than men are socialized early to be good listeners. However, women can also be very determined talkers.

The talkers usually experience – and later describe – strong negative or positive feelings as a result of the way their listeners respond to them. The listeners report how more or less easy they found it to obey the instructions on their paper, depending on the behaviour of the talkers.

You might like also to discuss the following:

- Human behaviour is a constant phenomenon whether the owners are conscious of it or not.
- People cannot *not* behave.
- People signal messages to each other all the time, even when they think they are doing nothing in particular.
- If people want to be leaders – to influence others – they need to become more aware that their slightest behaviour makes an impression of some kind on those who observe it.

Closing

The above should be enough to give you the general purpose of this exercise, which is one of the very few, if not the only one, in this book not allowing for observer roles as such. This is because it is important that everybody in the group experiences some kind of personal communication interaction.

26 WALK-ON

Time required Two class periods, back-to-back.

Aim To take participants through a learning cycle:

- first they have the *experience* of engaging in a group discussion;
- then they *watch* their own performances in video replay;
- next, they *reflect* on their observations and on the comments of the other viewers, in a supportive environment;
- finally, they *think* about ways to become more effective communicators through verbal and non-verbal behaviour.

Many people find the experience of being videotaped is quite stressful, and some people flatly refuse to allow it at all. Therefore you may find this exercise is not suitable for some groups of young people, or indeed adults, until they feel really comfortable with each other (and you).

Group size About 5 – 15 people.

Environment The classroom, with plenty of space in the middle of the room. At least three chairs, which are easily portable (you may have to provide relatively small, lightweight chairs specially for this activity; we sometimes use stools). Video recording facilities with monitor and playback.

Set up the room with a 'performance area' commanded by a fixed camera – unless you are fortunate enough to have a camera operator, in which case the replay will be more fruitful because there will be close-ups, etc. However, do not take on this role yourself. You need to observe the whole action. Outline the playing area with chalk or by some other means.

Procedure

(1) Divide the players into groups of 3 people.
(2) Ask them, one group at a time, to walk into the 'performance area', ie the designated space in the middle of the room which is in the camera's range.
(3) Ask each person to carry a chair 'on stage', to put it down wherever they want inside the chalk circle and then to sit down on it.
(4) Explain that the first round will be treated as a rehearsal, so everybody will know what is expected of them before videotaping begins.

(5) Just before each group goes on stage, give its members a discussion topic, for example:
- Should voting be compulsory? (If it is compulsory in your country, the question becomes: Why should voting be compulsory?)
- Why did you dress the way you did this morning?
- Are dogs more fun than cats as pets?
- Is it more convenient to live in a house or a flat?
- Should through-traffic be banned from suburban residential streets?
- Should young people in employment be paid less than adults?
- Is a staff canteen preferable to having automatic food and drink machines?
- Have anti-smoking rules gone too far?

Give each group a different topic. When the first group has discussed their topic, remind them this was a rehearsal, and that they will be required to go through the exercise again, on a different topic, when the other groups have finished.

(6) Ask the next group to go on stage. Then, if there is no camera operator, look through the viewfinder, check the picture and switch to record.

(7) Time each group's discussion for 3 minutes; then stop it, no matter what stage it has reached (unless something so interesting is happening, visually, that you want to let it run). If you have only a few people, you can allow 5 minutes per group, but they really do not need more. Don't forget to call the first group back, at the end of the session. Give them another topic to discuss, and record them.

(8) Replay the tape to the whole group, stopping at appropriate moments to lead a short session of discussion and feedback.

Evaluation The following are a few discussion points you may find useful for this or other activities concerning 'the presentation of self in everyday life' (Goffman, 1975). Novelists and dramatists portray three stereotypes in stories and plays: the hero, the villain and the fool, and behaviour that is seen as heroic in one culture may be classed as villainous in another. The Japanese view suicide as an honourable act, for instance, but Christian societies condemn it. Leaders can be represented in fiction as heroes – like Robin Hood –

or villains – like the plantation manager in *Uncle Tom's Cabin* – or fools – like the emperor who walked through the streets naked, thinking he was wearing new clothes. They are recognized in these roles by certain patterns of behaviour.

In real life, those who aspire to leadership roles – like politicians – assess the kind of behaviour their potential supporters and followers are likely to perceive as 'heroic' – and pattern themselves accordingly. The trick is to avoid transmitting messages whose sequence builds up to an image of aggression rather than assertion.

Closing John Gielgud has defined 'style' in acting as 'knowing what kind of a play you're in'. Assertive behaviour (including leadership style) comes partly from the ability to recognize what kind of situation one is in – to be able to send the appropriate sequence of signals, more effectively to gain control of the outcome.

27 THE HUMAN PYRAMID

Time required About 20 minutes.

Aims
- To give people practice in working together as a team on a specific task, making use of each member's special contribution.
- To increase individuals' willingness to make a commitment to the group to achieve a common task, even at the risk of some discomfort.

Group size Any number, divided in smaller groups if necessary.

Environment Preferably the open air – a park lawn, for example, or a children's playground: but any large open space, indooors or outdoors, will do providing the ground is not too hard.

Procedure

(1) Announce that the group will build a human pyramid.
(2) The criteria are that its apex must be higher than the height of the tallest individual in the group; that every team member must be part of it; and that it must be stable enough to stand for at least 30 seconds after completion. Don't say anything about using non-human supports such as chairs, ladders, etc. If you are asked, reply that you have set all the constraints; the rest is up to the group.
(3) Watch what happens without interfering. Note what concessions the group makes to individual needs (for example, if somebody is wearing white clothing that will become soiled easily; or tight clothing that prohibits climbing; or has a stiff knee and cannot kneel: does the group make allowance for these?). What use does the group make of individual strengths (for example, do the strong members act as supports for smaller and lighter team members to climb on? Does somebody demonstrate planning skills in organizing the pyramid? Who helps who and why?)

Evaluation After congratulating the group on their pyramid, share your observations of the activity with group members. Ask for their comments about teamwork. Who was team-minded and who insisted on remaining an individual?

Closing End with a general discussion about the nature of team-work compared to individual action. What are the differences? What are the strengths of a team compared with those of an individual? What are its weaknesses?

Chapter 10

Activities to explore competition and power

28 NEW YEAR'S EVE HAT

Time required About an hour and a half.

Aim To explore attitudes towards disadvantaged people in the community, in terms of competition and power.

Group size A minimum of somewhere between 8 and 12, but virtually any number of people can can take part, providing there is seating space for them.

Environment Materials must be provided so that every player can make a paper hat, but the makings can vary depending on budget. Basically, they should consist of:
(1) sheets of coloured crepe paper bought from any stationers;
(2) scissors;
(3) a roll of cellophane tape, a small stapler and staples, and a packet of pins (at least one packet, more if group numbers are large);
(4) depending on budget, packets of balloons (uninflated), ribbons, etc, for decorating the hats.

Provide materials to be ties and blindfolds. These should be soft enough not to bruise the players, but strong enough to bind them. Ideal materials are (new) babies' nappies, folded diagonally. They are large enough for either binding or blindfolding.

Procedure

(1) Explain to everybody that the scenario is of a group of handicapped and non-handicapped people who are going to make paper hats to wear in a fancy hat parade on New Year's Eve.

Describe the scenario with as much detail as your imagination can provide, stressing the social importance of the parade and the need for everyone to wear a beautiful hat (perhaps to impress the boss – a person's job may depend on it, for instance).

(2) The ratio of non-handicapped to handicapped players should be about 1 : 5. The handicapped players really are disabled. Get someone to help you if necessary, and tie a player's thumbs, fingers, wrists, and arms together, and/or tie someone's hand behind his or her back, or a player's hand to a chair; and blindfold one or more players.

(3) Other characters in the simulation are judges. If numbers are very small, there will probably be only one judge, but three judges provoke more controversy over judgement criteria. Once the judge-roles are decided, those players get together privately to decide their criteria.

(4) While the judges are discussing their roles, put the hat-makers at one large table or separate tables, and make sure that 4 out of 5 players are handicapped in any one group. Either the hat-makers are each given their own materials or there is a communal supply. If you provide communal hat-making materials, you force the players to share resources; then afterwards you can comment on how this was done, ie who was advantaged and who was disadvantaged even further in the process.

(5) Time the hat-making process carefully, giving players not more than 15 minutes at the most; 10 minutes is usually enough.

(6) Then the hat parade takes place with all the competitors parading past the judges in their hats. Make a note of details at this point, such as, how did the blind people handle the situation? Did anyone offer to guide them? If so, what happened? If not, why not? And how did the people manage who were tied to their chairs?

(7) The judges pronounce their verdict and the game is over. If the judges take for ever to make up their minds – and they often do – then allow the blind players to take off their blindfolds so they

can see the hats and generally feel that they are part of the action again. But point out afterwards that in real life people are often so eager to be 'fair' to handicapped people in the community that they add to their burdens – such as making them wait around in very uncomfortable conditions.

Evaluation One time when we played this game, a badly handicapped man and a non-handicapped woman collaborated so effectively to make their hats (she gave physical assistance, he advised about design) that their partnership became a joint entry in the competition – they created the headgear of a bride and groom. This was in stark contrast to the behaviour of a young woman, slightly handicapped, who became the protector of an older male player who was 'blind'. Her attitude was so maternal that he found himself acting like a child, finally demanding loudly to be taken to the toilet in the middle of the hat parade. Another woman refused all help, even though her hat collapsed just before the parade and she had to struggle slowly and painfully to remake it. A non-handicapped man neither offered help nor was asked for help by anyone. He worked in isolation, made a hat, then announced that he would take part in the parade 'just for fun', not as a competitor.

All these actions provoked heated discussion when the game was over. For example, one man strongly criticized the independent behaviour of the handicapped woman who had insisted on making her hat all by herself. He said: 'If it takes you half an hour to tie your shoelace, then it's better to let someone else do it for you, so you can spend your time inventing a better mousetrap.'

Everyone resented the 'patronizing' attitude of the non-handicapped man who did not want his hat judged with the others. This astonished him, for he had genuinely thought his action was right and just.

One seriously handicapped woman (she could not use one hand at all, and did not have the use of the thumb on the other) was frankly furious at the judges. They had ranked the handicaps in order of disability and marked the owners' hats up or down accordingly. The woman said: 'How dare you people, who have no handicaps, sit in judgement about whether it is "worse" to be blind or maimed?' One of the judges was so upset by this that he blamed us for 'making' him act as a judge. He said that he deliberately avoided judgement roles in real life, that he had not wanted to be a judge in the game, and that he felt betrayed that we had seduced him into uncharacteristic and humiliating behaviour. The whole group talked about its feelings for more than two hours after this particular game session, and members were still arguing, in twos and threes, as they went to dinner (it was a residential course).

Closing It is worth remembering that, as a general rule, a highly experiential simulation game will take twice as long to debrief as to play. The more guidelines you give the judges the more specific will be their value judgements about the hats, and some of the game's options will begin to close up. Thus at this early stage of the game it is within your control to keep the structure of the game open or to constrain the players within particular assumptions. Your decision will depend on what you want the players to 'know' at the end of the game that they did not know before.

For example, if you have a group of managers who work in the advertising industry, and you want them to become more aware of the commercial constraints under which they work and which limit their leadership power, then you might give the New Year's Eve Hat judges a list of criteria that emphasizes the saleability of the hats and makes no allowance for the handicaps of the makers. On the other hand, you might want a group of social workers to get a gut-level experience of the kind of social discrimination that handicapped people receive. In that case, you could give some of the hat-makers more colourful materials than the others, then make 'colourfulness' one of the judgement criteria, and ask the disadvantaged players afterwards how they felt. Another strategy you might want to try is to give a pair of children's blunt-tipped scissors to the 'blind' hat-makers. Then when you debrief the whole exercise, you can point out that the ways in which society protects its handicapped members from injury sometimes also increase their handicaps.

29 PONSONBY

Time required About 45 minutes.

Aims

- To study the effects of competition on individual and group behaviour.
- To examine how individual perceptions about a group task can affect the end result.
- To study the effects of competitive behaviour on group perceptions of the task.

Group size About 10 people to virtually any number. We have played this game with over 100 people.

Environment At a national conference on simulations and games we were asked to give an *ad hoc* demonstration of game design. We were inspired by the fact that one of the conference rooms in the hotel could be turned into a ballroom by the simple device of removing the carpet, which was laid on the floor in large squares. We watched a man come in one evening with a pushcart, load all the squares on to it, and wheel it away – and we promptly sat down and devised a game we called 'Ponsonby' because that was the name of the hotel.

When the time came to demonstrate the game to the conference, we moved everybody into the hall. The carpet squares, with the permission of the functions manager, had been arranged in advance. Half the squares were placed in heaps in a line along one wall of the room, the other half along the opposite wall, revealing the expanse of parquet flooring. We divided the parquet down the middle lengthwise with a chalk line.

If you don't have access to carpet squares you can substitute, for example by using chairs. You will need one chair per player; and half the chairs should be one colour and half another (or they should be distinguishable in some other way). Stack each set against two opposite walls of the seminar room. Prepare the following written instructions:

The coach for Team A
You must urge your team to win at all costs.

Impress upon them that this is a competitive situation and they are in it to win, even if this involves a certain amount of aggression – within the rules – towards the opposing team. *Do not reveal to the other team that you are prepared to win at any cost.*

The coach for Team B

You must stress that the object of this game is to study group processes, and that it has been designed purely as light relief in an otherwise demanding conference. The object is to observe players' behaviour during the course of the game, and to enjoy the game; never mind about the result; *but do not reveal to the other team that you know this.*

Procedure

(1) When the group has assembled in the seminar room, keep them standing while you explain the activity will be a competitive team game and ask for a coach for each team. Give each coach their respective instructions and ask them not to communicate with each other.

(2) Get everybody into two teams – one team to line up against one wall in front of one set of stacked chairs, the other team against the opposite wall. Draw a chalk mark or lay a tape down the middle of the room between the two teams. Thus the two teams will face each other across the room, a stack of chairs along the wall behind each team, and a chalk line or tape between them.

(3) Ask everybody to imagine they are two sporting teams who will play against each other. Introduce the respective coach to each team and let them get on with the business of privately coaching their teams according to their instructions.

(4) When the coaches are satisfied their teams have been sufficiently motivated, explain to everybody that the object of the game is that every team member in each team shall sit on a chair on their side of the room *but* the chair must be from the *opposite* side of the room. In other words, if Team A has red chairs and Team B blue chairs, then Team A must end up sitting on their side of the room on blue chairs. Team B must finish by sitting on red chairs. The winning team will be the first to be seated correctly.

The rules are that Team A members have to cross the floor, pick up a chair from Team B's side of the room – one chair per person – re-cross the chalk or tape to their own side, put down their chair, and sit on it. Then everybody sits on a chair and the task is complete. Team B has to do exactly the same with the chairs from Team A's side. This means that all players from each team have to cross sides, from their own territory, into the other team's territory and back again

(5) When you are sure everybody understands the rules, let the game begin.

Evaluation It is almost inevitable that team members who think they are playing a competitive game will begin rushing over and back across the dividing line, each carrying the chair as fast as they can. The non-competitive team members are much more likely to pick up their chairs quite casually, watching the other team with surprised interest. After a few seconds, however, the dynamic may change. The frenetic activity of Team A may communicate itself to Team B, especially as it becomes obvious that A will inevitably win the game if B continues its present behaviour. Then the game may turn into a race in which there is a lot of pushing and shoving as members from opposing teams pass each other.

On one occasion when we played Ponsonby with carpet squares, and as the floor became more and more carpeted, Team A looked certain to win because they had been competitive from the beginning: but then the going started getting rougher. One woman from Team B stood on a square to prevent a Team A man from picking it up. The man lifted her physically off her feet, none too gently, dumped her down on the floor, and picked up the square. From then on, that woman became one of the most aggressive players, but none of her team-mates were far behind her. In fact, Team B ended up being noticeably more belligerent than Team A, and 'won' the game.

During the debriefing the woman described how she had begun Ponsonby in a relaxed and contented frame of mind – grateful to it for giving her 'time out' from mental effort. She ended the game, she said, feeling that she would have killed to win, and feeling deeply resentful that she should have been 'made' to feel this way by the offensive behaviour of Team A. All the members of Team B expressed similar feelings and all blamed their feelings on Team A for being so 'pushy and horrible'. Team A at first could not see what all the fuss was about – which effectively opened up the debate along the lines of the game's objectives.

Closing Ponsonby was the highlight of the conference, and people talked about it all week. It had been a serendipitous combination of the three components of gaming: the people, the setting and the game. The game structure was dramatic – conflict of desires, reversal of expectations, action and suspense – and well suited to its objectives and the needs of the players. And all because we happened to see a man picking up carpet squares off a floor.

30 AUCTION

(Based on a gambling game called 'The Game of Life', in Michael Laver's 1979 book, *Playing Politics*.)

Time required About 45 minutes.

Aims

- To study cooperation versus conflict in group negotiation.
- To evaluate the extent to which people have to cooperate to survive but compete to win.

Group size From about 7 players to virtually any number.

Environment Ideally this is a money game. However, if there is some real obstacle to playing it as a gambling game, supply everybody with packets of colour-coated chocolates (Smarties or M&Ms). Otherwise provide £3 for each player. Don't worry about the money – you will get it all back.

All the players are seated at one table (though if there is a large number of people, several games can be played simultaneously at different tables). Either you will be the banker or some other disinterested party will be, who must then be briefed in advance. You should have prepared a list of rules of the game, one copy for each player, to read as follows:

(1) Each player receives £1 in change from the Bank of Life. Any currency may be used. If Smarties are used, give each player 10.
(2) At the start of each round, each player who wants to be in the game must put 10 pence (or one Smartie) in a central fund, which is placed in the middle of the table.
(3) The Bank will match these resources penny for penny, adding the money to the central fund.
(4) Players then bid for this fund. Players can bid any sum in multiples of 10 pence, but must place it in front of them on the table. If they wish to raise a previous bid, they must put the additional amount in front of them. No bid may be withdrawn once the money is on the table.
(5) The entire central fund is paid out to the player making the highest bid.
(6) All bids are then forfeited and returned to the Bank of Life.

(7) Deals and side payments between players are allowed, but *no deal is enforceable.*

(8) Bids may be made only by *individuals* and the central fund may be won by only *one person.*

(9) At the end of each round, once the pay-out has been made, and after a short period of negotiation, if the players want it, Round 2 will begin as in Round 1, starting at point 2 above.

Procedure Let us assume you are playing with a group of 20 people.

(1) Give them each £1 in small change (to be returned to you at the end of the game).

(2) Each person puts 10 pence in the central fund. This is not a bid; this sum is their contribution in order to be in the game.

(3) Thus, in this instance there is £2 in the fund, to which you, as banker, add £2 and then call for bids for this £4 pot.

(4) Sooner or later someone will bid, say, 10 pence by placing it in front of them on the table, and then the rest will start joining in. At this point, some agitated discussion usually begins as players seek clarification from each other about the economic possibilities of the game.

(5) When no one is willing to bid any more, you give the £4 pot to the highest individual bidder, and scoop up *all* the money on the table (including the successful bid). Keep referring people to the rules if you have any argument (see rule 6 in this case).

(6) Start Round 2 as soon as you can, pushing people along a bit if you have to (but allow them time to form coalitions. Some players may want to leave the room for a few moments for private bargaining; allow this). Again there may be £4 in the pot (or more or less, depending on whether some people who remained as observers during Round 1 now wish to play, or whether some players wish to become observers and conserve their resources).

Evaluation By now at least one, and usually more, of the players have realized that if everyone cooperates, they can break the bank quite quickly. All they have to do, each round, is to allow one person in turn – for as many rounds as there are players – to win the pot on a ten-pence bid. There are one or two minor problems: for instance, each player only has £1, so if their money runs out before it is their turn to win they will have to trust one of the winners to pay 10 pence in order for them to stay in the game. Nevertheless, in theory the above strategy will inevitably bankrupt the bank.

The first time we ever played the game, a couple of players started arguing along these lines, and we became afraid that, as the bank, we were going to be made fools of. We started thinking frantically about what sort of learning lesson we could draw from this humiliation, but it did not happen and now we can report, dozens of games later, that 'Auction' seldom works that way.

Some people can never resist the temptation to try and win more than the others, and so they make deals and then go back on them. Some people are mistrustful of others in the first place and refuse to allow them to win by default; and so on. The game starts with a group of isolated individuals. The players must cooperate or all will lose their money, but each must beat the others in order to win. It is a fascinating game to watch and listen to, especially when there is a really large group, say over 30 players. This is a game that can be videotaped very effectively. Factions form and re-form, leaders rise and fall, trust is established and then broken, sometimes later to be rebuilt, sometimes not. Players argue with each other, and sometimes become angry out of all proportion to the monetary value of the stakes.

The exceptions are Japanese players. They are the only people, in our experience, who have broken Auction's bank. This is not inevitable, however, because Japanese like to play power games as much as anybody else, and some groups of Japanese businessmen turn out to be more reckless gamblers even than Australians. Nevertheless, we remember in particular one Japanese group which realized very quickly how to win the game. One player was delegated (after discussion and consensus agreement) to be the only bidder while the others watched the inevitable result with keen interest. When the bank was broken, the winner scrupulously divided the spoils, the other participants carefully pocketed the money and then looked at us expectantly, waiting to be told what useful lesson they had learned.

Closing Once we played this game with a group of senior trainers, and when it was over we asked them if they thought it had any value for them as a diagnostic training device; but they had all become so involved in the game that it was difficult for them to regain objectivity (another example of the need for uninvolved observers of simulations, games, and roleplays as teaching tools). We replayed the videotape, which led to a revealing discussion. For example, one of the players – a training manager in real life for a large bank – said that it had been very interesting for her to observe the reckless behaviour of several people who apparently developed 'gambling fever'. They took money out of their own pockets to remain in the game after losing their initial stakes (in fact, this often happens but this observer could not have been expected to know that; she had herself been a very cautious player).

This woman concluded that games might be a valuable diagnostic tool within her own training programmes. For example, playing Auction had already given her the idea of designing a seminar to be called something like 'Human Factors in Funding Decisions', to be based on company policy. She said this kind of spin-off from games might raise her credit with her boss, who might regard her as being perceptive and innovative concerning company training needs.

31 MAKING MONEY

Time required Minimum 20 minutes, maximum about one and a half hours, depending on how many players there are and how many rounds you want to play.

Aim To evoke and study coercive behaviour.

Group size From about 7 people to virtually any number.

Environment A room where people can move about freely. About £1 per person, preferably contributed by group members themselves. However, for various reasons you may wish either to provide the money yourself or to distribute a handful of Smarties to each player (the same number for each). If you are using money, remember to have lots of small change. You will also need a blackboard or flipchart to record the results of each round.

Procedure

(1) Divide the players into groups of 3-7 people.
(2) Each player should begin the first round with the same individual stake, say 20 pence broken down into even smaller change, or 20 Smarties.
(3) Tell everyone that the person in each group (or maybe two people if the group is large) who has the most money (or chocolates) by the end of a 10-minute round will be the leader for the next round and will be able to set the rules for that round. Any form of trading, borrowing, gambling, stealing, begging, etc, is permitted.
(4) At the end of 10 minutes, call all the groups to order and post the sum of each person's resources. If there are a great many people, get someone to help you.
(5) Initiate a short discussion of the results. Then announce that this round has been a rehearsal; and now the game will really begin. Redistribute the money (or provide more chocolates; you will probably find most of them have been eaten).
(6) Begin Round 1, as for step 3 above.
(7) Repeat step 4.
(8) The richest people in each group are the leaders for the next round and they now have the right to set the rules of play; however, every player's objective will be the same as before, namely, to end the round with more money than anyone else.

Ask all the leaders to leave the room to discuss their strategies for the next round. They may choose any tactics to keep their leadership (and wealth), though we find that when we play Making Money with young people (in youth groups or schools, for example) we sometimes have to ban more violent forms of coercion by leaders and/or resistance by group members.

(9) Give the leaders 5 minutes or so to consider strategies, then recall them, put them back in their groups, give them a few minutes to explain to their members what the new rules are, and begin Round 2, announcing that the leadership may change at the end of the round, depending on the distribution of resources. Theoretically, the leadership should not change in any group, because the people who emerged as leaders should now formalize the rules so that inevitably they get richer and the rest get poorer. However, this does not always happen, usually because some group members become as smart at playing the game as the leaders, and find ways to circumvent the new rules in their own favour.

(10) Play as many rounds as the players ask for, or that you have time for.

Evaluation Debrief the game in terms of coercive and persuasive skills. You should be able to point out that the most successful leaders – that is, the ones who become richest – are those people who are best able to achieve one of two situations. Either their followers *actively cooperate* to enrich the leader because in return the followers get some kind of reward themselves, or they defer to the leader out of respect and/or fear.

In one game that we played, one man eventually became the manager of the whole group, not just his own sub-group, because he opened a 'Two-up' school. This is a very popular Australian pastime in which people bet on whether a tossed coin will fall heads or tails up – and the person who runs the school always takes a cut of the profits, so this man became very rich, but even more important, his team was happy with the process.

The other situation in which emergent leaders manage successfully to formalize their positions is through overt use of power, prestige, class or status, so that no one feels assertive enough to oppose them. This can happen, for example, if you are directing a group of employees of widely differing status within the same company. The junior trainees are not likely to oppose a bid for leadership if it comes from someone much older, or someone who has been with the company for 20 years (though it can happen, if the juniors are aggressive and ambitious). In an Australian setting, Asian students are less likely than the native white Australians to challenge an emergent leader, and so on.

Closing Plan for a fairly long debriefing period. This activity evokes a wide range of behaviour and response, which people like to talk about afterwards.

32 MONEY IN THE MIDDLE

Time required Anything from less than 5 minutes to nearly an hour, depending on how many people there are in the group and how quickly they reach consensus.

Aims
- To study the process of group decision-making.
- To evoke a range of value-judgements.
- To call into question decision-making processes at high levels, for example allocations of funds in large organizations.

Group size Any number over 5.

Environment This game can be played anywhere, so long as the players can sit in one big circle with the 'money in the middle'. It is not a gambling game, so no one should be offended when you ask each participant to contribute 20 pence – though they will not get the money back. If someone does not have twenty pence, *give* him or her the money (make it clear you are not lending it) to put in the pot.

Procedure

(1) Sit everyone in a circle; this is important.
(2) Put the money in the middle, visible to all and accessible to all.
(3) Announce that one person, and only one, will get it all, to spend as he or she likes, though not to return to the individuals who donated it. Then do not say anything else.

   After a silence, someone will probably ask who the lucky person will be. Answer that this is for the group to decide, but *there must be consensus*. Again, do not say anything more.

Evaluation Groups solve this problem in different ways. Sometimes an emergent leader or leaders devise some sort of game and give the money to the winner. This is the simplest, quickest, and most equitable solution, and one which is the most fun. We are always surprised that groups do not think of it more often. If people start talking about who deserves it most, for instance, they inevitably get bogged down and the discussion can last a long time.

Sometimes a person will just take the money and defy anyone to get it back. We remember a group of middle managers actually engaging in a physical fight because one of them put the money in his pocket – an example of a bid for power that was too overt to work *with that particular group*. The man was a poor psychologist. His bluff might have worked with a group of people who were not his peers, or who were not as assertive as he.

If a power play like this is successful, do not let it worry you. Just announce the end of Round 1 and start all over again. You will find the tension noticeably higher in Round 2 as the players start looking for ways to take revenge on the deviant.

When the decision has finally been made, ask the participants who or what the real decision-maker was. What happened? Help them retrace the argument and discuss their feelings. How were priorities established? Did any one person (or a sub-group of people) set them, openly or tacitly? There are other questions that can usefully be asked, concerning individual problem-solving styles, for example, enquiring who pressed for solutions and closure, and who widened the scope of the debate. Who spoke most? Who listened most? And what were people's feelings as the game was played?

Closing Allow enough time for people to think about these questions, bearing in mind that some people take longer than others to 'get going'.

33 THE FIVE-POUND NOTE

(A negotiation game adapted from a similar activity designed by R Meredith Belbin (1981).)

Time required About half an hour.

Aim To study the stages and processes of negotiation

Group size At least 5 people, up to virtually any number, provided the room is large enough.

Environment Classroom, seminar room, conference room. We call this game 'The Five-Pound Note' because when you play it you have to auction a £5 note.

Procedure

(1) Explain this is an auction. You will auction a £5 note and the successful bidder will really keep the money.
(2) The bids have to be in 10-pence offers. If players don't have enough small change, postpone the auction until everybody has a few 10p coins. Confirm that people don't have to bid unless they want to.
(3) All bids at the end of each auction are forfeit to you as auctioneer. Stress this; it is a critical factor.
(4) Start the auction. Give the note to the highest bidder, and keep all bids for yourself.
(5) Begin another auction of another £5 note.

Evaluation Belbin suggests that players may be more keen to make their opponents lose than they are to win themselves, but in our experience the players are torn between wanting to win and wanting to beat, not each other, but us. The Five-Pound Note is an entrepreneurial game because players recognize that it makes the best sense not to play; this, however, applies to the others as well, so maybe they should play after all.

Closing Belbin relates the outcomes of the game to real-world negotiations like trying to avoid or stop wars in different parts of the world, and union/management disputes. He suggests that these are the issues the game leader should raise with the group. You may want to do this; or you can offer the following discussion points:

(1) It is hard to let go of a situation in which you have already invested time and trouble, and in this case money. This feeling may tempt you to 'hang in there' longer than you can afford. On the other hand, if you are willing to invest your resources only up to a certain level, which you have decided in advance, you can relax, enjoy the activity and learn a lot about negotiation.

(2) If you are afraid you are getting in too deep, but feel it is too late to withdraw, your opponents will sense this and increase their bids. On the other hand, if you can bring yourself to withdraw when the going gets too hot for you, you may lose some money, because your bids will have been forfeited to the auctioneer, but you will have learned something about the other players, and yourself. In addition, you will know how to recognize in the future the characteristics of escalation games, so you can avoid them if you want to.

34 QUOTE ME A PRICE

Time required About 20 minutes.

Aim To analyse the verbal and non-verbal transactions that take place between a seller and a potential buyer.

Group size From about 5 people to almost any number.

Environment The classroom, seminar room or conference room. Bring some gold chains, costume jewellery, an old watch - anything that a second-hand shop would sell. Provide the video equipment if you want to record this activity.

Procedure

(1) Explain that you want to set up some roleplays about negotiation.
(2) Set up the video camera, if you want to record the action. Check through the viewfinder that the playing area is in range and focus.
(3) Put a player in a role as salesperson and create a 'shop' with tables, chairs, furnishings from around the room, bits and pieces of clothing and jewellery borrowed from players as well as the things you brought with you.
(4) Price everything. Ask the group to set a price on each of the items and post the list.
(5) Put somebody in charge as the shop owner. Ask another person to be a buyer who has seen an item in the shop window, has taken a real fancy to it and enters the shop determined to purchase it at less than the listed price.
(6) If you want to video the subsequent bargaining, switch the camera on now.

Evaluation The advantage of video is that you can play back the tape as a debrief of the action. You can fast-forward if the players were slow to get their act together; and you can stop the tape at places where you remember or can see something interesting.

For example, one buyer began by saying: 'I'll give you £1 for that paperweight'. The seller asked for the full price, £5, and rode out the buyer's derision. In fact this woman 'shopkeeper' handled the negotiation very well throughout the roleplay. When the purchaser dug his heels in, so did she, and she appeared willing to break off the negotiations if all he would offer was £1. He modified his stand and raised the offer to £1.50. At this point, the 'shopowner' called on the services of another player and announced him as a world authority on paperweights who would attest to its value. The buyer accepted the word of the disinterested expert but enlarged the scope of the debate by saying that he was a regular customer and it was in her interests to keep him satisfied. At this point the woman said that she would have to talk to her manager, and handed over the negotiations to another player. The manager expressed every desire to satisfy this valued client and added all sorts of extra information about the paperweight's previous owner, now unfortunately deceased but formerly a wealthy and discerning collector. He waxed eloquent about the quality of its glass and the beauty of its design until the customer raised his offer to £2. After that there was a pattern of negotiation with the manager suggesting £5.50 and the buyer £3, until eventually they agreed on the seller's original price of £5. It was interesting to see how the intervals of time between offers and counter-offers became less and less the nearer they got to agreement. Moreover, the manager helped the buyer to save face over having to pay the original price; he refrained from the slightest suggestion of gloating and congratulated his customer on having made an excellent purchase.

These players were all experienced negotiators in real life and it was enlightening to see how in turn each handled this roleplay. On another occasion, when the players were not so skilful, they were less able to signal their commitments and the transaction was in danger of foundering. We suggested that they might enlarge the scope of the discussion by adding a contingency arrangement, such as the possibility of the customer returning the paperweight if not entirely happy with it. This spurred the manager to offer to sell the paperweight at the lower figure if the customer would agree to purchase something else in the shop as well – which is what happened.

Closing This roleplay illustrates the basics of negotiation, which are:

(1) Beware of opening first with a concrete offer; it may 'anchor' your adversary's perceptions.
(2) Gauge your reactions to an extreme suggestion. Either break off negotiations until the other side modifies its stand, or make a

counter-offer and expect to end up somewhere between the two. Be aware of your own aspiration level, and protect your integrity.

(3) Keep reassessing your perceptions, and learn to recognize patterns of concessions. Your concessions should be paced and linked to those of your adversary. Note that the intervals between offers should become shorter as limits are signalled. Learn to handle stress.

(4) Signal your commitments. Make it clear when you will go no further (whether, in fact, this is true or not). Learn to communicate your intentions effectively with non-verbal behaviour as well as words.

(5) Introduce a disinterested or expert third party as a mediator.

(6) Enlarge the scope of the negotiation, for instance, by including contingency arrangements.

(7) If you want to avoid being pushed into a commitment, or if you want to change your mind, you can do several things. For example, you can:

- get yourself replaced by another negotiator;
- state that you have received new instructions and/or information;
- include new issues in the debate.

(8) Help your adversaries to save face. For example:

- agree that the circumstances have changed, even if they have not, which makes your adversaries' change of mind perfectly reasonable;
- accept that they were pushed for time and were not able to prepare properly to negotiate with you.

(9) Do not gloat.

35 PENALTY

Time required About 20 minutes.

Aims

- To illustrate some of the pressures on negotiators to reach compromise.
- To study bluff and other manipulative behaviour in negotiation.

Group size At least 4 people, preferably about 12–25 people.

Environment The classroom, seminar room or conference room.

Procedure

(1) Give any two players £2 between them, in small change.
(2) Ask them to divide the £2 between them, in front of the rest of the group as audience.
(3) Explain you will penalize one of them 5p per minute of negotiation and the other 10p per minute (it doesn't matter which is which).
(4) Give the signal to start the negotiation.
(5) When the money has been divided between the two players, allow a few minutes for discussion, then go through the process again with another two people. This time the results will almost certainly be quite different.
(6) Go through it once again, if numbers permit.

Evaluation This is an exercise for players to practise bluff as well as learning more about how to 'think on their feet'. The player who stands to lose more from delay (by being penalized for delay at a higher rate than the other party) is theoretically in a weaker bargaining position. This person often does end up with virtually nothing out of the £2.

Closing Players in this position sometimes think fast enough to say something like: 'The longer we stand here talking, the more money we both lose. How about if you take 10 per cent extra for your cut?' In this case they have a good chance of getting away with an 80p payout, which in other circumstances might have been a lot higher.

36 GET SMART!

Time required About 30–45 minutes.

Aims
- To simulate industrial conflict.
- To explore ways people can reconcile opposing aims.

We originally designed Get Smart! for occupational health students, to give them some experience of leadership in situations of occupational safety hazards when remedies are likely to be in opposition to management policy, ie when remedies are likely to interfere with productivity. It can easily be adapted to be relevant to any environment where workers' welfare and management aims are in opposition. It may seem a childish exercise to ask grown men and women to eat as many Smarties as they can – so maybe you will not want to play this game until you are on terms of high trust and esteem with your group – but we can practically guarantee that nobody will find it undignified.

Group size Minimum 8 to about 25 players (though it can be run with more).

Environment A room large and empty enough for players to move around freely. You will need to provide:

(1) A large number of packets of 'Smarties' (or M&Ms), many of which are going to be eaten. Fortunately they are not expensive.
(2) A large container of water or a soft drink (unless you want to supply alcoholic refreshment, in which case the game will take on an added dimension) and enough plastic cups for everyone.
(3) More plastic cups on the main playing table for people to use as containers for their Smarties.
(4) About £10 changed into 1-pence pieces (you may need more, but you will get it all back; we have commented before on the psychological advantages of using real money in these learning games).

Procedure

(1) Put any six players in roles as:
- 2 managers;
- 2 workers;

- a character who symbolizes the social pressures of a consumer society;
- a union representative, conservationist, environmentalist, or some such character who is concerned to protect workers and the general public from the forces of production.

If you have lots of people, create more social pressures and more workers before you add an extra manager. All other participants are consumers.

(2) The 6 main characters sit and stand round the playing table on which there is a large heap of Smarties. Note that the game works better when people are standing. They use more body language, such as gestures or touching each other, perhaps to restrain someone physically from eating the Smarties: and generally respond more overtly to the pressures of the game.

(3) The 2 managers are given all the money (they operate in partnership) and also a bag of Smarties in case the mountain becomes eroded and needs rebuilding.

(4) The consumers either sit in a larger circle around the table and its occupants, or they may prefer to wander around, watching and listening to the action.

(5) The refreshment stand is located somewhere off to the side, and we usually act as the waiters because we like to have a small piece of the action, but you may prefer to delegate this task to one of the observers.

(6) Explain that the aims and objectives of the characters are as follows:

- The managers want the workers to prepare Smarties for workers and consumers to eat (the managers do not eat Smarties themselves, because their job is to produce, not consume these lowly articles). They have to decide what wages to pay, but a good estimate is 10 pence for every 100 Smarties consumed.
- The workers have to collect as many Smarties as they think will be consumed, take the container to one of the managers for checking, and then either eat the Smarties themselves or offer them to the consumers. Before managers pay out the appropriate sum for the number consumed, they should keep an eye on the action to make sure no Smarties have been thrown away or otherwise illegally disposed of – they have to be *eaten*. You may prefer to keep track of this yourself, or to ask observers to see

that the people who take the Smarties actually put them in their mouths and swallow them.

The managers' most urgent priority is maximum consumption. As a bonus for good work, they can invite workers and/or consumers to be their guests at the refreshment buffet (only the managers can help themselves to drinks; others must be invited).

• The union representative (or conservationist or whoever) has read a report that the Smarties are carcinogenic, and does not want anyone to eat any more until extensive health tests have been carried out. Meanwhile, the production lines should be shut down. The most urgent priority is *nil consumption.*

• The character who symbolizes the consumer society wants to put as much pressure as possible on workers and consumers to eat more and more Smarties; this person goes around suggesting ways they can do so.

• The workers know that if their leaders become dissatisfied with their performance and dismiss them, there are plenty of consumers who are ready to take their place on the production line. Anyone can talk to anyone else; any syndicates, pressure groups, etc, can be formed; anyone can do virtually anything within the above general context.

You may want to write out all the main roles individually, adding any extra comments or colourful touches of your own, in which case presumably no one will start off knowing the motives of the other characters; or you can describe the scenario aloud to everyone in your own words; with as much eloquence as you can muster. We think it is more effective to describe everything verbally to everyone, but the really important thing is to motivate the participants to play their roles with enthusiasm. Thus, you should either write something to this effect into the roles or give the group a pep-talk before you start the game. In any case, the presence of the Smarties will add to your persuasions, because they always seem to exercise a powerful motivating force on the players.

• However you set it up, the result will probably be noisy, which is fine. You want the managers to encourage the workers to get more and more Smarties eaten – with offers of refreshments, higher wages, bonuses and incentives for increased consumption. They may set one worker in competition against another, and so on. On the other hand, the union representative or conservationist utters grim warnings; while all the time the consumer society tempts the workers to eat more and earn more. Everyone usually ends up shouting and frequently the observers join in.

• Let the game run its course. There are many possible outcomes. Maybe all the Smarties will be eaten, or they may be forgotten in the heat of debate. The workers and consumers may listen to the union representative, who may, as a result, succeed in getting the Smarties banned (and may even force the managers to suggest another form of labour); and so on.

Evaluation On one occasion when we played the game with a group of physical education teachers, the workers, under pressure from the consumers as well as the union representative, abandoned the Smarties and used sheets from their notepads to make paper hats to 'sell' for a 'crippled children's association'. They did so with the full cooperation of the management, who agreed to pay the same wages as before, and everyone ended up wearing a paper hat.

Sometimes people are swayed by the social pressures of the consumer society and eat the Smarties as fast as they can. The workers refuse to listen to any health warnings because they argue that otherwise they will lose their jobs and they cannot afford to be out of work. Sometimes a pressure group of consumers will side with the conservationist and get the workers 'laid off'; then they negotiate with the managers to make some nominal safety changes and take over the jobs themselves, and so on.

Closing The discussion afterwards is likely to be animated. We vividly remember one senior nurse on an occupational health course who played the role of a health officer (equivalent to the role of union representative). She completely failed in her efforts (which became quite frantic as the game progressed) to stop people eating the Smarties. This was largely because the woman who played the consumer society was very persuasive. She interpreted her role by presenting what were, in effect, a series of commercials about the lovely things the workers could buy with their wages, and how good chocolate was nutritionally for the consumers.

The nurse said afterwards that the game had given her such a sense of helplessness and frustration that she felt ready to burst into tears as the table became more and more empty of Smarties. She said she now felt much more able to identify with the efforts of conservationists and other members of the real-life community who work against all the pressures of a consumer society to protect the quality of people's lives. This kind of reaction, and the various responses of all the players and observers, can be related to the theme of power. Who controlled whom? Why? How did the various characters perceive their tasks? How did the consumers perceive the behaviour of the characters? Participants may discuss the socio-political contexts in which organizational power operates, and the extent to which individuals can control this context: which in turn governs the degree of power they can achieve.

Chapter 11
Negotiation activities

37 THE ROAD GAME

(Adapted from Lineham and Long, 1970.)

Time required About two hours.

Aim To increase people's awareness that there are *choices* involved, on several levels, in any development programme for a company, organization, neighbourhood, city or nation.

Group size You will need a large group for this activity: within limits, the more the merrier. It works well with a group of about 20 to 35 people, though it can be played with an absolute minimum of 8. Try to get hold of at least 12.

Environment The Road Game requires the following materials:

(1) Four sheets of thin drawing cardboard (20 x 20cm or any size convenient for you), the sort you buy from an art supply shop or from your local stationer. Each sheet should be a different colour.
(2) Sticky or masking tape to join the four sheets of cardboard together to make one big square. This is the playing board.
(3) Four fat felt-tipped pens, preferably in the colours of the four cardboard sheets, but not essential so long as they are each of a different colour.

This game is a good choice of activity for a conference, because you have access to numbers of people who will have the opportunity to discuss the experience at length, perhaps over several days.

© Elizabeth M. Christopher and Larry E. Smith, 1993. Published by Kogan Page.

Procedure

(1) The Road Game is best played with the big board on a carpeted floor with space all round for players to walk, kneel, or crawl as they feel like it. However, if there is no carpet on the floor, put the board on a table approximately the same size as the board, and let people stand around it.

(2) Explain that the four coloured squares on the board are four countries and the players are all citizens of one country or another. Let them divide themselves up any way they like; it doesn't matter if the populations are not evenly distributed.

(3) Every citizen of every country has to pay a capital sum into the World Bank - you can ask for any sum that seems suitable, from about 30 pence upwards. If you are playing with a group of people who don't have any money (for example, we have played this game with young people on a retraining programme in a reform school), you will have to put 30 pence per player in the bank yourself.

(4) Announce that each country has a **leader** and a **state engineer**; everyone else is an ordinary person. Countries can decide which sort of leadership to have and how they are going to decide on their leader and their engineer. Give them 5 minutes to do this.

(5) Announce that the object of the game is to build roads, and give a felt-tipped pen to each state engineer, emphasizing that only engineers can put pen to board.

(6) The rules are simple:
- Any completed road earns 20 pence from the World Bank to be paid to the country that built it.
- To be classed as 'completed', a road must begin somewhere in the country of ownership and end at the edge of the playing board *in someone else's country* (internal roads do not count).
- Before crossing any frontier, the road builders must first obtain the permission of the leader of the country into which they wish to extend their road.
- If road builders want to cross a road belonging to another country, *even if that road is on their own land*, the same negotiation process must take place.
- the number of completed roads will be tallied at the end of the game and the monies paid out. However, there will be an

opportunity for any country to protest that another country's roads were built illegally, and if the protest is upheld at the World Court, the relevant road will be erased and that country will not get the money.

- Only state engineers can draw roads, and only leaders can negotiate between countries.

(7) Strongly emphasize the game's few rules, and the definition of a completed road. You can write the rules down in advance if you like, and give everyone a copy.

(8) Then let everyone get on with it; do not interfere at all, even if the rules are being broken right, left and centre. The game will become a microcosm of power politics and is enthralling to watch and listen to. You may want to video part of it. Some countries are indifferent to anything except development, while others seek to protect their environment; and each country develops power plays that are worth examining in some detail afterwards.

Evaluation Probably the most effective way to offer suggestions for debriefing The Road Game is to describe the results of a game we played some years ago for an environment protection organization (Stone, 1981). The four countries, each with about 7 citizens, plus their leader and engineer, called themselves respectively Salami, Serenia, Beli Cose, and Kom Erse.

The people of Salami decided they were going all out to get rich quick. They would forget about social conscience, civic planning, and preservation of the environment. They did not bother to build any roads at all. Anyone could come on to their land and build roads wherever they pleased - for a price of 8 pence a road, payable in advance.

Serenia decided that it had plenty of natural resources and withdrew from the outside world - no roads in, no roads out. Its people spent the entire game happily breathing down the state engineer's neck while she crawled around drawing houses and trees to their instructions, and churches and hospitals, animals, and a countryside with lots of windmills and waterfalls and solar catchment areas.

The citizens of Beli Cose took a pragmatic stand: this is a game, they said. The object of the game is to draw as many roads as possible. 'Right,' they said, 'that's what we'll do.' Their leader soon found out that Serenia was not interested in letting anyone cross her borders, and that Kom Erse would consider roads only on a one-for-one basis, which left Salami. Both Beli Cose and Kom Erse fell on Salami with cries of joy when they realized she would agree to anything. Kom Erse tried to haggle over the price, however, which was a tactical error, because the leader of Beli Cose took 10 pence out of her own purse and gave it to the leader of Salami, saying grandly: 'Keep the change!' Then she rapidly moved her state engineer in, to draw a blue road in such a way that Kom Erse would have to cross it (and therefore would need Beli Cose's permission) to get to Salami's perimeter.

Kom Erse was furious and its citizens loudly abused their leader for being outsmarted. However, he was not far behind. He promptly paid for a road, so close to Beli Cose's borders that the balance of power was restored because Beli Cose would have to cross it to get virtually anywhere. After that the two countries worked out some kind of bargaining system in an atmosphere of 'cold war' negotiation.

In addition to getting him to draw roads, Kom Erse's citizens also kept their engineer busy siting cities and industrial centres and airports. But Beli Cose's leader loved the diplomatic process *per se* and spent all her time in close consultation with other heads of state. Her people saw very little of her. Her engineer tried to locate a site for a capital city but it never got beyond the planning stage because other considerations always came first with the leader, like trying to fit in another road without crossing an existing one. She kept making unilateral decisions and telling the people about them afterwards, when it was too late to protest.

At the end of about an hour we called a halt, even though the game had got to a stage where Beli Cose's leader was looking greedily at Serenia's empty spaces; but the debriefing of The Road Game is every bit as important as playing it, and we did not want to cut that time short by continuing to play. Salami was the official winner, with capital reserves of £1.28, and no one could accuse her of behaving illegally because she had not built any roads. However, ecologically it was a mess, with lots of foreign-built roads all over the place. Salami's citizens did not care. They announced that they were all in voluntary and luxurious exile in the Bahamas. Beli Cose came second, with £1.08 and a half-built capital city. They would have earned more, but Kom Erse protested that one of their roads had been drawn without consent, and Serenia and Salami upheld the protest. Kom Erse was third with 84 pence, but insisted it had won overall because it was the only country with an international road transport system, money *and* an environment. Serenia had no money at all, but was quite unrepentant. Its people had done their own thing and were feeling very pleased with themselves - though they looked rather thoughtful when the leader of Beli Cose reported she would have followed the call of *lebensraum* and invaded Serenia if time had permitted. The three 'losers' (but what does 'losing' mean in the context of The Road Game?) were unanimous in condemning Salami's foreign and domestic policies, in spite of (or because of?) the fact that Salami had 'won'.

Closing Debriefing The Road Game should be organized so that each country takes its turn to comment on the game and to complain, if they wish, about the behaviour of another country, or countries. When this happens the two countries who are not immediately involved in the dispute become the judges. They decide whether the relevant country gets paid for its roads. On another occasion when we played this game, a participant (a university senior lecturer) said derisively that crawling all over the floor was a game for children, that the activity was totally disorganized, and that no one could possibly learn anything from it. We asked him to be patient and listen to the discussion. By the end of half an hour he had quietened down considerably and when the seminar was over he stayed behind to ask if we knew any more political games.

38 THE PHOTOCOPY MACHINE

Time required About half an hour: up to about an hour if numbers are large.

Aims

* To study individual negotiation styles.
* To explore conflict resolution.
* To practise persuasion as a leadership skill.

Group size Numbers will depend on circumstances. Theoretically any number can participate in this activity as players and/or observers; but everybody must be in a position to see and hear the action.

Environment Virtually any classroom environment.

Procedure

(1) Make sure everybody is sitting comfortably and can see and hear you clearly.

(2) Give them this scenario:

'I want you to imagine that the photocopy machine broke down in your office this morning and has only just been repaired. It is now 4.30pm and normally everybody goes home at 5 pm. But by 8.30am tomorrow 150 folders have to be filled with 20 pages of material for a conference. It is your job as the office manager to persuade the relevant staff member to stay late and do the photocopying. Unfortunately your task is made difficult by your knowledge that this person has tickets for a one-night jazz concert tonight by an internationally famous overseas group. This staff member queued all night to get tickets and has been talking for weeks about the concert.'

(3) Ask one person to role-play the manager and someone else to play the subordinate.

(4) Help them only as much as needed to get them into role, then let them negotiate the situation.

(5) When the roleplay comes to a natural end (whatever the result); or when one player indicates they have had enough, ask two more people to assume the roles and let them see how far they

can take the negotiation. You may want to run the roleplay once more, with another pair, but we usually find three times is enough.

Evaluation At the end of each roleplay ask the audience: 'On the basis of what you've just seen and heard, do you think in this situation that the conference delegates will have their folders in front of them in the morning?' As an example, the following was an occasion when all participants replied: 'Yes!'

A man called Jim played the manager. He started off by saying to his 'staff member': 'Now, Tom, I'm not going to blame you. I know it wasn't your fault; it's just one of those things. It can't be helped.'

Tom found himself replying: 'Well, thank you, Jim, I appreciate that', even though it was Jim's unfounded assumption that Tom was to blame in the first place.

'Don't worry about it' continued Jim. 'I know you'll get the job done, just like you always do. You're one of the most reliable people on my team, and I've got total faith in you. And I'll tell you what I'll do – I'll phone my wife and tell her I'll be late. I know she's got a dinner party and she'll be furious with me, but that can't be helped. I'll stay and help you for at least an hour.'

Tom thanked him again with genuine gratitude and that was the end of the roleplay. Not only did Tom have no opportunity to mention the concert tickets, he did not even want to mention them. His boss had manipulated his feelings so successfully that he was willing, even eager, to do the job, and ended up thanking the manager for letting him do it.

During another roleplay a woman called Esther played the manager and negotiated rather uneasily for a while with her 'employee', who became increasingly insubordinate. Esther stopped, looked at us, and said: 'I'm finding this really difficult, and quite untrue to life, because in my office this kind of thing just would not happen.' We asked why not, and she replied: 'Because the minute that photocopy machine broke down, I'd have been on the phone to the nearest printing firm to arrange for them to do all the conference material.' She maintained that crises never happened in her office.

'Funny', said Jim. 'In my office they happen all the time!' Somebody asked Jim if he ever precipitated a crisis, just for the intellectual stimulation, and before he could answer, his accountant (who was one of the group members) replied with feeling, 'Oh, yes!'

Esther was frankly incredulous; she just could not believe that anyone would want to behave in so irresponsible a fashion. Ordinarily, she would dismiss such a person as incompetent but she could not react that way to Jim, who was plainly very competent indeed. The whole group began to discuss what it feels like when someone who hates a crisis, who plans carefully and avoids crises, has to work with (or is married to) a person who thrives on crises and will apparently wantonly destabilize a situation or a relationship just because of a need for the creative stimulus of restabilizing it in a different way.

Closing Ask participants:

- if they think the activity identified differences in individuals' negotiation styles;
- if it revealed ways to explore conflict resolution through compromise;
- what they have learned about persuasion as a leadership skill.

39 THEM AND US

(There is a similar activity 'Majors and Minors', in Joanne Hope's 1986 book, *Games Nurses Play.*)

Time required About 20 minutes, preferably a break period, or interval between two sessions.

Aim To explore some symbols of power and status, and their effects on people's behaviour.

Group size At least 10 people and preferably 15–25.

Environment This activity requires a setting in which refreshments are served, for example during a seminar in a hotel or conference room where participants break for coffee or lunch by going to a specially prepared dining room. Ask the functions manager to make the following arrangements for morning coffee:

(1) To group chairs at one end of the room only.
(2) To set up two tables:
   • one table near the chairs with a big (preferably silver or fine china) coffee pot, cream jug, sugar bowl, cups and saucers, cloth table napkins, and plates of biscuits;
   • the other table at the bare end of the room with nothing but a plain coffee urn and plastic cups.
(3) To label each table with a large, clear sign, one at the more heavily laden table reading '**US**' and the other one at the more modest table reading '**THEM**'. The details will vary, but the general effect should provide a sharp contrast in style and content between the two tables.

Take the functions manager into your confidence, explain why you want the room to be set up this way, and say that you would like the waiters and waitresses to restrict their service to keeping up supplies. (We remember one waitress who became so interested in the activity that she asked afterwards if she could give some feedback to the group, based on her observations of their behaviour. They listened with great respect to her extremely pertinent comments.)

Provide badges or some other form of visible identification for all participants. One set (or half the total group) should read '**THEM**' and the other '**US**'. Provide two sets of instructions, written on cards. One set each for half the total number of participants (see p. 187).

Procedure

(1) Shortly before the coffee interval, explain to your participants that this will be a working break.
(2) Divide them into two groups. If you are working with multicultural, multilingual, or otherwise mixed participants, you may want to divide them into two homogeneous groups. Or you may want males in one group and females in the other.
(3) Give each person a badge or some other form of visible identification. Thus half the whole group will be labelled '**THEM**' and half '**US**'.
(4) Give an appropriate instruction card to each player (ie an **US** card to all **US**s and a **THEM** card to all **THEM**s)
(5) Begin the coffee break by leading all participants into the dining room.

Evaluation When the players go into the coffee room and become aware of the inequality of the situation, they react in a number of ways, some of them extreme. For example it becomes obvious very quickly to **THEM** that if they want cream or sugar in their coffee, they are going to have to go over to the **US** table and ask for it – which will mean either grovelling or risking a snub. If the first few tentative attempts are met with patronage by **US** players, some **THEM** people will not persist; they would rather take their coffee black or drink nothing at all than be a participant in an unequal interaction.

This happened when we used this activity during an international conference in France, at which papers and discussions were presented in French and English, but where power games were being played between the French-speaking and the English-speaking participants over which language would be used for informal conversations. Since France was the host country, we gave all of the French speakers the status of NOUS LES FRANÇAIS and all the foreigners became NOUS LES AUTRES. We specified that the only language NOUS LES FRANÇAIS would recognize in the coffee room would be French. The French speakers were delighted with this chance to even up a few scores and behaved with a cool arrogance that LES AUTRES, especially the native English speakers, found annoying – so much so that none of them took any refreshment at all but stood around their table with their backs to LES FRANÇAIS, talking in carefully non-modulated voices.

Another example of an extreme reaction is when some players – Australians in particular – cannot handle the elitism of being US and walk over to THEM to make friendly conversation, only to become even more embarrassed when they are treated as visiting VIPs.

Closing After such encounters it is interesting to discuss the possibility that liberal-minded people are behaving simplistically if they seek to break down social and economic barriers by ignoring them.

HANDOUT
Them and us

US

During the following coffee break you will find yourself among members of an 'in-group' and an 'out-group'. You are fortunate to be a member of the 'in-group', which means that you are one of **US**, not **THEM**. You will recognize the others who share your exalted status by the **US** identification that they wear. Please join them at the senior managers' table and sit in the comfortable chairs. If any of **THEM** approach your table with a request of any kind, you will, of course, make sure that they behave respectfully or you will send them away.

THEM

During the coffee break you will all find yourselves to be members of either an 'in-group' or an 'out-group'. Unfortunately, you are one of the 'out-group', which is denoted by your badge, which says '**THEM**'. You may not take your refreshments from the table near the chairs – your table is the one in the corner. The chairs are reserved for the use of those whose buttons read '**US**'. You may sit on the floor if you wish. If you should need anything from the **US** table, you may go over and ask for it, but be sure that your manner is respectful and that you show by your behaviour that you understand the exalted status of **US** people. If by any chance an **US** person approaches your table, this is a great honour which you should acknowledge appropriately.

40 DIGICON

Time required One class period: about 40 minutes.

Aims

- To provide a planning exercise.
- To illustrate leadership behaviour.
- To explore the feelings of followers for their leaders, depending on the leader's behaviour.

Group size Digicon can be played with as few as 4 people and will still 'work', but its effects are much greater if there is competition between groups of players, and for that you need larger numbers, say 8 people upwards. There is no upper limit, providing you have plenty of space and can stand a lot of noise.

Environment You need no special materials, just ordinary classroom furniture. Each player should have a pencil and paper, and you must provide a large door key, because this is the most important 'prop' in the game.

Procedure Digicon involves people playing the roles of either prisoners or robots (ie who behave as mechanical figures). There is one robot for every 'cell' of 3-7 prisoners. Thus in a class of 12 learners there might be 3 robots and 3 cells, each holding 3 prisoners.

(1) Make sure everyone has a pencil and paper.
(2) Divide the players into groups of any number from 4 to about 8 – the groups do not have to be the same size.
(3) Ask for one volunteer from each group to play a robot. Ask the robots to imagine they are machine-made slaves who have to obey their masters. They can see, hear, move and respond like human beings, but cannot speak.
(4) Tell all the rest that they are prisoners locked in cells, and box each group into a corner or against a wall by pushing tables and chairs in front of them to represent their cells. Keep the cells as far apart as possible. The robots stand outside their respective masters' cells and await activation.
(5) Draw everyone's attention to a large door key that you have placed somewhere in the room in full sight.
(6) Describe the following scenario to everyone. It will seem complicated when you read it but it takes only a few moments

to explain and it seems difficult only on the first occasion that you direct the game. After that it gets easier each time, and you will find yourself adding all sorts of fancy touches.

Scenario

You are all characters in a science fiction story. You are either extra-terrestrial travellers (ETTs) or earth-bound robots. All the ETTs have been taken prisoner by earthlings and locked in cells. At any time you may be taken out by the guards and executed. Your only hope of escape is to order the robot slaves to bring you the key (which you can all see, wherever it is) which opens every cell door. But you must be quick, because you don't know if the prisoners in the other cells are friends or enemies.

Those who escape first may release the others, or they may murder them.

Those of you who are robots are free to move about anywhere except into the cells. Before the prisoners can use their respective robots they have to activate your memory-banks by giving you a list of commands. Write these words down. Unfortunately none of you are very efficient robots. Your memories can only hold 10 commands, each of not more than two words at the most. *These are the only sounds to which you can respond.* Moreover the command words cannot be in English or any recognizable language; they have to be nonsense-words like 'zin' for 'go forward' or 'chut' for 'go back'. This is because each cell is full of multicultural prisoners who have no common language and therefore they have to make one up.

Each group of prisoners in each cell will have to decide which commands will mean what, and then put them into their respective robots' 'look-up table', so that when the robot is activated it can be ordered to go and get the key and bring it to the cell. Thus the robots respond to a list of predetermined commands.

Once stored, these commands can be given in any order and used repetitively. *The stored lists in the robots' memories cannot be changed.*

(7) When you have explained all this, answer questions briefly, and make sure everyone understands what they have to do. Then give the prisoners 5 minutes to fill their robots' memory-banks. Each cell should begin discussing what words it will need to feed into its robot and as the prisoners decide each of the commands, they and their robot should write it down, with the English translations. Keep checking to see that this is happening but do not interfere in any other way, and above all, do not offer any suggestions. If you are playing with a multinational group you will almost certainly find that at least one group uses command words from a real – if obscure – language that one of its members speaks, like Basque or Tamil. Allow this.

(8) When the 5 minutes are up, send all the robots out of the room.

(9) Then announce that the guards have made some changes to the prison, and move the furniture around a bit – for instance, pull a table out into the middle of the room and explain that this is a tunnel that the robots will have to crawl through to get the key. Add some more obstacles, such as making it necessary for the robot to climb over something. You can move the key if you want to, and if you are playing Digicon with a very clever group you can afford to be really sneaky and hide the key where the robots will not be able to see it easily.

By this time, some of the prisoners will be very dismayed, probably because it did not occur to them to commit to their robot's mechanical memory any words that meant 'crawl' or 'climb'. Reassure them and tell them to do the best they can.

(10) When all the prisoners understand the sequence of actions their robots must perform to get the key, recall all the robots and stand them all together against a wall. Take their memory sheets away and mix them up, then return them so that no robot has its original list. This will probably cause something like panic in both robots and masters, but explain that as the robots are only machines, it does not matter which of them responds to whose commands.

(11) Announce that all robots are now activated and operational.

No one will know what to do at first, but sooner or later one or more prisoners will start calling out commands from their lists. The robots will each anxiously be scanning their own lists to find out what commands they contain, and what they mean. Eventually one of them will recognize a command and respond to it, which will cue other players; and the race will be on. There may be a lot of noise at this point, with everyone shouting out commands, insults and encouragement to the robots. If you have psyched the players into their roles, the robots will not cheat (much) and the prisoners will not walk out of their cells before they get the key. Under pressure and excitement the rules may get a little bent, so be on the watch to restrain the more enthusiastic players. You may have to push people back behind the barricades, scan the relevant vocabularies if you think any robots are responding to more than 10 command words, and forbid any command that sets one robot physically to attack another. The safest thing to tell a group of young players is that if one robot touches another they both have to 'freeze' until their controllers' commands separate them again.

You may need to use your own judgement about when to end the game, because even if one robot gets the key to one cell, the other prisoners may not notice it and may thus continue to direct their own robots. Even if they observe that the key has gone, they may still want their own robot to finish the course. The challenge of negotiating it through the various obstacles may be, for them, the nost important part of the game. On the other hand, some players may give up long before this point, because they know that their robot-vocabulary is inadequate. However this decision may be premature because the most pitifully limited word-list can be stretched to an amazing extent by creative thinking.

Closing Players usually find Digicon great fun, and the thrill of the chase makes it a good warm-up game at the beginning of a conference. On one occasion when we did this, the successful prisoners ran around the room after their robot gave them the key, 'unlocking' all the other 'cell doors' in quite a ritualistic way. One of the rescued said later that this behaviour had probably been a critical factor in setting a cooperative standard for the conference as a whole. Robots often report that the process of being programmed makes them feel they 'belong' to the group that programmes them; so it is a real 'culture shock' when they have to exchange vocabularies and discover themselves being directed by strangers. This comment is a good introduction to a discussion about the meaning and the power of organizational socialization.

Robots also develop strong opinions about who was 'really' in control during the game. Some robots argue that theirs was the real power, and they enjoyed it. If this happens you can ask: 'Surely all you did was obey orders?' Sometimes respondents report that their controllers would have been helpless if the robots had not interpreted the orders accurately. This can lead to an interesting debate about the division of labour in organizations – for example, whose is the real power, the people who give the orders or the people who have their hand on the switch? Other robots respond differently – with feelings of helplessness and frustration. They describe how angry they became at what one man described as: '. . . an awful feeling, when you know that the people who have power over you are totally incompetent!'

The prisoners who escape first usually do so because they possess one of two dominant group characteristics. Either they have a strong emergent leader whose competence operates the robot with maximum efficiency, or they are very democratic and task-minded prisoners who take turns almost intuitively to contribute to the action in a kind of brainstorming process. In these latter groups, members clearly recognize and use each other's problem-solving strengths. For instance, there was one prisoner in a cell of three who remained silent while the others programmed the robot (she said she recognized that they were quicker than she at doing this and was happy to let them get on with it). She quickly proved so efficient at operating the robot afterwards that the others willingly fell silent and became satisfied observers of her performance in achieving their common purpose.

As a learning method, Digicon fits quite well into organizational communication programmes, as well as for youth leadership training. For example you can use it to study power relationships between management and workers; or the dynamics of task-oriented small groups, including leadership behaviour, under pressure from the environment. Digicon also can be effective in cross-cultural contexts, for instance to promote understanding of different problem-solving styles between people of different national/ethnic/cultural backgrounds.

41 GERONTOLOGY

(This is a simplified version of a game of the same name in a book called *Australian Management Games* by Barry Moore (1978), based on an original idea by Fred Hollows, University of Michigan at Ann Arbor.)

Time required At least an hour. If the group is large, allow two to two and a half hours.

Aims

* To study how a community is created.
* To examine some of the problems of growing old in the community.

This is a game that can have a stunning effect on groups of social workers, bank trainees, public health students and other managers who work in government departments, the private sector or non-government agencies which have to deal with the aged and the poor. Players might also be leaders of church associations or youth groups because so many people in the community, young as well as old, are concerned with the problems of senior citizens' health and welfare, whether they be neighbours, family members or friends.

Group size At least 12 people. The game works best with at least 25 people, and as many as 50 can take part. None of the players should be old. We do not think this is a good game for elderly people, as it is, perhaps, a bit close to home for them. Even youngsters sometimes get very depressed about the game's implications and you may have to talk them through these feelings. Like New Year's Eve Hat (Activity 28, Chapter 10), Gerontology needs really sensitive leadership. It takes at least two hours to play and debrief.

Environment Beforehand, assemble the following:

* four small sheets of cardboard;
* four felt-tipped pens, preferably in different colours;
* lots of pencils and paper;
* several boxes of paperclips;
* a ball of soft rope. Cut the rope up in advance into a number of 1-ft lengths – at least three times as many pieces as you are going to have players.

- a pair of scissors;
- about 20 cards, the size of playing cards, to contain messages from Death, who in this game is called the 'Grim Reaper'.

Write a number of phrases on the cards, repeating each phrase on several. Here are some examples:

- You have had a stroke and your brain is impaired. Give your pencil to the Grim Reaper.
- You are very old and are losing your memory. Give your paper to the Grim Reaper.
- You have to pay your phone bill. Give one paperclip to the Grim Reaper.
- You have to buy a birthday present for your grandson. Give one paperclip to the Grim Reaper.
- You have arthritis. Give one length of rope to the Grim Reaper.
- Today you fell down and broke your hip. Give all your rope to the Grim Reaper.
- You are dying. You have one minute to make a will if you wish, which the Grim Reaper will execute on your behalf. Then you must die, and leave the game to become a heavenly observer of the remaining players.

When you have directed Gerontology a few times you may want to write more of these Grim Reaper messages, or alter some of them. You may also want to give the 'heavenly observers' some written suggestions about the kinds of interaction they might usefully look for in the players who are 'left alive' – but don't worry about that yet because the above are sufficient for a first attempt.

You need access to the game room a few minutes before the players arrive because you first have to arrange their chairs in special rows. Allow one chair per person, and 10 chairs to a row. Put most of them very close together with almost no room to move along the aisle between the rows. Arrange a few rows with chairs widely spaced with plenty of leg room. All the chairs represent residences. Some are in poor and overcrowded neighbourhoods while others are in salubrious suburbs with lots of space.

On each chair place at least one length of rope, a pencil, a sheet of paper and one paperclip. Put an extra piece of rope and two or even three paperclips on each of the widely spaced chairs. Ropes represent players' mobility, paperclips their money, and paper and pencil their knowledge and experience.

At each end of the room there must be a desk and chair, with the chair behind the desk, facing out into the room. If there are more than 25 players and the room is large, set up four desks. They represent banks and welfare agencies. Try to arrange them so they are as far as possible from the rows of chairs. The bank should be close to the 'good' neighbourhood, and the welfare agency should be relatively near the poor quarter; but they both (or all) should be at least one rope's length away from the nearest chair in the nearest row. On each desk put a sheet of cardboard, a felt-tipped pen, and (dividing out the supplies equally), the rest of the paperclips, pencils and papers. Put the remaining ropes *only* on the desk(s) of the bank manager(s).

Procedure

(1) When the players arrive, ask for two volunteers if you have a small group (say 10-15 people), and four volunteers if the group is larger. Ask the volunteers to sit at the desks and tell them that you will visit them later with their instructions.
(2) Ask all the others to find a chair, gather up and hold the ropes, paperclips, pencils, and papers that are on it and then sit down, but not to change the position of the chairs. Ask them to tie one end of a length of rope to their wrist and another to the leg of their chair.
(3) While they are doing this, go round to each of the volunteers. Tell those to whom you give the supply of ropes that they are bank managers. The ropes represent their clients' mobility, the paperclips are money, and the pencils and papers are for the managers to create any paperwork, special reference forms, etc, that they decide clients must complete before they borrow money. The ropes are for sale, for any number of paperclips each manager decides. In order to negotiate with the bank, a client has to keep one hand on the manager's desk at all times. Tell the bank manager that this rule should be strictly enforced. A manager may wish to make other rules as well, such as insisting that the client make an appointment, or show identification, or whatever. The managers should interpret their roles as imaginatively as possible, and are free to act virtually as they want.
Ask the managers to draw a sign on the cardboard with the felt-tipped pen, and prop it up on the desk, so customers will know the name of the bank, what the banking hours are, and so

on. Managers may leave their desks to visit anyone – for instance, the welfare agents – or just to take a break; but a responsible person must be delegated to 'mind the shop' while they are away, and the bank will he closed to customers during that time. There is an imaginary telephone on the desk, so enquiries can be called out to anyone in the room, and information called back in return.

The other one or two volunteers are welfare agency representatives. They are to assess the needs of any client who visits the agency, and can give money at their discretion. The agency does not have any ropes, which can be purchased only from the bank. Give the agent(s) all the instructions that you gave the bank manager(s), and suggest that they may like to prepare some questionnaires, etc, for the clients to complete before aid is given; or they might want to devise some other form of investigation and/or selection process. Ask the agent(s) to use plenty of imagination in interpreting the role.

(4) Address the room at large. Tell the group that they are all old people in the community. The chairs they are sitting on represent their homes, the paperclips their worldly wealth, the rope their mobility, the pencil and paper their knowledge and memory respectively. At all times they must have one end of a rope tied to their wrists and the other end tied to the chair, but two or more lengths of rope can be joined together. The chairs cannot be moved but players may negotiate to buy each other's houses if they wish to move to another neighbourhood, or to acquire property for speculation. In these cases they can move to the appropriate chair, even if it means displacing its occupant. If this happens (say because an 'old person' has been forced by poverty to sell his or her home), the homeless one must sit on the floor, with the end of the rope caught underneath the nearest chair.

Apart from these provisos the players can do anything they want, provided there is not a rule that expressly forbids it. The people at the desks represent banks and welfare agencies, who are there to serve this community of senior citizens. They should be approached for advice and assistance when these are required.

(5) Ask if anyone has any questions about what you have said so far. Repeat anything you have to. When everyone is silent, tell them that the game can now begin.

(6) Once the action is well under way, you should move quietly among the players. Your role is that of the Grim Reaper. Whenever you see anyone who appears to be rather too active – or for any other reason that seems good to you – give that person a card out of your pack. You may want to let players select one at random, or you may want to give them a specific handicap, or kill them off altogether, after which they have to leave the game and become observers. We dislike this role very much because players quickly learn to greet the Grim Reaper with open dread, even hostility. We remember one man – a senior government employee – who shouted, 'Get away from me, you bitch!' when he saw one of us coming. It was unthinkable that he would speak like that to her in real life and after the game he was very apologetic. We reassured him that his reaction was a real tribute to the power of the game. All the same, we usually hand over the Grim Reaper role to the first player we decide should 'die' – which has the added advantage that it brings this person actively back into the game.

Evaluation After you announce the beginning of the action, almost invariably people wait for you to tell them what to do next. Pretend to be busy with the video camera or something, or just sit there. Probably someone will ask eventually: 'What are we supposed to do now?' In which case you reply: 'How you play the game is entirely up to you. All I have done is set the scene for you; now you have to create the action.'

Sometimes they then call out to the bank manager, for instance, asking what they can do. The manager may mime a telephone call in order to reply that the client must personally visit the bank. People will begin to negotiate, to beg, borrow, or steal more paper clips and extra lengths of rope if they need them to reach the bank or the welfare agency. Gradually a society begins to emerge out of this collection of individuals. It is up to you to assess the nature of that society. Is it individualistic or communal, capitalist or with some other form of economic structure? Within it, how are the old people treated and how do they behave towards each other? Are the bank and welfare agency very bureaucratic? Do people have to stand in line for government aid? Who gets rich and who stays poor? Why?

You will find that the group dynamics are different depending on whether you allow a significant number of players to remain 'alive and well' long enough to get themselves organized and start having a good time. For instance, in one game we left players alone until several people found themselves 'jobs', like dusting people's chairs, and some others joined ropes together to make a community bus to visit housebound citizens. The bank manager was extremely obliging about overdrafts and the welfare agent dispensed paperclips on a regular basis.

Players' responses afterwards to a game like this are likely to be very positive. They will make statements to the effect that getting old is not all that bad, because there is always work to be found if you want it and anyway a community looks after its own. On the other hand participants' reactions will be much more negative if you have ensured that most players died, one by one, from various depressing illnesses, so that those left behind found themselves wandering about aimlessly in an empty world with a great deal of money and mobility but no incentive to do anything. It may occur to them to criticize the attitudes of society in real life that allow old people to wither away unnoticed and uncared for.

On one occasion a woman called Beth decided to 'commit suicide' (ie leave the action and become an observer) because, she said, she was 'starving to death' in her home. The Grim Reaper had struck her down, first with a severe illness so she had no mobility, and later with loss of memory so she had no paper and pencil. She had lent her sole remaining paperclip to a neighbour who had not returned it; in addition, the players in the chairs around her were busy chatting to each other, ignoring her. In the debriefing, Beth made it quite clear that she was still annoyed and hurt by the way her fellow players (in real life her fellow health administration graduate students) had treated her. For example, 'the woman next door' had acquired many lengths of rope but refused to give even one to Beth without payment even though it was obvious Beth could not afford to pay. Beth now asked this player: 'Why wouldn't you lend me even one rope, so I could move?' The woman, plainly disconcerted, replied that she had not wanted to restrict her own mobility and added, 'Why are you taking this so seriously? It was only a game!' Beth retorted: 'If it was only a game, why should it matter to you how many ropes you had?' We think this is a good example of how scarcity of resources and constrained circumstances can put pressures on people to behave in antisocial ways.

Closing These are the kinds of responses that make Gerontology an effective problem-solving game in appropriate learning circumstances, but again it is one we recommend for experienced game-directors only. Its open-ended structure generates not only strong but very diverse and complex feelings.

42 MODEL AEROPLANES

(There is a much more elaborate version in *Organizational Psychology* by Kolb, Rubin and MacIntyre (1984) but you will find ours is equally good for a comparative study of team efficiency.)

Time required At least an hour, maybe more, otherwise don't play it. The discussion afterwards is when the real learning occurs.

Aims

- To illustrate the importance of teamwork in quality assurance programmes.
- To identify the critical components in quality assurance.

Group size From 8 to any number of people who can work comfortably in small groups at tables in the one room. Ideally you need at least two groups and preferably three, each of about 3 – 5 people.

Environment A large room in which players are free to move about. Tables and chairs for the aeroplane builders. Provide lavish quantities of paper – recycled paper is fine, but you will be surprised sometimes at how much is used. You can devise a price list if you want to (Kolb, Rubin and MacIntyre's lists are quite complex). If you are lucky enough to have an economics expert to play the role of PO (see below), so much the better. When the game gets going, ask that person to work out a discount price for bulk orders of paper, or any other refinement he or she cares to invent.

Procedure

(1) Form all the players except two (or more than two if group numbers are large) into teams of 3 – 5, though you can form groups of up to 7 people.
(2) Tell them each team represents an aircraft manufacturing company whose business is to make and sell model aeroplanes, which will have to pass a quality control test (ie they must fly) before a government purchasing officer will agree to buy them.
(3) Ask each company to give itself a name, which you post.
(4) Each team has to choose a general manager (GM) to be in charge of purchases and production; and an assistant general manager (AGM), who is responsible for quality control and sales. The other members are assembly-line workers. Post the

name of each group leader under the appropriate company name.

(5) Introduce the two people you have kept in reserve as, respectively, a purchasing officer (PO) and a quality control manager (QCM). Explain that the QCM has to test the model aeroplanes, and those that pass are handed on to the PO for purchase.

(6) Explain that paper sheets with which to make the aeroplanes can be bought from the PO at 10 pence a sheet, and the aeroplanes (which can be made from a single sheet) will be purchased for 15 pence each, providing they pass quality control.

(7) Give everybody half an hour to play the game. You can issue a standard model aeroplane design, if you like, which everybody has to follow, or you can say that any design will do, providing the planes will fly. (How 'fly' is interpreted depends on the QCM. This game leaves a lot of responsibility to the players.) Note that if you insist on a standard design, some teams will negotiate with the PO to accept another. Whether or not this strategy is successful will depend on the PO.

We think the game works better this way because it stretches the players more, but the process will take longer than if you leave the design open.

(8) Having set the whole thing up, you can afford to relax for half an hour and amuse yourself by watching the show. Sometimes the air becomes so thick with flying aeroplanes that you have to watch out you don't get one in the eye. Frequently the assembly-line workers spend as much time in testing their planes as they do in making them.

Evaluation Eventually you get everybody's attention (which may be difficult) and post the results. One team will emerge as the winner as far as profit is concerned but the really interesting part is discovering how the various team dynamics worked and how the companies ran their businesses.

Closing Government employees are often made very thoughtful by this game because they are not used to working to an economic bottom line (which tells us something about criteria for public expenditure) and it gives them valuable insights into private sector thinking. Some companies will not hesitate to cheat, for example, by forging the QCM's signature to get a faulty plane accepted by the

PO. When this happens, we like to start a discussion about business ethics.

In most playings of the game, profitability seems to depend on good design rather than careful construction – why, we we do not know; but time and again a team-member will come up with a brilliant design that wipes the floor with all competitors. All in all, Model Aeroplanes is rich in human potential. When we played it on one occasion on the first day of an intensive residential course for senior government officials, the course organizer told us later that it provided a benchmark for everything that came later.

43 WIN OR LOSE

Time required About 45 minutes.

Aims

- To recognize the advantages and disadvantages of teamwork.
- To help individual players recognize their own preferred behaviour as team members and as leaders.

Group size This game requires a fairly large group, say from 16 people upwards. You can play it with as few as 8, but it's not so effective.

Environment The classroom. Prepare a copy of the Win or Lose sheet (see p. 205) for every participant. If possible, advise all participants in advance that this will be a gambling game and they should bring a sum of money with them, small enough to lose without distress. If you can't do this, or don't want to, provide yourself with a float of about five pounds. This game works best when people actually stand to win or lose real money, even if a very small amount; but if you don't have a petty cash account for game materials and don't feel sufficiently altruistic to donate a sum out of your own pocket, make it clear that any money you hand out during the game has to be returned to you afterwards.

Procedure

(1) Without announcing the aims of the activity, tell people this is a gambling game, and divide them into four teams by arbitrarily designating everybody as 1, 2, 3 and 4 respectively, then putting all the 1s, the 2s, the 3s and the 4s together. It doesn't matter if you only have two or three 4s; but if there's only one, you may prefer to start again, and form teams with 3 people in each.

(2) Give each person in each team a Win or Lose sheet.

(3) Start the game by asking the team nearest you whether they want to choose X or 0? They are almost certain to protest that they haven't had time to decide, in which case allow them, and the other teams, the stipulated 2 minutes. But at all times push for consensus as quickly as possible within teams.

(4) Play the game, round by round. It is obvious from the beginning that if all four teams vote X in every round, every participant will win 10p each time. However in our experience this never

happens! At least one team always tries to outsmart the others and win more money for its own members, for example by voting 0 in round 4. If team representatives want to negotiate with other teams, allow this. If they want to negotiate in private, let them leave the room. But always insist on the time limit and enforce the penalty if any team has not made up its mind when time is up. Create as much tension and competitiveness as you can.

Evaluation When the game is over, survey the results. Did one team emerge as 'the winner', ie with more money than the others? In which case why? Or if not, why not? What were the incentives to cooperation? The incentives to competition?

Conclusion Ask everybody how much your own leadership style affected players' behaviour. Did you succeed in setting up assumptions that this was necessarily a competitive game? Initiate a discussion about accepting other people's assumptions about the nature of a situation, and how this can constrain your decision options. Relate the discussion to the aims of the activity.

HANDOUT
Win or Lose

SCORE SHEET

IF ALL FOUR GROUPS CHOSE 0 (ZERO)	ALL GROUPS LOSE £1
IF THREE GROUPS CHOSE 0	THEY EACH WIN £1
AND ONE GROUP CHOSE X	IT LOSES £3
IF TWO GROUPS CHOSE 0	THEY WIN £2 EACH
AND TWO CHOSE X	THEY LOSE £2 EACH
IF ONE GROUP CHOSE 0	IT WINS £3
AND THREE GROUPS CHOSE X	THEY LOSE £1 EACH
IF FOUR GROUPS CHOSE X	THEY ALL WIN £1

Win or Lose round	Time allowed	Choice		£won	£lost	Balance
1	2 minutes	X	0			
2	1 minute	X	0			
3	1 minute	X	0			
4	1 minute	X	0			
5	3 minutes	X	0			
6	1 minute	X	0			
7	1 minute	X	0			
8	3 minutes	X	0			
9	1 minute	X	0			
10	3 minutes	X	0			

44 WHO WANTS THE JOB?

Time required About one and a half to two hours.

Aim

- To identify problems in the recruitment process.
- To recognize strategies for 'selling' your company to the most suitable potential applicants.

Group size Any manageable number, divided into sub-groups if necessary. Ideally the class should consist of at least 9 people.

Environment An ordinary classroom with each group seated round a separate table. Prepare a copy of the scenario for each participant and at least one copy of the guidelines for each role.

Procedure

(1) Give everybody a copy of the scenario on p. 208; give them time to read and absorb it, and to ask any questions.

(2) Ask for volunteers to play the union representative, the recruitment manager and the equal employment opportunity (EEO) officer. Give these people each a copy of their respective roles (see p. 209) and suggest they leave the room or at least retire to a quiet corner to discuss their roles for about 10 minutes.

(3) Meanwhile discuss with the human resource management (HRM) officers what recruitment methods they might use.

(4) When everybody is back together again, set up interviews between the roleplayers and the HRM officers. You may find that some participants would rather not take active roles; in which case ask them to act as observers and give them a complete set of roles for background information.

(5) As class leader you will play the role of chairperson. Begin by seating the active players at one big table (pull several small ones together if necessary) and sit yourself at the head of it.

(6) Announce that the reason for the meeting is to decide, as a matter of urgency, how most effectively to recruit at least two accountants.

(7) Introduce everybody, clockwise round the table, by saying aloud their name and job position (invent names for them if you prefer).

(8) Ask each person in turn to state their case and give them 3

minutes each to do so. Interrupt them courteously and move on to the next person if anybody goes over time.

(9) When all have spoken, throw the meeting open to 15 minutes' general discussion. You may have to offer suggestions to help things along (especially if you are working with inexperienced participants). Some suggestions might be to:

- recruit book-keepers instead of accountants, to work under the accountants currently employed;

- provide the new book-keepers with formal and on-the-job training to upgrade their skills;

- invite current employees in the finance department to undertake multiskilling programmes to equip them to handle basic accounting responsibilities as well as their original jobs (with appropriate re-writing of job descriptions and renegotiated salaries).

- initiate a job-sharing scheme: recruit two part-time accountants.

(10) Keep control of the meeting by posting all definite proposals (to be voted on later) and by restating at intervals the reason for the meeting: to find an urgent solution to the problem of an acute skills shortage in a specific area. Don't allow people to get distracted. One strategy is to suggest that all important but irrelevant issues should be postponed to a subsequent meeting.

(11) After about 15 minutes ask the committee to vote on all proposals that have been put forward.

(12) Finally ask the observers, if there are any, to offer any comments that occur to them: and these end the activity.

Evaluation
- Ask each roleplayer in turn what insights they have gained to the recruitment process through playing their roles.
- Post several key comments; and ask whose objectives were achieved and why.
- Were there any negotiation tactics or arguments that proved to be particularly successful?

Closing Ask the class which of the posted comments they think are critical.

HANDOUT
Scenario

You are human resource management (HRM) officers in a company where a vacancy for a cost accountant has been outstanding for six months. Two offers have been rejected and one appointee has resigned after six weeks. She complained to the placement agency that her colleagues discriminated against her because of her colour. The agency telephoned you to warn you.

Not only this agency but all the others have no more applicants on their books and the recruitment manager has come to you in a state of distress and frustration. Moreover the senior financial manager has approached you about two other vacancies for qualified accountants at a salary which unfortunately is below market rate.

She tells you the job can be carried out by someone who is not professionally qualified if they have the experience of a qualified accountant. The job carries the same grade as that of qualified accountants. To complicate matters further, the union representative has confirmed it is company policy to consult the union before placing job advertisements but the recruitment manager refused to do so when advertising for accountants. The union rep has heard that non-qualified people may be employed in positions at the same grade and the same salary as qualified accountants and is concerned about this possibility.

Faced with this situation, you need to talk to the recruitment manager, the union representative and the equal employment opportunity (EEO) officer; and then decide how to go about recruiting some accountants – fast!

HANDOUT
The Roles

The Union Representative

As described in the Scenario, you are shortly to be present at a meeting between the Recruitment Manager from the Personnel Department, the EEO officer and several personnel management officers to decide, as a matter of crisis, how to recruit some accountants. You have previously had a very unpleasant meeting with the Recruitment Manager, who continues to dispute your right to be consulted over the wording of job advertisements. At this meeting you are determined to accomplish two objectives: (1) to obtain formal recognition of your right to be consulted over job ads, as agreed between your company and the union. You are quite prepared to recommend industrial action (ie some kind of work stoppage, or even a full strike) if necessary to uphold this agreement. (2) to ensure that non-qualified people are not recruited to positions of the same grade and salary as qualified accountants.

The Recruitment Manager

As described in the Scenario, you are shortly to meet other personnel managers to decide, as a matter of crisis, how to recruit some accountants.

The union representative and the EEO officer will be present at the meeting. You met the union rep recently, when you made it clear that the personnel department will not tolerate interference in its recruitment methods.

The rep tried to insist that there was a company agreement with the union to this effect; but to your knowledge there has been no written directive to confirm this. You are not prepared to consult with the rep on this matter until you get something in writing to say you have to.

You are aware that the EEO officer is concerned not only with appropriate pay scales but also that equitable treatment be given to non-Caucasian and female employees. This is the result of one unfortunate incident when a very aggressive new recruit, who happened to be female and black, had to be put in her place. She chose to resent it and left. At this meeting you are determined to accomplish two objectives: (1) to make it clear that in all matters of recruitment and human resource management the personnel department is legally and morally above reproach; (2) to devise some strategy to advertise for accountants that appears to have a good chance of success.

The Equal Employment Opportunity (EEO) Officer.

As described in the Scenario, you are shortly to attend a meeting with the recruitment and other managers of the personnel department.

The union representative will be at the meeting, which is being held to decide, as a matter of crisis, how to recruit some accountants. You have been concerned for some time that recruitment advertisements do not make it sufficiently clear that EEO principles and practices will be observed; and you, like the union rep, are concerned that unqualified accountants should not be given the same salary and grade as CPAs (Certified Public Accountants).

At this meeting you are determined to accomplish two objectives: (1) to obtain an agreement that all advertised job vacancies, from now on, will state explicitly the EEO aims and objectives of the company; (2) to obtain the formal agreement of the personnel office, as represented by the officers at the meeting, to promote actively a policy to encourage women to achieve career positions and to ensure that all staff give courteous and supportive treatment to members of disadvantaged minorities.

45 EMPLOYMENT CONTRACT

Time required About 45 minutes.

Aim To illustrate some aspects of negotiation about remuneration between a contracted employee and the contracting employer.

Group size Any manageable number.

Environment The classroom. Prepare a copy of both roles (pp. 212–13) for all participants.

Procedure

(1) Describe the aim of the activity and initiate a brief discussion about the problems participants may have encountered in negotiating a fee with a client or a remuneration package with an employer.

(2) When everybody is talking easily and people seem relaxed, ask two volunteers to demonstrate some of these problems by means of a roleplay. Give each participant one of the roles; and copies of both to all the observers.

(3) Ask the volunteers to come to the front of the class, or otherwise position them in some way so that everybody can see and hear them.

(4) After the volunteers have had time to read and understand their roles, let them interact in role for about 10 minutes.

(5) Repeat the process with at least two more volunteers before beginning a discussion about what happened during the roleplays, and why.

Evaluation

- Can participants identify the major factors to take into consideration when negotiating an employment contract?
- Can they identify where problems are likely to arise?
- Do any participants have direct knowledge and experience of negotiating remuneration packages? If so, ask them to address the class for a few moments on what they consider to be key factors in the process.

Closing Encourage the discussion to become general. Draw on the resources of all the participants.

HANDOUT
Role A

At a conference you met the human resource development (HRD) Director of a large corporation. This director seemed impressed by your qualifications, your experience in cross-cultural and international management training; and the paper you presented at the conference, about the problems of working with people of different nationalities and cultures.

The director asked if you would be interested in running a three-day residential workshop on cross-cultural negotiation. The participants would be middle-to-senior managers in the company, which is based in New Zealand and organizes oil exploration expeditions all over the Pacific. Company managers have to liaise and negotiate with people in many different Asian countries at every level, from senior government officials to local workers; and apparently they find this very difficult and need some training.

The following week you submitted a proposal in writing and quoted a fee that would vary depending on the number of participants; and whether or not you had to make administrative arrangements such as organizing the location for the training, the catering, and so on.

The next week you received a simple contract in the post. Although you felt you could meet its terms, you did not think you should accept it as written because your fee was described as being payable 'subject to satisfactory completion of the course'; and there was nothing written about your fee being variable depending on the situation.

You requested an appointment to discuss the matter and today you are to meet again with the HRD director. You intend to clarify what 'satisfactory completion' means; and exactly what you are expected to provide under the terms of the contract.

HANDOUT
Role B

You are the human resource development Director of a large corporation, based in New Zealand, that organizes oil exploration expeditions all over the Pacific.

The company managers have to liaise and negotiate with people in many different Asian countries at every level, from senior government officials to local workers; and sometimes they find this very difficult.

At a conference recently you met a consultant with outstanding qualifications and experience in cross-cultural and international management training. This consultant presented an excellent paper at the conference, about the problems of working with people of different nationalities and cultures.

You asked if this consultant would be interested in running a three-day residential workshop for overseas managers, on cross-cultural and international negotiation.

The following week you received the consultant's proposal in writing; and you arranged that the consultant should be sent a copy of the simple training contract you started using when you first took over your job. It allows the contracted trainer to fill in a number of items at will – such as location, training aids required, and so on.

The consultant has since requested an appointment to discuss the contract, though you can't see what there is to discuss; and today you are to meet in your office.

Chapter 12

Activities for cross-cultural communication

The following four activities are roleplays whose time-frames, aims and procedures follow the same pattern.

Time required About 30 minutes.

Aim To practise negotiation with somebody from a different culture, orientation or background.

Group size If you want everybody to play a role, not more than 4 people for a half-hour session. If you are willing to choose a few people from the group to demonstrate the roleplay while others watch and later comment, numbers can be much larger, say up to 25 or even 30 people.

Environment Classroom, seminar room, conference room.

Procedure At the end of a session (before a lunch break, for example) select two people from the group. Tell them you will ask them, during the next session, to conduct a roleplay. Give them each one of the following outlines to read during the break.

Alternatively you can form small groups and distribute all the roleplays among them, give everybody a few moments to read, absorb and maybe discuss the roles; then ask two **volunteers** at a time to demonstrate the roleplays.

(1) Explain the activity will be a roleplay to demonstrate some aspect of cross-cultural communication (however you want to define the phrase).
(2) Ask the two roleplayers to come to the front of the room where everybody can see and hear them; and to negotiate the roleplay.
(3) Initiate a general discussion afterwards.
(4) Ask two more people to take over the roles and afterwards discuss with the group the differences in their handling of the situation compared with the first roleplayers.

46 WAITER, THERE'S A FLY IN MY SOUP!

HANDOUT

Role A

You are travelling in a foreign country. Today, while eating out in a fairly expensive restaurant, you found what looks like part of an insect in your soup. You complained about it to the waiter but he insisted it was spice, not an insect. You do not agree, and have requested to speak to the manager. The manager is coming to your table now.

Role B

You are the manager of a very good restaurant. The prices may seem high, but the quality and the service make them extremely reasonable. Your restaurant has a good reputation and attracts many foreigners. Today a foreign diner came to your restaurant and one of the new waiters served the customer with soup. There seemed to be some complaint; and now the waiter has told you the foreigner wishes to speak to you. You are going to the table now.

Evaluation

(1) Did A complain? Cancel the order for the rest of the meal? Refuse to pay for the soup?
(2) Did B listen to the problem? Correct any misunderstanding? Express regret sincerely? Make apologies gracefully?
(3) Were both parties able to give and receive explanations and find solutions to the problem mutually?
(4) Was A able to make a complaint objectively and effectively? The roleplay can be used to demonstrate the culture-specific nature of people's behaviour. For example, do men and women adopt different behaviour when making the same complaint?

Closing Nobody can make value judgments about the 'best way' to handle communication problems in foreign environments but discussion of this roleplay may help participants to identify a broad spectrum of possibilities.

47 I DON'T BELIEVE IT!

HANDOUT
Role A

You are Korean. You have worked for IBM for about 15 years and have a good position in Korea as a local IBM manager. You are now in Japan on a technology transfer training project. You will be in Japan for one month and will then return to your own country to train Koreans in how to use this new machinery. Your instructor, a person who is very friendly and capable, and about your age, is from Singapore. You like Singaporeans in general and are impressed by their working style, but yesterday something happened which puzzled you. After the instructor had explained a rather complicated operation, he said: 'What do you think? Any questions?' You were really impressed that a machine could perform such a sophisticated procedure, and said: 'I don't believe it!' The instructor made no verbal response to your enthusiasm but later he asked to see you privately. You are going to see him now, but you are not sure why.

Role B

You are a Singaporean who has worked for IBM International for 15 years. You are responsible for a technology transfer project, in which you are training international IBM employees. After this training with you, the participants will return to work at IBM companies in their home countries. You have a good reputation among your colleagues for being honest, friendly, and capable. Yesterday something happened that upset you. After describing a rather technical operation with some new machinery, you asked: 'What do you think? Any questions?' A Korean trainee replied: 'I don't believe it!' You were angry at being told politely that you are a liar, and after the session you asked to see the trainee. Now you are about to meet with this Korean, who is about the same age as you, in an equivalent position with IBM, and with about the same number of years experience. You want this person to know that you do not like being called a liar.

Evaluation Cross-cultural communication theory suggests that the first thing both parties should do is to seek clarification of the other person's intended meaning. Therefore, the trainer from Singapore, who feels the injured party, should find out exactly what the Korean meant by the remark 'I don't believe it!' before getting upset. In fact the expression is common among English-speaking Koreans and means no more than 'Wow!' or 'That's great!' If the Korean in this story can be made to realize that offence has unwittingly been given, explanations can be made to clarify the situation and perhaps to compliment the Singaporean as a good trainer.

Closing This roleplay can be adapted to other situations, for example between a young trainee who expresses enthusiasm in jargon currently popular with his peers but which may be misinterpreted by a much older trainer.

48 MEET THE WIFE!

HANDOUT

Role A

You are a Thai legal advisor to an American import/export firm in Bangkok. You are in your forties, married, and have four children. You were educated in Thailand and your foreign travel has been limited to driving to surrounding countries (Malaysia, Singapore, and a few years ago an attempt to go to Laos but the roads were too bad for your car). Motor cars and driving are your main interests. You bought a new Mazda recently for three times what it would cost in Japan. To prevent it from being stolen, you had a special alarm system installed which sends a signal to your office, your home, and a bleeper which you carry with you at all times. Mostly you drive alone, though occasionally you invite a friend. Today you are attending a reception for the new American managing director of your firm. You have heard that his Corvette is being shipped from the States and you are eager to tell him of your interest in cars and about the new security system that you have for your car. Perhaps you can plan a trip together. You hope that there will be a chance someday to drive his Corvette.

Role B

A week ago you arrived in Bangkok to become managing director of an American import/export firm. You and your wife are staying in a hotel until your furniture and car (a Corvette) arrive next week. Today the firm has invited all employees to a reception in your honour. You are American, in your forties, married with two sons at universities in the United States. Your wife is an artist who in the last two years has had several exhibitions and won two outstanding awards. She is hoping to find a suitable studio and gallery in which to continue her work here. One of your sons is at Princeton University, majoring in international law. He has a very fine record and is vice-president of his class. The other son is studying American literature at Brown University, is editor of the student newspaper, and has sold one article to *Esquire* magazine. You are proud of your family and would like your staff to meet your wife soon, and your sons when they arrive for the Christmas holidays.

Evaluation If the roleplayers follow the above guidelines they will almost certainly be talking at cross purposes and probably becoming irritated with each other. Both characters need to learn appropriate topics of conversation and the kind of small talk in which business people engage at social functions.

Closing You can adapt this roleplay to relate to any two people who have very different interests, for example somebody who is mad on sport and a video games freak.

49 THE COMPANY PIN

HANDOUT
Role A

Before coming to Japan as an American office manager for a joint American-Japanese company, you did a lot of 'homework' in order to understand Japan, the Japanese, and their business practices. One of the things you learned was the obligations that exist both ways between company and employees. For example, Japanese workers are proud of their employers and take pride in wearing the company pin. Most companies require that it be worn during working hours, but many wear it all the time. At your office, you have noticed that a new secretary is not wearing her pin. When you asked her why, she said that she had not received it yet. You asked your personal assistant to see that she got one, and your PA said that she would take care of it. Two days later, you saw that the new secretary was still not wearing the pin. This time your PA said that she would get it later. Wanting to show your understanding of Japan and your concern for the company, you got a pin and gave it to her. You are now about to meet the personnel director to check the background of your personal assistant, who seems not to be following your orders.

Role B

You are the Japanese personnel director for a joint Japanese-American company. An American office manager, recently arrived in Japan, noticed that one of the new secretaries was not wearing the company pin. This manager got a pin and told the young woman to wear it whenever she was in the office. It is your duty to explain to the manager that the pins are not given to new employees until they have been with the company six weeks. Then the pins are presented during a small ceremony when the new employees are made 'family members'. Your job is to explain the situation supportively to the foreign office manager, yet to correct the mistake; and to explain why the manager's personal assistant did not tell him about the ceremony.

Evaluation In this case, the office manager's personal assistant would have felt it presumptuous to argue on her own initiative with her superior's commands, however inappropriate she felt them to be. The manager would have behaved more effectively by asking the PA if she knew why the new employee was not wearing a pin, before acting in an autonomous way that is quite uncharacteristic of Japanese companies.

This role-play offers a good illustration of the value to newcomers of 'informants' within an organization – people who have worked there for some time, who know the ropes and can explain how things are done.

Closing All the above role-plays were designed to reveal particular areas of cross-cultural communication in the broadest sense where misunderstandings frequently arise.

50 THE GLOBAL WORKPLACE

Time required About an hour.

Aim To discuss how training programmes can help to build a united organizational culture with workers of cultural diversity.

Group size About 8 – 28 people.

Environment The classroom. Prepare the three critical incidents (on pp. 225–7) one copy of each for each participant.

Procedure

(1) Announce the aim of the activity and initiate a brief discussion to ensure that everybody understands the topic. Make it clear that though the discussion relates to sexual harassment, this is only one example of a huge range of organizational behaviour for which a multicultural workforce has to find a common standard. If you prefer, you can write a different kind of cross-cultural critical incident as a discussion-starter, perhaps using ours as a model.

(2) Distribute the three critical incident sheets and ask everybody to read them. If you want to, you can then ask for three pairs of volunteers, give each pair the roles in one of the critical incidents, and ask each pair in turn to enact them. With a willing group you can have a lot of fun.

(3) Whether you lift this exercise into a 'moved reading' or allow it to remain at the level of discussion only, encourage the group to express opinions about the content of a proposed training programme on the avoidance of sexual harassment in a workplace in which all three critical incidents ocurred.

Evaluation What key points emerged about problems of training a multicultural workforce?

Closing Broaden the discussion to include other factors to consider when employing people from many different national, ethnic and religious backgrounds.

HANDOUT
Critical Incident 1: Girl Talk

Kurt is a German working as a consultant for the UK office of a German company. Alice is the office manager, white, UK-born; and Maria, a West Indian immigrant, is her assistant.

ALICE: When I walked into the office this morning it seemed to me Kurt was making himself very unpleasant to you. Was he sexually harassing you?

MARIA: It's OK, Alice, I can handle Kurt.

ALICE: That's not the point. You shouldn't have to put up with rude behaviour. I'll speak to Kurt.

MARIA: Oh, Alice, please don't make such a fuss about it, you'll only get me into trouble.

ALICE: No I won't. It's his behaviour that's against the law, not yours.

MARIA: It may not be, where he comes from. And anyway, I've got to work with him, haven't I? So I don't want to get his back up. Besides, he's only here for a few weeks.

ALICE: But the more you put up with it, the worse his behaviour will get – and he'll never learn how to treat British women.

MARIA: We immigrants are used to this sort of thing. We learn not to make a fuss or we'll lose our jobs. It's no big deal, honestly, Alice, just leave it alone.

Questions
- Is Alice exaggerating the situation? Is there really a problem here?
- If so, whose is the problem?
- What should be done about it?

HANDOUT
Critical Incident 2: Shop Talk

Ali is a departmental manager and Ben is one of his supervisors. Both men are Turkish nationals who work in the Izmir branch of a multinational corporation. Ali has asked Ben to come into his office for a private talk.

ALI: Ben, I've had a complaint about your behaviour from one of the Australians.

BEN: What do you mean? I always get on well with everybody. Who's been complaining about me?

ALI: Sheila Kelly, the secretary from Sydney. She says you look at her rudely and make suggestive remarks.

BEN: What? That's ridiculous, she's the one who makes suggestive remarks to me. She puts her hand on my arm and looks boldly into my eyes – she's quite shameless, always talking about her boyfriends. None of the other secretaries behaves like that. Yesterday she asked me to stay late, after the others had left the office, to talk about one of the projects, she said, but I know better.

ALI: Well, the other secretaries are local, they know how to behave. Sheila is a foreigner – maybe they all behave like that in Australia. We don't want her complaining to head office. You should be more discreet.

BEN: But she is gorgeous, man. Can you blame me?

ALI: No, but be careful!

Questions
- Do you think Sheila wanted to encourage Ben to make advances to her?
- What further action do you think Ali is likely to take?
- What further action, if any, should Ali take?
- What is likely to happen, if the situation is allowed to continue as it is?

Critical Incident 3: The Perfect Secretary

Mayumi is a Japanese secretary in a Tokyo bank. Ned Baker is the New York manager of one of the bank's affiliates. He is in Tokyo for a banking conference. This is his first visit to Japan, he thinks he has been well briefed and knows how to behave.

NED: Mayumi, please Xerox this for me.

MAYUMI: Yes, Mr Baker.

NED: Do you know you have the most beautiful eyes?

MAYUMI: No, no, Mr Baker.

NED: Please call me Ned.

MAYUMI: Yes, Mr Ned.

NED: I love when you smile. How about a drink after work?

MAYUMI: I have to meet my friend.

NED: How about tomorrow?

MAYUMI: I have to shop.

NED: Friday?

MAYUMI: I visit my mother

NED: Well, you name the day.

MAYUMI: Er...well...

NED: How about next Monday?

MAYUMI: Well...I don't think...

NED: Fine! I'll come by your office at five pm Monday and pick you up.

MAYUMI: Yes, Mr Ned.

Questions
- Does Mayumi really want to go out with Ned? How do you know?
- Do you think Mayumi can be taught the kind of assertive behaviour that Western women practise? Or do you think she is so much a Japanese woman that she must find her own tactics to cope with foreign men like Ned?

51 SPIKED PUNCH

Time required About 30 minutes.

Aim To sensitize participants to cross-cultural communication problems in a multicultural workforce.

Group size Any number, divided into sub-groups if needed.

Environment The classroom, seminar room, conference room, etc. Prepare a copy for each participant of the Case Study, the Suggested Answers and the Comments Sheet.

Procedure

(1) Announce the aim of the activity.
(2) Distribute copies of the Case Study and Suggested Answers. Ask people to read them, and to work as individuals for 10 minutes to rank-order the suggestions in order of probability (1 is the lowest score; 5 is the highest).
(3) Ask everybody to form small groups (say 3 people in each group) to compare scores for 10 minutes.
(4) Get everybody together in a plenary session. Distribute the Comments Sheet and initiate a discussion about the comments.

Evaluation Did most of the participants agree with the remarks on the Comments Sheet? If so, why? If not, why not? What other comments did people make about the case study? What have participants learned from the activity, about working with people from different backgrounds?

Closing Initiate a general discussion about dietary and other restrictions familiar to group members. Do they have anecdotes about personal frustrations at being unable to find the food or drink, or indulge in the behaviour, of their choice? What compensatory behaviour do they use? How can we help ourselves and others to become more sensitive to people's needs that are based on cultural values other than our own?

HANDOUT
Case Study

Ahmed has recently emigrated to Australia and has found a management position in a fairly small, competitive private company that makes electronic equipment. He is a very smart man with an attractive personality and the company feels it is lucky to have hired him.

Last Sunday he was invited to an office barbecue to celebrate a large new contract. It was a lavish one with angels-on-horseback and other exotic hors-d'oeuvre, various salads, rum trifle, and a whole roast pig on a spit. Alcohol flowed like water – beer, spirits and a punch generously spiked with vodka.

The general manager, who held the barbecue in his garden, did his best to see that Ahmed had a good time. He knew Ahmed was battling bravely with culture shock in his new country, and trying hard to make friends and do a good job at work: but today Ahmed was impossible.

For a start he arrived alone and made no mention of his wife, though the general manager knew he was married and took it for granted, not yet having met his wife, that Ahmed would bring her along to introduce her to everybody. Then, after saying how hungry he was he refused to eat or drink anything and left the party after about 20 minutes with only the curtest apology. Moreover Ahmed's bad temper continued the next day in the office. The general manager began to think Ahmed would never fit in. What on earth was wrong with him?

Suggested Answers

Answer A: When Ahmed saw that his colleagues were accompanied by their partners at the barbecue, he was offended that his wife had not been formally invited.

Score out of 5?

Answer B: Ahmed did not bring his wife because his marriage is breaking up; which is why his behaviour was so unfriendly.

Score out of 5?

Answer C: Ahmed was offended by the presence of the secretaries and other support staff at the party, which he had assumed would be for managers only.

Score out of 5?

Answer D: Ahmed is experiencing much more culture shock than even his boss is aware of. He is so worried about his environment that he cannot relax and enjoy himself.

Score out of 5?

Answer E: Ahmed is Muslim. When he discovered there was virtually nothing he could eat or drink at the barbecue he left because he was so hungry. He was aware his behaviour seemed impolite and the next day in the office his behaviour was still constrained because he didn't know how to explain his problem without making too big a 'thing' of it.

Score out of 5?

Comments Sheet

Suggestion A: This is unlikely. It is more probable that Ahmed would think it inappropriate to bring his wife to an office function, however informal the function. He was not at the party long enough to find out which guests were company employees and which were not.

Score: 1

Suggestion B: This is possible, though we have no evidence for it. It seems more likely, in the context of the case study, that the reason for Ahmed's displeasure was more directly connected with what happened at the barbecue.

Score: 2

Suggestion C: This is possible; but no matter how hierarchical his previous organizational experience may be, Ahmed is a smart man. He has had time to appreciate the relative informality of office life in Australia. Also it is very likely that he heard the secretaries discussing the barbecue the previous week.

Score: 3

Suggestion D: It seems likely that Ahmed did suffer some kind of culture shock at the party, but what was it? We know that he seems to have settled down well at work and is valued by the company. Having accepted the invitation in the first place, it seems unlikely that he would feel so unwelcome he would leave again so soon; especially as the general manager went out of his way to look after him. Therefore what happened to offend him, to the extent that he was still angry at work the following week?

Score: 4

Suggestion E: This is by far the most likely explanation. Practising Muslims don't eat pork, nor do they drink alcohol. If Ahmed was in any doubt about the content of the hors-d'oeurvre (and in fact angels-on-horseback are made with bacon), the salads or the punch, he would not have touched them. Moreover he might well have felt offended that his hosts were so indifferent to his cultural and religious beliefs. Nowadays more Australians (traditionally great meat-eaters) are deliberately providing vegetarian dishes at their parties in deference to Australia's increasingly multicultural population.

Score: 5

52 MADE IN JAPAN

Time required About 30 minutes.

Aim To explore some issues of equal employment opportunity (EEO).

Group size 10 – 30 people.

Environment

(1) Prepare the Discussion Notes (see p. 234).
(2) Prepare a set of 5 headbands. You do this by folding an A4 sheet of white paper in half longways, then in half again to make a strip. Write one of the following in thick black letters on each of the strips:
 ● **Minority** (Note: you may want to write **Black, Hispanic, Indian, Asian, Aboriginal** or some other specific word to denote the kind of minority group member who is particularly disadvantaged in your community.)
 ● **Woman**
 ● **Union Rep**
 ● **MCP** (Note: this stands for 'male chauvinist pig'; but you may like to indicate this mindset with a different word or short phrase.)
 ● **EEO** (Note: this stands for Equal Employment Opportunity Officer.)
 When you have labelled the paper strips, fasten the two ends of each together with tape and then cut down the long folded edge to make the five headbands (measure one on your own head to make sure of the fit).
(3) Get rid of all the tables in the classroom.
(4) Set up five chairs in a circle in the middle of the room. This will be the 'fishbowl'.
(5) Group all the other chairs around the fishbowl, enough for all observers to be seated.

Procedure

(1) Explain to everybody that a fishbowl exercise consists of a small group of volunteers discussing a topic while everybody else acts as audience. The only variation here is that you will stop the discussion from time to time, so members of the audience can change places with the 'fish'.

(2) Co-opt 5 volunteers and give them each a headband to wear. Ask them to behave as they would in real life, if what is written on their headband were true.
(3) Seat them in the fishbowl, and settle everybody else round them.
(4) Announce the setting. Distribute a copy to everybody of Discussion Notes.
(5) When the discussion has got under way (say about 5–7 minutes), call a halt and ask one or more members of the audience to change places with one or more of the fish by taking their place in the circle and assuming their headband. However each newcomer is to interpret the role as they wish. You can choose individuals to change places if you want or you can ask for volunteers.
(7) Start the discussion again from the point where it left off. Give it another 5 minutes or so.
(8) Repeat steps 6 and 7.
(9) You can continue to repeat these steps every 5 minutes, if you like, until all the fish have been replaced at least once; but if so, the exercise will take more than half an hour.

Evaluation Declare a formal end to the activity, then ask the class if they think they have learned anything from it. If they have, what is it? If they have not, why do they think the activity was ineffective?

Closing Ask individuals at random if they can offer an example known to them, of prejudice in the workplace on grounds of gender, colour, etc. Help the class to summarize the basic tenets of an EEO policy.

HANDOUT
Discussion Notes

There has been a merger of two companies. A Japanese manager has taken over your (British/US/Australian/etc) company. He is not anti-women or against any minority group; but it just doesn't occur to him to promote them because they wouldn't get promoted in a Japanese company. There are vacancies for three middle managers. The Japanese chief executive officer (CEO) will follow his usual procedure and give first preference to internal candidates; but he will only consider white males to be eligible. How can you convince him that at least one woman and one member of a minority group should be considered? A group of you have met informally to discuss strategy.

You are, respectively: a member of a disadvantaged minority group; a woman; a union representative; a traditional male (or a woman who holds traditional views about the division of labour between the genders); and an EEO (Equal Employment Opportunity) Officer.

These are some of the points you want to discuss (and you will probably think of others):

- How best to remind the CEO of the company's EEO policy?
- How most effectively to ensure that other candidates are considered besides white males?
- What kind of affirmative action can the group promote?
- What kind of training programmes might be started in the company to promote the career development of currently disadvantaged employees?
- What evidence can the group provide to demonstrate to the CEO that company interests would be served by advancing the position of women and minority employees?

53 AFFIRMATIVE ACTION

Time required: About 45 minutes.

Aims

- To enhance understanding of what affirmative action means.
- To assess the extent to which the organization implements affirmative action in its recruitment methods.

Group size Virtually any number from about 3 people upwards. Large groups can be split into discussion teams.

Environment The classroom. Prepare copies of the case study, one for each participant.

Procedure

(1) Form small discussion teams if necessary.
(2) Announce the aim of the activity; distribute the case study and ask participants to discuss it briefly, as a trigger to think of ways in which affirmative action is or is not implemented in their own organization(s); and how an affirmative action policy could be introduced or improved. Ask a recorder in each team to take notes.
(3) After about 15-20 minutes, call a plenary session and ask recorders at random to read out the notes they have made on their team's suggestions.

Evaluation The aim of this activity is to give participants the opportunity to assess their organization on its affirmative action policies. What was the result? How did the organization in each case emerge from this scrutiny?

Closing Initiate a general discussion, if there is time.

HANDOUT
Case Study: Lady of Spain

The Opiate Pharmaceutical Company (OPC) is located in a city containing a large minority of immigrants from the Middle East, Asia and South America. OPC has a policy of recruiting salespeople from these backgrounds; but so far has been unsuccessful in finding anybody suitable from South America. Recently a Mexican Spanish woman applied for a sales vacancy, along with several other candidates. The recruitment manager is keen to hire her. However, her English is not good and she has very little sales experience in pharmaceuticals; whereas at least one of the other candidates – a native English-speaking man – has these qualifications. Should OPC hire the woman?

Advantages of hiring her:

(1) Her employment would increase the percentage of women and of Latin Americans in OPC; thus supporting OPC's equal employment opportunity policy and at the same time filling a gap in the sales force.
(2) After training, she could become a sales representative to Spanish-speaking sections of the community.

Disadvantages of hiring her:

(1) She would need instruction in English as a second language.
(2) She would need sales training in pharmaceuticals.

Both kinds of training would be expensive and time consuming; and would have to be set against her usefulness to OPC. Moreover the male candidate for the job has expressed a willingness to learn Spanish.

54 TALKING HEADS

Time required The game takes most of one day to play and the debriefing runs throughout the game instead of being restricted to the end, which has the effect of breaking the action up into sessions. This arrangement enables you to maintain control of the simulation by the simple device of stopping the game every 20 to 30 minutes in order to comment on the players' behaviour.

Perhaps surprisingly, these artificial and periodic interruptions – rather like the commercial breaks in a television programme – do not seem to affect players' concentration when they resume their roles. Nevertheless, you should be aware that your 'interference' will to some extent (more or less, depending on the group you are working with) impose your value judgements on the game. Thus when the action starts again you will have given the players a push towards particular kinds of behaviour. Therefore, you want to be sure that this is the way you want the action to go – which implies that you should be well informed on the subject of international and intercultural business negotiation before you direct this game.

Aims

- To make players more aware of a range of important factors that affect the conduct of a business meeting involving people of different cultures.
- To promote greater cross-cultural sensitivity, no matter what the cultural background of the participants. The roles are not cultural stereotypes; they focus on general issues for leaders in international settings.

Group size Virtually any number of players can take part because, if the roles run out, the remaining participants can be observers and their information can be used as feedback to the players at the end of each session.

Environment You will need a committee-style set-up, ie a number of chairs set round a boardroom table or its equivalent. Prepare copies of the instructions and roles as described below (pp. 243–59). To give you some sense of what the game is about, the following is a brief summary:

In 1950 Saito Corporation, a petrochemical company, had an export department which took care of its foreign business, which was only about 7 per cent of its total. However, in the 1960s, Saito began to make major foreign investments and in 1965 the company was restructured according to geographical region.

Today all country managers outside Japan report to and are supervised by an international vice president. Each country is managed largely with local staff. Company reports and all international letters are written in the local language with a translation in Japanese.

Further market expansion has now led to the creation of more divisions within the international section, more and more involved with one another, and much confusion has resulted.

Reorganizing for Greater International Productivity

The President and Board of Directors are now considering a proposal for an organizational restructuring. Under this new plan it is suggested there be five vice presidents: one each for North America, South America, Europe, Asia, and Japan. All individual national divisions are to be directed by managers who will report directly to their respective vice president.

The goal of the reorganization is to coordinate production and marketing efforts across the entire corporation. Furthermore, many company leaders believe that a single language must be chosen as the international language of Saito if that goal is to be achieved. In the roles of national division managers the players are invited to meet in order to decide on this international language for Saito and to review the proposed organizational changes for the company. The scenario specifies that recommendations made by this group will be sent to Saito's President and Board of Directors, and are likely to be followed. (Note: all this may seem very complicated if you don't have a business background, but you will find any group of managers will grasp the essentials very quickly.)

Procedure

(1) Give a copy of the scenario on pp. 243–6 to each participant and give them plenty of time to read it. The players also receive a copy each of the three figures referred to and a copy of the 'conference agenda'. They each get a copy of their individual role instructions (see pp. 247–59).

(2) Explain they have two tasks:
- To make recommendations concerning proposed changes for Saito Corporation;
- To recommend a single corporate language for Saito Corporation's international dealings.

They will be required to adopt certain positions, which are outlined on the cue cards they will receive at the beginning of the game.

These roles may or may not accord with opinions held by the roletakers but nevertheless it will be their task to argue in support of them as effectively as they can.

(3) Most players seem to have no difficulty in assuming their roles as the respective national managers for Korea, Thailand, the Philippines, Singapore, the Netherlands, France, India, the United States, Brazil, Great Britain, Taiwan, Germany and Italy (if you have fewer players you have fewer roles. Pick the ones you like best).

Evaluation Basically what the players have to do is sit around the 'conference table', ostensibly to discuss the ramifications of the proposed organizational changes to Saito Corporation and to decide on a single international language for all its future negotiations. However, all the delegates have hidden agendas as well, because the game setting ensures they will all have strong vested interests in both the organizational structure and the official language of Saito's huge international branch.

For example, the manager from Korea wants the international arm of Saito to drop its attachment to Japan and the Japanese language, which Koreans do not like, and to adopt English as its international language. The manager from Thailand is not really interested in either of the conference objectives, but is far more concerned to bring up more important matters, such as his or her personal problems in managing cultural differences. The representative from the Philippines is a Japanese national, since no Filipino has yet been found who is qualified to be manager. Therefore this representative wants Japanese to be the company's official international language; and likes the proposed reorganization of Saito's international branch since it will make this person a manager, and if s/he does a good job s/he will get back to the home office in Tokyo. On the other hand, the manager from Singapore thinks the proposed reorganization plan is far too complicated and will cause more problems than it tries to solve; and English has to be Saito's international language because, even though Singapore has four official languages (Malay, Tamil, Mandarin and English), everybody knows that English is the international language of business.

And so it goes on. Everybody has some sort of personal stake in the outcome of the conference, and the unfortunate chairperson has to try and get all the participants to some form of consensus on the two agenda items. As game leader, your role is to hold a watching brief and halt the debate at what you decide are critical moments. This requires a high degree of concentration and, as we have said before, considerable experience of international negotiation.

This does not have to be direct experience. You may be a university lecturer, a director of international training programmes, an expert in teaching English as an international language, an organizational orientations manager, or some variant of any of these positions.

These are some of the things you need to consider when you are deciding whether to interfere with the behaviour of the players during Talking Heads:

(1) The emergence of 'hidden agendas'.
(2) Whether you should add extra information from your own knowledge, perhaps about the cultural imperatives of the represented nations.
(3) What strategies are being employed by the chairperson to achieve consensus and whether, in your opinion, they are working.
(4) The chairperson's management of time.

You may have to interfere with the game's 'real time'. That is, you may decide to ask the players to assume that a certain stage has been reached in the negotiation, even if it has not. For instance, you might feel that discussion has gone on long enough over Item 1 of the agenda, the proposed reorganization of the company. In that case, do not hesitate to move the players on by restating the scenario to include an imaginary vote by the players on this motion, which has been passed or rejected, and therefore the players can now proceed to debate Item 2.

You may meet with opposition from one or more of the players to your authoritarian handling of the game. This is all to the good because the objections will increase players' commitment to the game. Remember that people are likely to make a fuss about something only if the matter is important to them. Therefore, hear them out and be prepared to submit to their point of view if it seems reasonable.

During one playing of the game, the player who had the role of the manager from Thailand became really obstructive. You will remember that this role has the hidden agenda that cross-cultural communication problems shall be discussed at the meeting even though the topic is not part of the official proceedings. The man who assumed the role was so determined to adhere to it that the conference at one point came virtually to a standstill because the chairwoman did not seem able to handle the disruption. Yet in real life she was a senior manager who presumably was more than capable of such a task. We needed to clear the bottleneck, so we stopped the action and asked this woman what she would do if the situation was real. This freed both her and the 'manager' to discuss their feelings. He was mildly resentful of our interference and insisted that his behaviour was in keeping with his role. Having clarified this, we allowed the dramatic action to continue but the chairwoman, now forearmed by the realization of what she was up against, was able to deal much more firmly with the situation, and the business of the meeting continued.

Closing The roles are gender-free and have no names assigned to them, though players will probably want to invent names that are appropriate. Players never seem to find it difficult to assume the role of a nationality other than their own, but sometimes we find ourselves involved in a discussion of role-playing in general.

We have always adopted the view that nobody can 'be' anybody else, not even professional actors. If a man plays the part of Othello, he does not have to be a real-life murderer. He calls on those emotions and feelings common to all of us that, taken to extremes, could theoretically end in murder. Thus in effect he plays himself (or a part of himself) in a simulated scenario.

When real-life students or business people are asked to play a simulation game, and to assume a role with a name and a background different from their own, they are not being asked to be other than themselves. They are asked to follow the 'script' and the rules and to interpret them from their total life experience, direct and indirect, of the real world. Simulation games are no more and no less than their name implies: the players put themselves under the general guidance of a game leader, assume an imaginary situation or event, behave as they would if it were real, and observe the consequences.

HANDOUT
Background

In 1950 Saito Corporation, a petrochemical company, had an export department which took care of its foreign business. The company had only two small overseas branches and foreign sales accounted for about 7 per cent of its total business.

The manager in charge of the export department was supervised by the vice president for marketing as shown in Figure 1. The language was, of course, Japanese. This organizational structure worked well until the 1960s when Saito began to make major foreign invest-

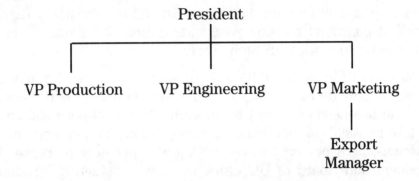

Figure 1: Saito Corporation 1950

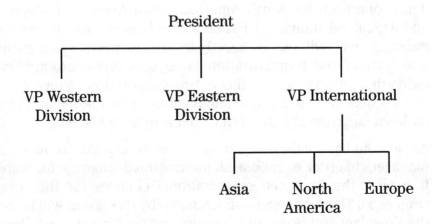

Figure 2: Saito Corporation 1965

ments. In 1965 the company was restructured as shown in Figure 2.

The 1965 reorganizational structure, which remains today, was carried out according to geographical region, with vice presidents for major Japanese areas as well as an international vice president. Presently all country managers outside Japan report to and are supervised by this international vice president. Each country is managed largely by local staff, using the local language. In a few cases the manager is a Japanese national. Company reports and all international letters are written in the local language with a translation in Japanese.

A few years ago major problems began developing within the international section. The expansion of markets led to the creation of more divisions, and these divisions have become more and more involved with one another. The US division now communicates frequently with the German division, while the Taiwan division is frequently in contact with the French and Italian divisions. There is a lack of coordination, however, and confusion is common as the divisions try to work with each other.

As shown in Figure 2, in 1965 there were only three foreign divisions but now there are 13 with sales amounting to 50 per cent of the total business of Saito Corporation. Of this 50 per cent, 25 per cent is in Asia, 14 per cent in Europe, and 11 per cent in the Americas, ie, 8 per cent in the USA and 3 per cent in Brazil. The President and Board of Directors are now considering a proposal for an organizational restructuring as shown in Figure 3.

Under this new plan it is suggested that there be five vice presidents: one each for North America, South America, Europe, Asia, and Japan. All individual national divisions are to be directed by managers who will report directly to their respective vice president. The goal of the reorganization is to coordinate production and marketing efforts across the entire corporation. Many company leaders believe that a single language must be chosen as the international language of Saito if that goal is to be achieved.

As a country manager, you have been invited to meet other managers in order to choose an international language for Saito and to review the proposed organizational changes for the company (Figure 3). The recommendations made by this group will be sent to the President and Board of Directors and are likely to be followed.

Figure 3: Saito Corporation's proposed reorganisation

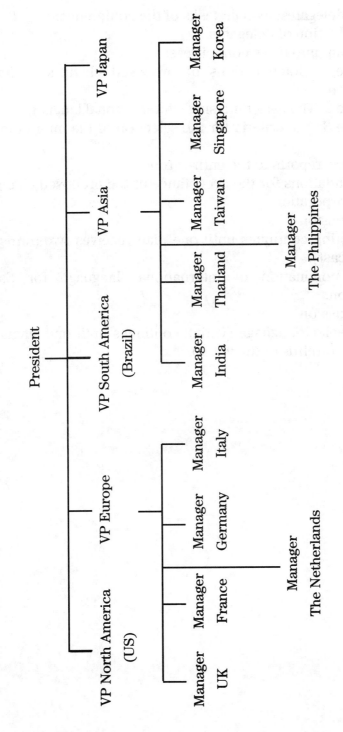

Agenda

(1) Welcome delegates; explain tasks of the conference.

(2) Self-introduction of delegates.

(3) Divide group into three committees:

Committee 1: Ramifications of proposed changes in Saito Corporation

Committee 2: The uses for a single international language

Committee 3: The criteria for the selection of the international language.

(4) Committees' reports to the entire group.

(5) Recommendations for the acceptance of the proposed changes in Saito Corporation.

(6) Open discussion.

(7) Voting (voting continues until one plan receives two-thirds of the votes cast).

(8) Call for nomination of international language for Saito Corporation.

(9) Open discussion.

(10) Voting to select language (voting continues until one language receives two-thirds of the votes).

HANDOUT
Participant cue card

for manager from Korea

You are a member of a conference which is to make recommendations to the Head Office (the President and Board of Directors) in Tokyo on the proposed changes in the corporate structure, and in the selection of an international language. Your particular concern is to ensure that the following are adequately incorporated into the suggestions for the corporation:

(1) Dealing with the proposed reorganization:
   The plans for reorganization seem to be simple and to involve few major changes. It seems to you that these plans merely reflect the present corporate structure and that is good.
(2) Dealing with the selection of an international language:
   You like very much the idea of having a single international language. You believe it is time for Saito (at least internationally) to drop its attachment to Japanese. If a single language is chosen, it will help your situation in Korea a great deal. Koreans are still unhappy about the Japanese occupation of Korea and they do not like to speak Japanese although many are still able to do so. If Saito is going to grow in Korea, a single language policy is necessary. You believe English would be the best choice.

In order to make certain that your points are properly dealt with by fellow delegates of the conference, it may be necessary to bring them up several times during the discussions. Be prepared to make and suggest compromises if necessary.

HANDOUT
Participant cue card

for manager from Thailand (who is a Japanese national, since no Thai manager has yet been found)

You are a member of a conference which is to make recommendations to the Head Office (the President and Board of Directors) in Tokyo on the proposed changes in the corporate structure, and in the selection of an international language. Your particular concern is to ensure that the following are adequately incorporated into the suggestions for the corporation:

(1) Dealing with the proposed reorganization:
This reorganization does not deal at all with the problems you are having in Thailand. The Thai attitude towards work is very different from that of the Japanese, and although you have learned to speak a little Thai, you still have real trouble in supervising Thais. They do not seem to know how to take the hints you give and when you speak directly to them in any negative way, they become insulted. In the three years you have been there you have had eight translators leave the job. The ninth one presently seems to be under a great deal of stress. You would like this conference to deal with this reorganization plan quickly and then discuss the more important matters of managing cultural differences.
(2) Dealing with the selection of an international language:
Your choice is Japanese or English, maybe both, but no other single language or combination of languages is possible for you.

In order to make certain that your points are properly dealt with by fellow delegates of the conference, it may be necessary to bring them up several times during the discussions. Be prepared to make and suggest compromises if necessary.

HANDOUT
Participant cue card

for manager from the Philippines (who is a Japanese national, since no Filipino has yet been found who seems Qualified to be Manager)

You are a member of a conference which is to make recommendations to the Head Office (the President and Board of Directors) in Tokyo on the proposed changes in the corporate structure, and in the selection of an international language. Your particular concern is to ensure that the following are adequately incorporated into the suggestions for the corporation:

(1) Dealing with the proposed reorganization:
    You like the plan. If you do a good job you can get back to the home office in Tokyo. You have been in the Philippines for two years and you are ready to go home. Your wife is homesick and your two children, aged five and seven, must now get a Japanese education or they will find it difficult to fit into Japanese society when they do return. Your friend is presently the vice president of the Eastern Division in Japan and he has said that if you do well as manager for one more year, he believes he can get you a place with his division.

(2) Dealing with the selection of an international language:
    You are aware of the problem because you face it every day. Your position is that Japanese should be the language of Saito – not only the international language but also the in-country language. Presently Saito has the policy of using the local language whenever possible and this has created many problems for you in the Philippines. It would be much better if Japanese was the only language to be used. That is your suggestion.

In order to make certain that your points are properly dealt with by fellow delegates of the conference, it may be necessary to bring them up several times during the discussions. Be prepared to make and suggest compromises if needed.

HANDOUT
Participant cue card

for manager from Singapore

You are a member of a conference which is to make recommenda-tions to the Head Office (the President and Board of Directors) in Tokyo on the proposed changes in the corporate structure, and in the selection of an international language. Your particular concern is to ensure that the following are adequately incorporated into the suggestions for the corporation:

(1) Dealing with the proposed reorganization:
   You feel this is a very poor reorganizational plan. No flow chart should be so complicated. You think the present corporate plan, which was drawn up in 1965, is much better and should be kept. This new plan will create more problems that it solves.

(2) Dealing with the selection of an international language:
   There is no question in your mind. The language has to be English. Singapore has four official languages (Malay, Tamil, Mandarin and English) and one national language (Malay). However, everyone knows that English is the international language of business. Saito should have made it the single inter-national language from the beginning. You are pleased that it can do so now.

   In order to make certain that your points are properly dealt with by fellow delegates of the conference, it may be necessary to bring them up several times during the discussions. Be prepared to make and suggest compromises if necessary.

HANDOUT
Participant cue card

for manager from the Netherlands, (who is a Japanese national, since no Dutch Manager has yet been found)

You are a member of a conference which is to make recommendations to the Head Office (the President and Board of Directors) in Tokyo on the proposed changes in the corporate structure, and in the selection of an international language. Your particular concern is to ensure that the following are adequately incorporated into the suggestions for the corporation:

(1) Dealing with the proposed reorganization:
    This seems like a very poor plan to you. There are too many vice presidents and it is not clear if they are equal in power or not. It seems strange that although Japan is in Asia, there is a vice president for Japan and another vice president for Asia. You think it would be wiser if the leaders of the North American, South American, European and Asian divisions be called directors instead of vice presidents, and keep only two vice presidents, one for the entire international division and one for Japan.
(2) Dealing with the selection of an international language:
    Your choice is French, Spanish, or English if it is necessary to have one single international language, but you would prefer a multilingual policy which allows for many languages to be used officially within the corporation.

In order to make certain that your points are properly dealt with by fellow delegates of the conference, it may be necessary to bring them up several times during the discussions. Be prepared to make and suggest compromises if necessary.

HANDOUT
Participant cue card

for manager from France

You are a member of a conference which is to make recommendations to the Head Office (the President and Board of Directors) in Tokyo on the proposed changes in the corporate structure, and in the selection of an international language. Your particular concern is to ensure that the following are adequately incorporated into the suggestions for the corporation:

(1) Dealing with the proposed reorganization:
    You like it and you want to keep it exactly the way it is. You know you have a good chance of becoming the first vice president for Europe and you want to do a good job at this conference to impress these company managers, for you would like to become the vice president for International Affairs in the next few years.
(2) Dealing with the selection of an international language:
    Your choice is French and you will suggest it, but not push for it. The selection of a language is not very important to you and you will go along with what you think is the majority view on this issue.

    In order to make certain that your points are properly dealt with by fellow delegates of the conference, it may be necessary to bring them up several times during the discussions. Be prepared to make and suggest compromises if necessary.

© Elizabeth M. Christopher and Larry E. Smith, 1993. Published by Kogan Page.

HANDOUT
Participant cue card

for manager from India

You are a member of a conference which is to make recommendations to the Head Office (the President and Board of Directors) in Tokyo on the proposed changes in the corporate structure, and in the selection of an international language. Your particular concern is to ensure that the following are adequately incorporated into the suggestions for the corporation:

(1) Dealing with the proposed reorganization:
   The plan is OK but you feel it would be better to have Asia divided into different divisions, in order to encourage future expansion. You will suggest that the reorganization replaces Asia with South Asia, Southeast Asia, and East Asia, with vice presidents for each of them. This will more nearly parallel the North American and South American divisions. You also feel that Japan should be a part of the East Asia section and should not have a separate division with its own vice president.
(2) Dealing with the selection of an international language:
   Your choice is Hindi. It is an ancient language with a great literature. It is spoken by many millions of people in India and is studied as a foreign language by foreign students worldwide. The written script is difficult but will add prestige to the corporation.

In order to make certain that your points are properly dealt with by fellow delegates of the conference, it may be necessary to bring them up several times during the discussions. Be prepared to make and suggest compromises if necessary.

HANDOUT
Participant cue card

for manager from the United States

You are a member of a conference which is to make recommendations to the Head Office (the President and Board of Directors) in Tokyo on the proposed changes in the corporate structure, and in the selection of an international language. Your particular concern is to ensure that the following are adequateiy incorporated into the suggestions for the corporation:

(1) Dealing with the proposed reorganization:

You completely agree with this proposal. In fact, you were on the committee which drew up these plans. As is clear from the proposal, you will be the vice president for North America; and, since you expect Canada to join the corporation soon, you will automatically be in charge of all the offices in both these countries.

(2) Dealing with the selection of an international language:

You support the selection of English, because it is already the international language of business and, of the 14 countries which are members of Saito's international division, five of them use English in an official or semi-official way. Those countries are the United States, Great Britain, India, Singapore, and the Philippines. You feel English should not be just the international language of Saito but its only language.

In order to make certain that your points are properly dealt with by fellow delegates of the conference, it may be necessary to bring them up several times during the discussions. Be prepared to make and suggest compromises if necessary.

HANDOUT
Participant cue card

for manager from Brazil

You are a member of a conference which is to make recommendations to the Head Office (the President and Board of Directors) in Tokyo on the proposed changes in the corporate structure, and in the selection of an international language. Your particular concern is to ensure that the following are adequately incorporated into the suggestions for the corporation:

(1) Dealing with the proposed reorganization:
It looks very good to you, and you would like to keep it just the way it is. You do not want to be a part of the North American division and are very pleased that North America and South America have been kept separate.

(2) Dealing with the selection of an international language:
Your choice is Japanese, which is spoken widely in Brazil. You believe that since Saito is a Japanese company, all official business should be conducted in Japanese.

In order to make certain that your points are properly dealt with by fellow delegates of the conference, it may be necessary to bring them up several times during the discussions. Be prepared to make and suggest compromises if necessary.

HANDOUT
Participant cue card

for manager from Great Britain

You are a member of a conference which is to make recommendations to the Head Office (the President and Board of Directors) in Tokyo on the proposed changes in the corporate structure, and in the selection of an international language. Your particular concern is to ensure that the following are adequately incorporated into the suggestions for the corporation:

(1) Dealing with the proposed reorganization:

You do not like the idea of the French manager becoming vice president for Europe, and having to work under him, so you are opposed to the present proposed reorganization plan. Of course, you cannot say that directly, so you must think of other reasons why you do not approve of the present plan. Since the US and UK divisions have always worked closely together and speak the same language, you suggest they form one division by themselves, perhaps called the 'English-speaking division'.

(2) Dealing with the selection of an international language:

You feel there should be four languages of Saito rather than one, in order to correspond to the four divisions of the company. You propose an English division for the USA and the UK (see above for reasons), a Spanish division for South America, a French division for Europe, and a Japanese division for Asia.

You believe that if the company tries to limit itself to one international language now, it will result only in more confusion and hard feelings among the different divisions.

In order to make certain that your points are properly dealt with by fellow delegates of the conference, it may be necessary to bring them up several times during the discussions. Be prepared to make and suggest compromises if necessary.

HANDOUT
Participant cue card

for manager from Taiwan

You are a member of a conference which is to make recommendations to the Head Office (the President and Board of Directors) in Tokyo on the proposed changes in the corporate structure, and in the selection of an international language. Your particular concern is to ensure that the following are adequately incorporated into the suggestions for the corporation:

(1) Dealing with the proposed reorganization:

You like it, except for one thing. You want to suggest the name of your country to be changed from Taiwan to China, so that when mainland China is opened to Saito, you will have a good chance to take over that very large division. Of course, you cannot tell the conference participants this, so you will say instead that there is only one China and that Taiwan is only a part of that China. Therefore, the name of the division should reflect the name of the country as other divisions do.

(2) Dealing with the selection of an international language:

You do not like the idea of choosing only one international language. You like the present policy of using the local language whenever possible and sending reports and all correspondence in the local language as well as Japanese.

If it is necessary to have fewer company languages, you will suggest that there be three: English for North America and Europe; Spanish for South America; and Standard Chinese (Mandarin) for Asia. Everything would continue to have a Japanese translation as well. In Asia, Mandarin is already used in Singapore and Taiwan, with many speakers of Mandarin in Hong Kong. Many Koreans and Japanese can read Chinese already, so that should not be a problem. If Standard Chinese is chosen, mainland China will be impressed, and it will be easier to establish a division there. That is important because of the cheap labour as well as the large potential market (population is one billion).

In order to make certain that your points are properly dealt with by fellow delegates of the conference, it may be necessary to bring them up several times during the discussions. Be prepared to make and suggest compromises if necessary.

HANDOUT
Participant cue card

for manager from Germany

You are a member of a conference which is to make recommendations to the Head Office (the President and Board of Directors) in Tokyo on the proposed changes in the corporate structure, and in the selection of an international language. Your particular concern is to ensure that the following are adequately incorporated into the suggestions for the corporation:

(1) Dealing with the proposed reorganization:
It appears reasonable to you, but it is certainly clear that a single language must now be found as an international language for Saito, or the company will not be able to expand. There are already too many languages in use and this is the absolute limit of expansion until a single language is chosen.

(2) Dealing with the selection of an international language:
German is your choice, and you will nominate it, but you do not really expect it to be accepted. You will accept any language, but you do not want it to be English, since the Americans and the British seem so arrogant about speaking English.

In order to make sure your points are properly dealt with by fellow delegates of the conference, it may be necessary to bring them up several times during the discussion. Be prepared to make and suggest compromises if necessary.

HANDOUT
Participant cue card

for manager from Italy

You are a member of a conference which is to make recommendations to the Head Office (the President and Board of Directors) in Tokyo, on the proposed changes in the corporate structure and in the selection of an international language.

No one at the conference knows this, and you do not plan to tell anyone, but you have agreed to accept a job as president of an Italian company within six months. Your new firm will not be in competition with Saito, so you felt you could come to this meeting, but you are reluctant to make any suggestions about either the proposed changes or the selection of a language. You have worked for Saito for five years and are glad to be leaving it, because there is so much internal competition between the divisions.

Chapter 13

Activities for the management of conflict

55 INFERNAL TOWERS

Time required About an hour.

Aim This is a team-building activity that attempts to demonstrate conflict due to communication barriers between team members. These barriers are argued to arise because people, generally, accept their perceptions of the world as valid; therefore if others perceive the same phenomena differently, those others are mistaken, misinformed, irrational – even malicious. 'Infernal Towers' takes this concept and uses it to encourage players to think about the factors that promote team-building and those that deter it.

Group size The instructions below are for a group of at least 12 people (ie two teams, each of 6 people). If for any reason you want to have more or fewer than 6 people on each team, you can vary the number of instruction cards. Virtually any number can play, providing there is room for them.

Environment A classroom, seminar room or conference room in which there is a minimum of furniture. Players must be able to gather together in teams to build their constructions.

Procedure

(1) Divide the group into teams of 6.

(2) Give each team a large quantity of Lego or similar interlocking building bricks. Explain that they have to build a tower.

(3) Give each member of each team an instruction card bearing a specific piece of information regarding the task. Stress that no one else is to know this information.

(4) Announce that the game will be played in silence, and let the players get on with it.

The following are suggestions for the instruction cards, but feel free to write your own. The only criterion is that the respective instructions must be conflicting:

- The tower must contain 20 blocks.
- The tower must be 10 levels high.
- The tower must be built of white, red and yellow bricks only.
- The tower must be built of blue and yellow bricks only.
- The sixth level of the tower must be a different colour from the rest.
- It is your task to build the tower. If other members of your team try to handle the bricks you must stop them and insist on doing all the actual building yourself.

Evaluation Infernal Towers is fun to watch (video it if you can) because of the evident confusion, bewilderment and frustration of individual players as they attempt to carry out their instructions only to find themselves obstructed by the behaviour of their team members. Expectations are confounded as people begin by assuming that they are all working together on a common task only to discover they seem to be doing no such thing. Examples are that one player attempts to place a blue brick, only to have it removed, with apparent indignation, by another player. A third will try to stop anybody else from doing anything, and so on.

We recorded one playing of Infernal Towers in a television studio for an educational television programme and the camera operators were all laughing at the action. Anybody who has ever had anything to do with television will know that these are the hardest people in the world to impress, so we chalked up another 'plus' for the game.

Closing One of a number of situations tends to repeat itself from game to game, which is useful for discussion afterwards:

(1) The player who is instructed to be the sole builder succeeds in being so. This happens when a forceful person is given the role, one who is effective in body language and who makes it plain that s/he will brook no opposition. In these circumstances the other team-members sit back, more or less patiently, depending on their individual temperaments, and watch the self-designated builder. All goes well until this person does something contrary to another player's instructions: the player gives silent protest and usually the builder heeds it and alters the design accordingly. When two protestors are in conflict with one another (perhaps because one wants no red or blue bricks) the builder often experiments by trying one brick after another until both protestors indicate that they are satisfied – for instance, when the yellow bricks are used exclusively.

This team behaviour often works well and when there are several teams a group such as the above may be the first to complete their tower, in which case they are likely to feel very pleased with their performance, the product (the tower) and each other. This is probably because nobody has lost face. The initial humiliation felt by team-members at not being allowed to touch the bricks is overcome by the builder later heeding their instructions as to how it should be built. This is another instance of leadership being a trade-off between leader and followers.

(2) The self-designated builder is overcome by powerful opposition from other players who insist on handling the bricks. This behaviour usually leads to a considerable amount of conflict. We have known people use force to snatch bricks from each other or to remove bricks already laid. When things develop this way, it is unlikely that the tower will be completed.

(3) There is a combination of the above strategies. A time-consuming process of negotiation takes place between would-be builders which continues throughout the construction. Every brick becomes the subject of non-verbal debate, sometimes heated. Given time, the tower will eventually rise, but a team which behaves like this will not, usually, win the game against one which adopts strategy (1).

56 & 57 EMPLOYER BEWARE!

Time required About 20 minutes for each ice-breaker.

Aim To learn from each other by sharing knowledge and experience of industrial relations negotiation.

Group size 5–25 (approximately).

Environment Classroom, seminar room, conference room. Prepare copies of the case studies for each participant; and provide writing materials for everybody.

Procedure

(1) Distribute one of the case studies. Ask everybody, when they've read it, to jot down any brief comments that occur to them. Give everybody about 6-7 minutes to do this.
(2) Ask for a volunteer to 'start the ball rolling' by offering a comment on the case study, preferably based on their own knowledge of industrial relations. Encourage general discussion for about 15 minutes.

Evaluation This exercise is particularly fruitful when working with groups of supervisors from different organizations; also before an in-house session on handling interpersonal, inter-group or intra-group conflict. The case studies are designed to provoke controversial comment and thus reveal areas of conflict.

Closing Use these activities as a lead-in to a seminar on industrial relations and/or conflict in the workplace.

HANDOUT
Case Study 1: Missing Evidence

Bill was hired by a hardware company to work in the timber yard. He has an excellent knowledge of timbers and customers value his advice.

However Bill is a thoroughly incompetent worker. He is often late, takes longer breaks than anybody else, works very slowly, makes lots of mistakes and leaves other people to clear up after him.

The manager, Ken, put up with Bill for two years until finally he found an adequate replacement. Then he tried to fire him. But Bill complained to his union that his dismissal was unfair because he had never had a performance appraisal to warn him that his work was unsatisfactory. In fact, he said self-righteously, in the absence of a formal appraisal he felt entitled to assume his work was well up to standard.

The company does have an annual written performance evaluation system – but Bill's immediate supervisor, Jane, just never seems to get round to doing the appraisals; and in fact hasn't done any for the last three years.

The question now is, what arguments can Ken and Jane come up with, to satisfy the union representative that Bill's dismissal is justified? Can they do it? Or will they be stuck with Bill for ever?

Case Study 2: The Unfair Dismissal

Joe has been with the company for 30 years. Last year his supervisor changed and Joe is now supervised by Mel, a young woman of 28, who appears to have a clear preference for younger men.

Poor Joe received a very negative performance appraisal, in all respects; and as a result he didn't get his usual annual bonus.

He appealed to the anti-discrimination board that he was discriminated against on the grounds of age.

If you were Mel's manager, how would you handle an interview with the representative of the anti-discrimination board (knowing that this person's adverse report could result in a large fine for your company – which would mean your head on senior management's block)?

58 THE UNCOOPERATIVE EMPLOYEE

Time required About an hour.

Aim To demonstrate effective ways of handling performance problems

Group size From about 5–30 people

Environment The classroom. Prepare a set of the 2 roles for each participant.

Procedure

(1) Explain the aim of the activity.
(2) Suggest that participants demonstrate how to handle a performance problem by way of a roleplay. Request two volunteers to play the manager and supervisor; and two people to play the staff members. Give them copies of their respective roles; and the full set to everybody else.
(3) When the roletakers have had a few minutes to read and absorb the role guidelines, ask them to act them out in front of the group.
(4) If the 'interview' has not ended after about 10 minutes, call a halt and thank the players. After minimal discussion, ask another 4 people to repeat the roleplay; and again another 4, if the group is large.

Evaluation What tactics did the supervisor use to persuade B to discuss the problem frankly? Did any of the B players try to conceal the fact they had taken a second job? What were some unsuccessful tactics that A and B used? What tactics worked best?

Closing Initiate a general discussion about supervisory problems and how to handle them.

HANDOUT
Role A

For the last two weeks your administrative assistant's job performance has fallen off badly. This person seems irritable, tired and nervous all the time, is getting behind with work assignments, and is upsetting the rest of the staff. You take pride in running a happy office where everybody gets on well with each other. The changed behaviour of the admin assistant has affected adversely the whole working atmosphere – everybody seems miserable. You have to find out what the admin assistant's problem is; and you are prepared to be supportive – but things must improve within the next few days.

Role B

You have been an administrative assistant in the same company for the last five years. You like this job and your co-workers. Two weeks ago you took a second job in the evenings, after your normal working hours, because you need the money to repay debts. By the time you get home after midnight you are completely exhausted; yet you have to get up at 5.30 every morning to commute to work.

You are constantly in danger of getting behind with your work because you are slow, being tired all the time. You are short-tempered with your colleagues and of course you don't have time to spend with them at the pub after work like you used to. You no longer take coffee breaks with them, and you eat a sandwich at your desk instead of going to the canteen for lunch and socializing.

Now the supervisor has asked to see you privately; and you are sure you are going to get into trouble for poor performance. Normally you take pride in your work and all this hassle has really made you miserable, but no matter what, you must keep the second job for one more month. Then you should have the cash you need to pay off the loan; and you have vowed never, never to borrow money again!

59 THE LIBRARIAN

Time required About half an hour.

Aim To explore the difficulties of a group having to 'sit in judgement' on an individual member.

Group size This is a small group discussion, but you can divide up a large number of people into smaller groups, provided they are not sitting in fixed seats, for example in a tiered lecture theatre.

Environment The classroom, with tables and chairs café-style.

Procedure

(1) Give everybody a copy of 'The Librarian'. Ask groups to discuss it among themselves for 10 minutes or so.
(2) Get everybody's attention and ask for general comments. What was the decision of each group?

Evaluation Why did groups decide as they did? What has this exercise taught participants about their own objectivity or lack of it, in making decisions about other people's future? To what extent do participants think group decision-making is more or less likely to be reasonable and just, compared with individual decision-making?

Closing Ask participants to share any real-life examples this activity reminds them of.

HANDOUT
The Librarian: a case-study

You are a librarian who works with a small team in a large city library. You have been asked, as a team, to provide a performance appraisal of the work of one of you, Joyce. What form this takes is up to you, provided you all agree on it.

Joyce is due for promotion to another library in the city, where she would be working with quite a large staff, including relatively young and inexperienced librarians; and librarianship students, including some from overseas.

The desire of all of you is to promote each other's careers. However, you all have some major reservations regarding Joyce. She does her work well, and is helpful when her advice is asked; but her communication skills are not good. She comes from a different ethnic background from the rest of you and maybe this difference accounts for her lack of ever saying 'please' or 'thank-you', or of observing other small courtesies. She maintains very little eye contact; often interrupts colleagues in a loud voice; and generally gives the impression of being sulky.

Joyce is away today, therefore you and your colleagues have taken the opportunity to meet together to decide what your joint appraisal will be. You are aware that the Senior Librarian is very much influenced by peer-group assessments when considering employees for promotion.

60 THE LONE WOLF

Time required About 30–45 minutes; longer if the group is large.

Aim To illustrate the advantages of collaborating with other members of the organization to get your job done, rather than ignoring their problems in pursuit of your own aims.

Group size From 4 to about 25 people.

Environment The classroom. Prepare copies of both roles for each participant (see pp. 272–3). If you are working with a group whose individual members might be really intimidated by having to enact an individual role in front of the whole class, you can rewrite the material to make each a team role, ie A can be a group of 2 or 3 managers and B a group of several employees.

If you want this to be a cross-cultural study, you can adapt the roles, for example, to turn 'London Incorporated' into 'Yamamoto Inc' and to make A a Japanese role. 'Midland' can become a US company and B an American; and the whole roleplay can be given a setting such as Hawaii. The phrase 'cross-cultural' includes 'cross-gender' because it can be argued that in every society men and women are socialized so differently they can be said to belong to two different cultures. If you want to, you can turn this exercise into a cross-gender activity by casting one role as male and the other as female.

Procedure

(1) Explain the aims of the activity; and that the group will enact a short roleplay to illustrate these aims.
(2) Ask for two volunteers (or two small teams) to be the first to enact the roleplay. Give one the guidelines for A's role and the other the guidelines for B. Give all other participants copies of both roles.
(3) Give everybody time to read the roles and ask any essential questions. Stress that the roles should be played as the actors perceive them.
(4) Ask the first pair (or small team) to come to the front of the class where everybody can see and hear them clearly. Allow them to negotiate their way through the roleplay without interruption.

(5) Call a halt after 10 minutes, no matter what stage they have reached. Ask another pair, or team, to repeat the process. Repeat as often as you want to, or have time for.

Evaluation

What happened? Did A fire or relocate B in any of the roleplays? Did B resign?

What kind of arguments were put forward by A? By B?

What negotiation tactics did the class find most effective? Why?

Was compromise possible? Do participants believe that in real life this problem of clash between personal and organizational or team needs can be avoided?

(This question becomes particularly relevant if the roleplay has been enacted with a cross-cultural group, or as a cross-gender exercise.)

Closing

Allow the discussion to become more general, to include participants' anecdotes of experiences they have had, of individualism versus teamwork (and of working with people across gender, and/or from other nationalities and cultures).

This activity leads comfortably into a discussion or seminar on team building and group dynamics.

HANDOUT
Role A

Six months ago London Incorporated, which manufactures computer systems and components, took control of Midland Systems. Three months ago you were made general manager of Midland. When you first took up the post you met the key personnel in the company and gave a party for all its employees. Everybody attended except B.

B's name also came up several times in your discussions with key people. They complained that B expected special treatment all the time; though they all admitted B was very valuable to the company. In your interview with B you were not favourably impressed with this employee's manner and style of dress. It surprised you to learn that B is the best salesperson for Midland Systems; a brilliant systems analyst who is highly valued by client companies.

Complaints from other staff members have continued. They say B promises clients early installation, though knowing the company does not have enough technical people to implement such promises. Currently there is a shortage of technical staff and it is difficult to employ more, since they command such high salaries. One field manager has threatened to resign unless something is done to make B more aware of the need to consult with technical staff before making rash promises to clients.

You realize that to lose B would be extremely costly for the company, especially at this critical time of growth after the takeover by your company, London Incorporated. You see this problem as an important challenge for you to prove yourself as a manager who can deal successfully with the former Midland personnel. You have asked B to come to your office to discuss the situation. B must realize that things cannot remain as they are. For the good of the company, B's behaviour must be modified. Your goal is to make the situation clear to B, that working as a team member is most important. You have the power to dismiss B if this employee is unwilling to change, or you may transfer B to another branch of the company in another area. However you would much prefer that B remain here, as a more cooperative staff member.

Role B

Six months ago London Incorporated, which manufactures computer systems and components, took control of Midland Systems which has employed you for the past year as a salesperson and systems analyst. The new general manager is now A who has been in the job for three months. You met together when A first took up the post and interviewed all key personnel but have not seen A since. You know A gave a party for all ex-Midland employees but you didn't attend. You don't have time for parties, you don't like to 'dress up' and you are not interested in socializing with company co-workers.

Basically you enjoy your work, you like the challenge of solving clients' system design problems. You know you are the best salesperson in the company and that your clients recognize you as a brilliant systems analyst. There have been complaints from the technical staff that you don't consult them enough, particularly before you give a definite installation date to clients for new equipment. It's true there is a shortage of technical people to carry out the actual installation but that's no reason to disappoint customers. It's a problem for the personnel department. It's all very well for personnel to say they don't have the budget to hire more technical staff because they can command such high salaries. That's nothing to do with you.

A has asked you to come to his office today. You are not quite sure why, but suspect it may concern this argument. You know that one field supervisor has threatened to resign unless something is done about your independent stand on the matter. Your goal is to make the situation clear to A, as you see it:

(1) The company needs more installation technicians.
(2) They should be hired, no matter what the cost. Profits will be higher in the long run because more customers can be serviced more quickly.
(3) You are not a team member and don't want to be. You are a very good systems analyst and a very effective salesperson for the company; and you work best alone.
(4) If A doesn't agree with you, you are prepared to leave the job; but this would be a last resort: you would much prefer to remain with the company and continue to work as you have done in the past.

61 IT DEPENDS ON THE SITUATION

Time required About an hour and a half.

Aim To compare and contrast team members' individual value-systems.

Group size Any number from about 8 people upwards, divided into four sub-groups, each of a minimum of 2 people.

Environment The classroom. Prepare the questionnaire, one per participant.

Procedure

(1) Explain the aim of the activity.
(2) Put people into four groups, or multiples of four. If you want to form, say, six groups, give the 'odd' two groups repeat copies of two of the questionnaires.
(3) Distribute the questionnaires, a different one to each of the four groups. Give everybody time to complete them according to the instructions (probably about 15 minutes).
(4) Ask all groups to exchange questionnaires; and repeat the process. Continue until all groups have answered all four questionnaires.

Evaluation How did individuals' first answers compare to the eventual group consensus? Did people find their attitudes changed from questionnaire to questionnaire?

Closing Initiate a general discussion about ethical values in the workplace.

HANDOUT
The Ethical Dilemma Questionnaire 1

INSTRUCTIONS

(1) Read the Summary of Situations.
(2) Use the Score Sheet to mark your individual responses. You are asked how you think the described behaviours would be viewed by different sections of the community; and how you would view them. Put a cross in the appropriate place.
(3) Compare your score sheet with those of your team members. Is it possible to reach consensus?
(4) When you have finished, exchange your questionnaire with that of one of the other groups, and repeat steps 1–3.
(5) Repeat Step 4 until you have answered all four questionnaires.

SUMMARY OF SITUATIONS

1.1. Elizabeth is an academic staff member of a large university. Because she needs to be able to talk to students on distance-learning courses she has the special facility of being able to make long-distance calls from her desk telephone. She also uses this facility to make personal calls during office hours.

1.2. An Australian businessman, Brian, wants to open an office in an Asian country. He understands that the law in that country forbids organizations from taking bribes to award contracts to foreign companies. However his Asian representative assures him that he will not get any contracts there unless he pays a large cash sum to each company he wants to do business with. Brian makes sure he is not offending any Australian regulations, then pays the bribes as required, through his Asian representative.

1.3. Bob is a self-employed plumber, who carries out installations, repairs and so on in customers' private homes. He does not report cash payments on his income tax return unless they are larger than £100. This provides him with non-taxed extra income of around £6,000 each year.

1.4. Janice is a student who has started a part-time job in the kitchen of a local restaurant, to earn money she desperately needs to support herself. She is glad to have the job because it is hard to find work within walking distance of where she lives. However the kitchen is very dirty, with cockroaches running all over the food. She puts up with this, but one day she hears some of the students mention that they became ill after eating in this restaurant. Janice decides to say nothing, for fear of losing her job.

Score Sheet 1

	Most business people	Most members of the general public	Your group's opinion	Your own opinion
Perfectly all right				
1.1				
1.2				
1.3				
1.4				
Some small reservations				
1.1				
1.2				
1.3				
1.4				
Major reservations				
1.1				
1.2				
1.3				
1.4				
Not right under any circumstances				
1.1				
1.2				
1.3				
1.4				

The Ethical Dilemma Questionnaire 2

INSTRUCTIONS

(1) Read the Summary of Situations.

(2) Use the Score Sheet to mark your individual responses. You are asked how you think the described behaviours would be viewed by different sections of the community; and how you would view them. Put a cross in the appropriate place.

(3) Compare your score sheet with those of your team members. Is it possible to reach consensus?

(4) When you have finished, exchange your questionnaire with that of one of the other groups, and repeat steps 1–3.

(5) Repeat Step 4 until you have answered all four questionnaires.

SUMMARY OF SITUATIONS

2.1. Elizabeth is an academic staff member of a large university. She has a budget to organize weekend residential schools for students, which includes a cash sum for catering. She helps herself liberally to this money for her own private use; and cuts down accordingly on meals and refreshments for the students.

2.2. An Australian teacher, Brian, is in an administrative position in the New South Wales Department of School Education. He accepts an expensive leather briefcase as a Christmas present from a paper supplier to whom he gave a large contract during the year.

2.3. Bob is a self-employed plumber, who carries out installations, repairs and so on in customers' private homes. He is paid mostly in cash and has to do very little paperwork, but for tax purposes he claims a small room off his garage as an office; and his teenage daughter as his secretary. These claims substantially reduce his taxable income.

2.4. Janice is a sole supporting parent with three small children. She is desperate for accommodation but finds most landlords don't want to rent their houses to people with several children. She goes to an estate agent in another neighbourhood, states that she has no children, and is able to rent a two-bedroomed flat at a reasonable figure. She leaves the children with her mother for a few days after she moves into the flat, then quietly brings them to their new home.

Score Sheet 2

	Most business people	Most members of the general public	Your group's opinion	Your own opinion
Perfectly all right				
2.1				
2.2				
2.3				
2.4				
Some small reservations				
2.1				
2.2				
2.3				
2.4				
Major reservations				
2.1				
2.2				
2.3				
2.4				
Not right in any circumstances				
2.1				
2.2				
2.3				
2.4				

HANDOUT
The Ethical Dilemma Questionnaire 3

INSTRUCTIONS

(1) Read the Summary of Situations.

(2) Use the Score Sheet to mark your individual responses. You are asked how you think the described behaviours would be viewed by different sections of the community; and how you would view them. Put a cross in the appropriate place.

(3) Compare your score sheet with those of your team members. Is it possible to reach consensus?

(4) When you have finished, exchange your questionnaire with that of one of the other groups, and repeat steps 1–3.

(5) Repeat Step 4 until you have answered all four questionnaires.

SUMMARY OF SITUATIONS

3.1 Elizabeth is an academic staff member of a large university. She collected some money from a group of students to pay for a farewell present for a departing teacher. Each student contributed £5 out of their slender budgets; but the gift Elizabeth buys, though expensive-looking, did not cost as much as expected and she finds herself able to refund £2 to each student. However, she doesn't see them regularly and can't be bothered to seek them out, so she takes no action.

3.2. An Australian businessman, Brian, has contracted to build a set of townhouses. All plans were approved by the local council but the work took longer than expected and a recently introduced regulation stipulates the need for more car-parking space than Brian has allowed for. He goes to see the town clerk and offers her one of the townhouses rent-free for a year if she will backdate the completion date of the complex to before the new regulation was introduced.

3.3. Bob is technically out of work and regularly draws unemployment benefit. When the employment officer sends him for job interviews Bob deliberately dresses so poorly and presents himself so badly that he never gets the job. Meanwhile, since he used to work in a hardware store, he does odd plumbing jobs in people's houses. He gets paid in cash and doesn't declare this income to the unemployment office.

3.4. Janice is a student who does well in her studies but has started a part-time job to earn money to support herself. This overloads her to the extent that she has no time to finish a term paper before the due date. The lecturer is strict and will not accept a late paper, so Janice copies a paper that her boyfriend has written for another class and hands it in as her own.

Score Sheet 3

	Most business people	Most members of the general public	Your group's opinion	Your own opinion
Perfectly all right				
3.1				
3.2				
3.3				
3.4				
Some small reservations				
3.1				
3.2				
3.3				
3.4				
Major reservations				
3.1				
3.2				
3.3				
3.4				
Not right in any circumstances				
3.1				
3.2				
3.3				
3.4				

The Ethical Dilemma Questionnaire 4

INSTRUCTIONS

(1) Read the Summary of Situations.
(2) Use the Score Sheet to mark your individual responses. You are asked how you think the described behaviours would be viewed by different sections of the community; and how you would view them. Put a cross in the appropriate place.
(3) Compare your score sheet with those of your team members. Is it possible to reach consensus?
(4) When you have finished, exchange your questionnaire with that of one of the other groups, and repeat steps 1–3.
(5) Repeat Step 4 until you have answered all four questionnaires.

SUMMARY OF SITUATIONS

4.1 Elizabeth is an academic staff member of a prestigious and very expensive training institute for senior managers. The institute regularly holds receptions for incoming groups of managers, graduation parties and other functions. The food and wine is always very good; and Elizabeth makes a habit of attending every function, whether or not any of her students are involved.

4.2 An Australian businessman, Brian, invites a very fitness-conscious senior police officer to be a guest member of his company's 'outward bound' training week in the mountains, which includes skiing, mountain climbing and other fun activities. During the week, Brian mentions casually that he was booked for speeding the other day and is rather worried about it because he may stand in danger of losing his driving licence.

4.3 Bob is a caddy at the local golf club, which is patronized by very wealthy golfers. He regularly receives large tips, only a fraction of which he declares on his income tax return.

4.4 Janice is a student who went bushwalking with a group of friends. When they stop for lunch somebody lights a fire to boil water for tea. Janice notices a big sign: 'EXTREME BUSHFIRE HAZARD; NO FIRES ALLOWED' but does not want to offend her friends and since they say nothing, neither does she.

Score Sheet 4

	Most business people	Most members of the general public	Your group's opinion	Your own opinion
Perfectly all right				
4.1				
4.2				
4.3				
4.4				
Some small reservations				
4.1				
4.2				
4.3				
4.4				
Major reservations				
4.1				
4.2				
4.3				
4.4				
Not right in any circumstances				
4.1				
4.2				
4.3				
4.4				

62 THE DIFFICULT CLIENT

Time required About 20 minutes.

Aim To brainstorm ideas about how to manage difficult clients.

Group size Minimum of 15, to any number.

Environment Classroom, seminar room or conference room. Two whiteboards with erasers and a good supply of pens for each.

Procedure

(1) Explain this is an exercise to get everybody in a creative frame of mind to begin the course/seminar/conference/etc. You will ask three questions; and reporters will record as many answers as they can in 3 minutes to each of the questions. (Note: You don't have to use the questions we suggest. Feel free to think of your own!)

(2) Ask for six volunteers to be reporters. You need people who can write fast and legibly on the whiteboards. Ask for three more volunteers to be editors who will direct answers to each reporter in turn, to avoid duplication of records.

(3) Ask the first two reporters to stand at their respective white-boards. Make sure they have several pens in case one runs dry. Ask the first editor to stand between them, facing the audience, and ready to direct one answer in turn to each of the reporters for recording. When these arrangements are in place, ask the first question of the audience in general. Don't worry if answers are slow in coming at first; audience members will soon get the idea. Time 3 minutes on your watch, or set up a clock.

(4) After 3 minutes, call a halt and allow a further 3 minutes for general discussion of the ideas recorded on the boards.

(5) Ask for a round of applause for the editor and reporters, make sure they erase their boards, supply more pens if necessary and ask two more reporters, and a second editor, to get ready to repeat the process.

(6) Ask the second question, allow 3 minutes for the answers, and repeat steps 4 and 5. Ask the third question and repeat steps 4 and 5 again.

Evaluation Did the audience respond with creative ideas?

Closing Which ideas did participants think were the most innovative?

Difficult client questions

(1) What do you do when the client is slow to pay?
(2) How do you steal a client from a competitor?
(3) When do you reduce your price?

63 MISSED OUT!

Time required About an hour.

Aim To practise correcting management mistakes.

Group size About 6–24 people.

Environment The classroom. Prepare a copy of each role for each participant.

Procedure

(1) Divide the group into paired teams A and B or multiples of A and B if the group is large. It doesn't matter if there are more people in one team than another, though try to keep the numbers as even across teams as possible.

(2) Distribute Role A to team(s) A and Role B to team(s) B. Ask them to read and discuss it among themselves and to work out some tactics for dealing with the situation.

(3) After 15 minutes or so, ask one volunteer from Group A and one from Group B to come to the front of the room and play out their roles, with everybody else as observer. If you have more than one Group A and B, you will have to pick two groups at random. If there is time, you can give every group a go.

Evaluation What happened? How did A and B reconcile their difference (if they did)? What kind of amends did B offer to make? What action was finally decided upon by both parties?

Closing Close with a short discussion on 'saving face' and methods in general of coping with the results of one's oversights.

HANDOUT
Role A

Six months ago you started work as a training officer for an institute that conducts cross-cultural training courses for business and government people. Your work has been good but you are considered to be an ideas person and an assistant to others, without enough initiative to work on your own.

You hear on the grapevine that there will be budget cuts soon; and you fear that unless you prove yourself to be a self-starter you could lose your job.

You have designed a workshop which the training manager has agreed to run, even though the cost to the participants will be higher than usual.

This means that effective advertisement and promotion of the workshop will be crucial to its success; but today, when you received a copy of the quarterly brochure advertising all the company's programmes, you find there is no mention of your workshop.

You go to see the editor responsible for the brochure's publication. This person has been with the company for about five years and is older than you; but you play on the same football team and get on very well together.

Role B

You are the editorial manager of an institute that conducts cross-cultural training courses for business and government people. You have been with the company for five years.

One of your responsibilities is to prepare and send out the institute's brochure every three months, that lists all their programmes. The latest brochure was sent today, covering the next three months.

Reading the copy again, you suddenly realize it fails to announce a workshop next month, to be conducted by a rather new training officer. This person has only been with the company for about six months and is younger than you; but you play on the same football team and get on very well together.

The institute is planning serious budget cuts and the training officer's job may be in danger if this new programme is not well attended.

On the other hand, you made a couple of rather serious mistakes earlier in the year. If this latest error gets to the ears of the institute's director, you could be out of a job yourself.

Chapter 14

Activities for management training

64 APPLIED METALS

Time required About half an hour.

Aim To practise the organization of budget priorities.

Group size Any convenient number from about 3 people.

Environment Classroom, seminar room or conference room.

Procedure

(1) Form small groups and ask each group to agree on an annual budget for the engineering department of a medium-sized construction company, Applied Metals. The budget must include the salaries of three engineers (the same amount for each), one supervisor and two support staff; and anything else the group cares to think of (suggestions might be travel, office supplies, capital expenses, etc). Stress that this is not real life: the budget can be as fanciful as they like and only the broad outlines are required. Give everybody about 10 minutes to work them out and write them down. It doesn't matter that probably all teams will come up with different budgets: they work independently on this exercise.

(2) Distribute the Memo From Head Office (one copy per team). Give all teams a further 10-15 minutes to adjust their respective budgets.

(3) Initiate a general discussion of the results.

Evaluation How did the teams variously manage to find Ms Hightower's salary? Did any team refuse to find it? What were the priorities of each group? For example, did some teams economize by getting rid of one of the currently employed engineers to make room for Ms Hightower? Or did they cut down on capital expenditure or other materials rather than let people go?

Closing Call on the knowledge and experience of the group to discuss what might happen in this situation in real life.

HANDOUT
Memo From Head Office

To: Engineering Department   *From:* General Manager

The Personnel Manager recommends we offer an employment contract to Ms Harriet Hightower. She is a well-qualified and ambitious young engineer who applied for a job both with us and with our biggest competitor, Steel Incorporated. We and Steel both accepted her, but Steel's salary offer was higher than ours. We offered her the same salary as all our engineers are currently paid.

However, apparently Ms Hightower has heard on the grapevine that we have a very cooperative working atmosphere and an attractive bonus system based on achievement. She has told the Personnel Manager that if we will make a 10 per cent increase on our offer, she would prefer to work for our company, but otherwise intends to turn us down.

Frankly, we need Ms Hightower. Not only are her qualifications and credentials first class, but being female she will help to earn us a reputation for equal employment opportunity and affirmative action. Our most lucrative client in the near future may very well be the Equal Employment Opportunity Commission (which as you know intends to contract for new premises to be built). It would be very much to our advantage to put a female engineer on the job, and to our disadvantage if she goes to Steel and is in competition with us.

I realize your budget may be rather strained by having to find Ms Hightower's salary; but if you can manage it for this year, I promise to give first priority to enlarging your budget after that, to the extent at least of her salary.

Thank you for you cooperation in this matter.

65 FLEX-TIME

Time required About half an hour.

Aim To provide practice in the collaborative management of employee grievances.

Group size Any manageable number from 4 people upwards.

Environment The classroom, set up café-style. A copy of the Scenario for everybody.

Procedure

(1) Give everybody a copy of the Scenario and a few minutes to read it. Answer questions, clarify any ambiguities.
(2) Divide the class into two groups (of 4, 6, 8, etc, depending on the size of the class); there should be multiples of two groups and at least 2 people in each group.
(3) Designate each group (or pair of groups if you are working with multiples) as B and C respectively, one to discuss the arguments B might use, and the other the arguments for C. If you are working with small numbers and/or have confident participants, you may prefer that B and C be individual, rather than collective, roles. Our experience is that the discussion is more profitable with collective Bs and Cs; but no doubt this depends on circumstances. For the purpose of describing this activity, we refer throughout to collective roles.
(4) Bring Bs and Cs together. If you are working with multiples of groups, deal with one team of Bs and one team of Cs at a time. Ask the two teams to engage in general discussion of the Scenario, speaking in their respective collective roles. The remaining paired groups of Bs and Cs (if there are any) await their turn, meanwhile acting as observers.

Evaluation How do participants think the supervisors would have negotiated with each other in real life? In people's experience, would the supervisors tend to be collaborative or competitive?

What are the advantages of collaboration between supervisors? What are the disadvantages? Did any Bs ask the Cs about the apparently real need to provide constant supervision for the workers under C's control? Why not multiskill or otherwise train the workers until they require less supervision?

Did anybody raise the question of organizational hierarchy? For example, in real life, an attempt by a worker to get one supervisor to collaborate with another might appear to be going over the head of the one to appeal to the other? If this was not mentioned, you might like to bring it up yourself.

Closing What was the general opinion of flex-time? Ask everybody, if the subject has not been discussed, what alternatives they can think of to flex-time. Ask them who benefits most from flex-time working hours (eg women as primary child-carers and home-makers; part-time workers; workers on study courses). Is flex-time part of the whole issue of discrimination in the workplace?

HANDOUT
Flex-time Scenario

(1) In the department where s/he works under supervisor B, A has been accustomed to working flexible hours. Supervisor B is accommodating and the workers are very satisfied with the arrangement.

(2) A has been moved to another department where there are no flex-time arrangements, and is now supervised by C. A requests of C that flex-time working hours be permitted in the department.

(3) C rejects A's request. C doesn't want flex-time. All the jobs in C's department require close supervision, which is not possible under flexible working hours, since C has no replacement.

(4) A refuses to accept C's refusal. A goes to her former supervisor, B, and asks B to intercede with C.

(5) B goes to see C and they talk about the advantages and disadvantages of flex-time.

66 LUNCH AT THE CLUB

Time required About 30 minutes minimum, but this activity can usefully be run over a more extended period. It always evokes an interesting discussion.

Aims
- To identify assertive behaviour in a context of power politics.
- To differentiate power games from genuine issues of authority and control.

Group size From about 5–25 people.

Environment The classroom. Prepare a copy of the Scenario for each participant.

Procedure

(1) Announce the aim of the activity and initiate a short discussion of the phrase 'the dignity of one's office'. In the armed forces, for example, 'officers' are distinguished from 'men' by uniform, badges of rank and a code of behaviour dependent on rank. How are junior managers distinguished from senior managers in business and government settings?

(2) Distribute copies of the Scenario and ask people to discuss it in small groups. Then ask two volunteers to come to the front of the room and improvise a dialogue based on the given situation: then two more, and so on, until time runs out.

Evaluation What priorities motivated the roleplayers? Did Sim intend, at some level, to humiliate Uri deliberately (some psychologists argue that we only forget about things we want to forget!). Did Uri feel humiliated? What strategies did Sim and Uri adopt for saving face? Did either feel the need to save face? If so, whose?

To demonstrate the ownership of power, is it necessary to disempower others?

Closing Recommend that participants read Machiavelli's classic work *The Prince*.

HANDOUT
Lunch at the Club Scenario

Sim is a bright young executive, moving up fast in the company. When still a new recruit Sim was mentored by Uri, an 'old hand', and profited greatly from Uri's knowledge and experience. Now, two years later, the wheel of fortune has turned and Sim is senior to Uri, whose career has stagnated after a brilliant beginning. They haven't seen much of each other recently, but the other day Sim asked Uri to lunch at the Royal Country Club – of which Uri could never afford to be a member.

The appointment was made for 12 noon, at the club, which is about 15 minutes' drive from the office. Unfortunately Sim was busy as usual on the telephone and completely forgot about lunch until 12.45. Then Sim had to think fast what to do. Meanwhile Uri arrived at the club at 11.55 am and had to wait in the reception area because only members are allowed upstairs. At 12.30 Uri checked with the elegant receptionist that there was no message from Sim. Uri wonders what to do. The chairs in reception are not very comfortable – though they look expensive: is Uri to wait indefinitely? If so, what is Uri going to say to Sim, if and when he arrives? Or should Uri stand on dignity and go?

67 VALUE STATEMENTS

Time required About 30 minutes.

Aim
* To discover some of the reasons why employees might not feel comfortable in their organization and seek to leave it.
* To provide information to assist workforce planning. Exit interviews can be valuable tools for this process because when people know they are leaving anyway, they are likely to be fairly frank about their reasons for quitting the job. The feedback they provide can help those who plan human resource management to find a better fit between recruitment, orientation and reward systems and the kind of person they want for the job.

Group size If the questionnaire on pp. 299–301 is used as part of an exit interview, by definition it will probably be administered to one person or at most two or three at a time. However, this activity is productive as a group training session; in which case any manageable number of people can take part, divided if necessary into small groups.

Environment A room where respondent(s) can sit and write comfortably.

Procedure Explain your reasons for asking the respondents to complete the questionnaire and ask for their cooperation. Give them as much time as they need to complete it and thank them for taking the time to do it.

Evaluation How do the respondent's scores match up with what you know to be the organization's workforce needs? For example, does the respondent emerge as highly individualistic in an organization that values good teamwork? Or perhaps a respondent may score highly on the need for power, and in fact may be leaving the job because it doesn't offer enough opportunity for promotion.

In this case perhaps the job can be enlarged to provide this person with more autonomy and control, which might satisfy the need for power, at least temporarily until a promotional opportunity appears?

Closing

It is to be regretted when an efficient employee leaves the company. All information you can collect on the way people feel about their workplace may be of value in planning to acquire and keep the kind of people who will want to go on working there. Even if it is not directly useful in persuading the person in question to stay, their feedback can alert you to employment disadvantages of which you may not have been aware; or whose seriousness you have previously discounted, but which you can now plan to alleviate.

Scoring the questionnaire

The scoring system for this questionnaire assumes five orientations for people's behaviour: affiliation; power; action; individuality; and reflection.

Affiliation. People in this classification have a relatively strong need to 'belong'. That is, they feel comfortable in environments where they work with congenial colleagues and a shared set of beliefs and values, in the expectation that 'the boss will take care of them'. Organizations that meet these criteria are likely to be small family businesses; large-scale but conservative manufacturing companies; federal and state government departments. Affiliative employees are likely to be unhappy in competitive, cutting-edge industries where the only loyalty their managers expect from them is that they work on their own, make impersonal decisions (for example about buying and selling shares on the stock market), generate large profits and subscribe to only the most pragmatic ethical beliefs.

Affiliative respondents are likely to score high on items 1, 3a, 4, 5a, 6, 7a, 8, 9, 10a, 11a, 12, 13a, 14a, 15, 16, 17a, 18, 19, 20a, 21, 22, 23, 24 and 25.

Power. People who have a strong need for control are not likely to fit well into egalitarian work environments where teamwork is valued and emphasis is on consensus and harmony. They tend more to enter competitive settings where personal achievement is rewarded directly, for example by leadership status or cash bonuses: or in organizations such as a university with a strict hierarchy of authority in which they can negotiate their way up the career ladder on rungs of ever-increasing power.

People who need power are likely to score high in the values questionnaire on items 1a, 2, 3, 4a, 5a, 6a, 7a, 8, 9a, 10, 11a, 12a, 13, 14a, 15a, 16a, 17, 18, 19a, 20, 21, 22, 23, 24a and 25.

Note that Questions 4, 4a, 5 and 5a refer to class systems and role hierarchies. In societies with a rigid class structure, people who need power, yet were not born to it, are disadvantaged by class. Therefore they would rather have no class system and prefer non-equality in role relations to be based on criteria other than birth and breeding (for example, education), which gives them more opportunities to acquire power.

Action. Action-minded people require a stimulating – though not necessarily competitive – work environment where a wide variety of problems often arise unexpectedly and have to be solved quickly by flexible thinking based on practical knowledge and experience: for example a garage that services racing cars. They thrive in an atmosphere where deadlines have to be met, frequently under difficult conditions, and success is measured tangibly in terms of quality and productivity of output and material rewards for task accomplishment. Such environments might include journalism, aviation, being a croupier in a casino, or investment brokerage. People who like to be where the action is are not likely to feel at home in slow-paced organizations like research institutes where data is accumulated patiently, results are not expected for a long time and there is little overt feedback on personal achievment.

On the values questionnaire, action-minded respondents are likely to score high on items 2, 9a, 10, 11, 12, 13, 14, 15a, 16, 17, 18, 20a, 22, 23, 24 and 25.

Individuality. People who exhibit this characteristic to a high degree are not necessarily competitive or action-minded; but they like to do things their own way and can be perceived as stubborn, even obstructive. They pay attention to detail, make careful plans, and can become resentful, even hostile, if their plans are thwarted. They tend to be relatively inflexible thinkers, but powerful in the management of quality control. People with this profile work comfortably in organizational environments such as an archives department, where policies and rules are cut-and-dried; where quality is measured in terms of objective, professionally accepted standards and criteria, where careful planning is valued and change is slow-paced. They are not likely to be happy in more spontaneous settings of rapid change where 'the customer is always right', such as a computer software retailer, that requires adaptability to market forces.

On the values questionnaire they are likely to score high on items 1, 2, 4, 5a, 6a, 7, 8a, 9a, 10a, 11a, 12a, 13a, 14a, 15, 16a, 17, 18, 19a, 20, 21a, 22a, 23, 24a and 25a.

Reflection. Reflective problem-solvers like to work in environments that encourage innovation and experiment, such as a design company. They can be driven almost to distraction in settings that require them to push for consensus, as in selling property or second-hand cars, for example. They work at their best when required to think of alternative ways of doing things, such as computer programming.

Reflective employees are like to score high on the values questionnaire in items 1, 2, 3, 4a, 5, 6, 7, 8, 9, 10a, 11a, 12, 13, 14a, 15, 16, 17a, 18, 19a, 20a, 21a, 22, 23, 24a and 25.

The Values Questionnaire

(1) I identify with the group I work with

(1a) I see myself as an individual

3	2	1	0	1	2	3

(2) Thinking is more important than doing

(2a) Doing is more important than thinking

3	2	1	0	1	2	3

(3) I thrive on competition

(3a) I value cooperation

3	2	1	0	1	2	3

(4) I feel comfortable as part of a class system

(4a) I don't believe in class systems

3	2	1	0	1	2	3

(5) I believe in equality in role relationships

(5a) I believe in a hierarchy of role relationships

3	2	1	0	1	2	3

(6) I would rather lose an argument than a friend

(6a) I would rather lose a friend than an argument

3	2	1	0	1	2	3

(7) I value my independence

(7a) I am dependent on others and they on me

3	2	1	0	1	2	3

(8) I am influenced a great deal by my family

(8a) My immediate (nuclear) family exercises the most influence on me

3	2	1	0	1	2	3

(9) Time is to be enjoyed

(9a) Time is to be managed

3	2	1	0	1	2	3

(10) Education is a system whereby we learn to recall principles and practices at need

(10a) Education is a process of experience, discussion and problem solving

| 3 | 2 | 1 | 0 | 1 | 2 | 3 |

(11) I am direct in my encounters with others

(11a) I tend to be indirect in my encounters with others

| 3 | 2 | 1 | 0 | 1 | 2 | 3 |

(12) Human beings are in harmony with nature

(12a) Nature has to be brought under control

| 3 | 2 | 1 | 0 | 1 | 2 | 3 |

(13) I am innovative

(13a) I am slow to change

| 3 | 2 | 1 | 0 | 1 | 2 | 3 |

(14) I am direct in the way I think

(14a) I tend to think about things in roundabout ways

| 3 | 2 | 1 | 0 | 1 | 2 | 3 |

(15) I tend not to interact very much in public with people of the opposite sex

(15a) I tend to interact quite a lot in public with people of the opposite sex

| 3 | 2 | 1 | 0 | 1 | 2 | 3 |

(16) I believe that fate determines the future

(16a) I believe that the future is affected by careful planning and hard work

| 3 | 2 | 1 | 0 | 1 | 2 | 3 |

(17) I believe success is measured in terms of achievement (professional status, material wealth, etc)

(17a) I believe success is measured in terms of harmony with nature and others

| 3 | 2 | 1 | 0 | 1 | 2 | 3 |

(18) I'm happy to take life at a slow pace

(18a) I like to live life in the fast lane

| 3 | 2 | 1 | 0 | 1 | 2 | 3 |

(19) I require very little personal space

(19a) I need a great deal of personal space

| 3 | 2 | 1 | 0 | 1 | 2 | 3 |

(20) I think I am quite a formal person

(20a) I am an informal person

3	2	1	0	1	2	3

(21) I like to have many superficial relationships

(21a) I prefer to have only a few deep relationships

3	2	1	0	1	2	3

(22) I don't feel the need to put everything into words: people don't need to spell things out to let me know how they feel.

(22a) I like to say straight out what I mean, otherwise how do we know we understand each other?

3	2	1	0	1	2	3

(23) I often find myself acting as mediator in disputes

(23a) I am usually capable of direct reconciliations

3	2	1	0	1	2	3

(24) If I'm in charge, I take responsibility even for the mistakes of others under my control

(24a) Even if I'm in charge, I can't take responsibility for mistakes made by my subordinates

3	2	1	0	1	2	3

(25) I tend to avoid eye contact

(25a) I tend to use good eye contact

3	2	1	0	1	2	3

68 THE TIME AND THE PLACE

Time required About 45 minutes.

Aims
- To identify the kind of behaviour by male managers that does not amount to sexual harassment, nor is intended as such, but nevertheless detracts from women's dignity in the workplace.
- To develop some tactics to deal with this kind of behaviour.

Group size Any reasonable number, divided in sub-groups of 3 – 5 people.

Environment Classroom or other working area. All participants should have writing materials. Prepare one copy per participant of the critical incident 'The Time and the Place'.

Procedure

(1) Divide participants into small groups of 3-5 people and ask each group to choose a representative to speak for them.
(2) Distribute the critical incident, one copy to each participant. Give all groups about 15 minutes to note down the key points from the incident.
(3) Bring all groups together. Ask each group leader in turn to summarize their group's discussion. You may like to ask volunteers to post key points on a blackboard, whiteboard or flipchart and/or make notes yourself. Try to record at least five separate and different comments.

Evaluation Go through the five key points that have been recorded from each group leader's report. Ask participants to rank-order them informally according to their perceived order of importance. Broaden the discussion, especially if both women and men are present, to include put-downs that young men receive from older men at work, such as 'sonny' or 'young fellow'.

Closing What advice have participants for each other, on how to avoid or minimize well-meant and unintended put-downs that relate in a derogatory way to gender, age or other personal characteristics?

HANDOUT
The Time and the Place: a critical incident

The company where Liz works has a reputation for treating its employees well; but yesterday Liz gave in her notice. Liz's manager was upset because there was important work she would leave unfinished and she was one of the best secretaries he had ever had. He asked Liz why she was leaving but she refused to tell him. He offered her more money if she would stay, but again she refused and was obviously determined to leave.

The company made it a practice to hold exit interviews. In her exit interview Liz confided to the personnel officer that the manager continually offended her by calling her 'little girl' and 'darling'; and she couldn't stand his patronizing behaviour any longer.

'There's a time and a place for everything,' she told the personnel officer. 'I don't mind being called 'darling' by my boyfriend; but not in the office, and under no circumstances by my manager. I'm on a career path to become a Programme Officer. How can I expect anybody to take me seriously if my own boss calls me "little girl"?'

The personnel officer, with Liz's rather reluctant permission ('I don't want to hurt his feelings; he's a nice old thing') discussed Liz's comments with the manager. The manager was surprised and distressed to learn that his behaviour, which he meant kindly, had been misinterpreted. He apologized to Liz, who agreed to stay on. Their working relationship become more colleague-like and three months later he recommended her for promotion to the position of Programme Officer.

Alternative Ending The manager was furious that Liz should be so childish and said 'Good riddance'. The personnel officer hired an older woman as the manager's secretary who enjoyed being called 'darling' and had no career ambitions.

The personnel officer also asked the training manager to run a course on 'What is sexual harassment and how can it be avoided in the workplace?' and arranged for the manager to attend it.

Liz found another job, with a merchant bank; and within a year she had begun training to be a financial adviser to corporate clients.

69 NO SEX PLEASE, WE'RE WORKING!

Time required About 45 minutes.

Aims
- To discuss the topic of sexual harassment constructively rather than prescriptively.
- To discuss the need for women and men to find new kinds of behaviour towards each other in the workplace, based on their emergent relationships of greater equality.

Group size Any manageable number, divided in sub-groups of 3 – 5 people.

Environment Classroom or other working area. Prepare a copy of the mini-lecture for each participant.

Procedure

(1) State the aims of the activity; and initiate a short discussion to ensure everybody is aware that:
- some countries (not all) provide legal protection for individuals who are annoyed, theatened or intimated by having sexual attentions thrust upon them against their will by people in authority over them;
- whether legal sanctions are in place or not, sexual harassment is offensive behaviour which has no place in the employment contract, yet is frequently difficult to identify. Sometimes offenders are not aware their behaviour is causing resentment or distress; and those who are offended do not always know how to deal with the situation: or do not wish to complain for fear of reprisals such as being passed over for promotion, losing their job, and so on.
- therefore the object of this discussion-starter is to get people taking about what constitutes sexual harassment, and what can be done to prevent, avoid and stop it by finding new ways to relate to each other at work.

(2) Read or talk-through the mini-lecture; then initiate a discussion of its contents. Distribute copies.

Evaluation Do men and women need to find new ways of relating to each other in their more equal roles at work? Do men and women need to find new way of relating to each other at work, full stop?

Closing Draw on participants' personal experiences. Emphasize any positive comments that are made.

HANDOUT

No Sex Please, We're Working!
– A Mini-Lecture

Probably the simplest way to define sexual harassment is derived from relevant US legislation which can be paraphrased as follows: 'Sexual harassment is any personal attention that is resented by the individual to whom it is offered; and who has legal redress against it, provided the individual first makes it clear to the person offering the attention that it is unwelcome.'

Many men claim not to understand what sexual harassment means; and often one must feel sympathy for this confusion, particularly when men have to work with women as peers in traditionally male occupations such as mechanical and constructional engineering, management, architecture and so on.

For example, a garage manager in a country town was willing to offer three mechanical apprenticeships to girls who had completed a basic course in car maintenance at a local technical college. This was a generous and innovative offer, since many school leavers, particularly girls, find it difficult to get work in country areas. However, the girls only served a month of their apprenticeships before they were 'let go' by the manager. The careers officer at the technical college called round to find out what had gone wrong. There was nothing wrong with the girls, the manager assured him. On the contrary they were very good workers, smart, enthusiastic and quick to learn. 'Then why on earth get rid of them?' asked the careers officer. 'Because they distracted the boys!' replied the manager: 'I couldn't get any work out of them, once the girls arrived. They spent all their time trying to get off with them!' Apparently it did not occur either to the manager or to the careers officer to get rid of the boys and keep the girls.

It is not only boys and girls at work who find it difficult to keep their minds on the job with each other around. Grown men and women have the same problem. For example, how are young professional women with comparatively little worldly experience to prevent themselves falling in love with their male mentors? These men are willing to go out of their way to help their less experienced colleagues, male and female, and generally to behave in supportive and caring roles. It is not surprising that some women will perceive this behaviour towards them to be not only lovable but loving.

How are men to treat their emergent female colleagues? Can they put a hand on their shoulder and suggest a quiet drink after work? This is acceptably friendly behaviour between male co-workers but will women see it the same way? Dilemmas like these create inhibitions between men and women in the workplace that hinder constructive professional relationships. Male managers know how to treat their secretaries, their wives and daughters, the wives and daughters of their colleagues; but how are they to treat women as managers? And maybe they have to find new ways now to treat secretaries?

Many men, perhaps most men, genuinely want to accord equal status to female colleagues; but equally genuinely they don't know how to behave appropriately towards this new breed of women when all their socialization has been to look after them, make decisions for them, tell them what to do and generally take care of them.

Conversely, how are women managers to behave towards their male colleagues? Traditionally women have been taught to seek men's advice, defer to their judgement and act on their orders concerning the planning, controlling, organizing and directing of life's events (the classic management functions). How can a young female manager, after listening to an older male colleague, reject his advice and follow her own ideas without feeling she has behaved badly? (Not to mention his feelings of rejection.)

The topic of sexual harassment has received a great deal of publicity in recent years, and rightly so. But we must not allow this to distract our attention from the less dramatic and unpleasant but no less important matter of our day-to-day relationships as men and women at work. It is fairly generally agreed nowadays that the 'Me Tarzan, you Jane' model of male–female behaviour is irrelevant. It is the responsibility of women as much as men to find a new paradigm that fits the times we live in and the kind of work we do.

70 CHILD CARE

Time required This simulation is conducted over at least three sessions, each at least a week apart. Each session will last something between one and two hours.

Aim To give participants the experience of being involved in a quality circle (QC); as part of a total quality management (TQM) programme.

Group size Any manageable number. Ideally, participants should come from a variety of organizational backgrounds; but the activity will also serve as an in-house exercise.

Environment The classroom. You may want to supply some literature about the concepts of TQM and QCs. You may also want to provide different research questions for your participants.

Procedure

Week 1

(1) Divide the groups into small teams of about 5-7 people.
(2) Explain the aim of the activity and its scope. Everybody will have the opportunity to find out what it would be like in real life to belong to a QC.
(3) Stress that a QC is not merely a discussion group. It is a research team whose objective is to gather hard evidence to prove the existence of a perceived problem or to monitor some policy, process or product quality. It is part of an organization-wide programme, spearheaded by senior management, in TQM.
(4) The research question all QC members will attempt to answer is: 'Other things being equal (eg funding, etc, being available) would total product quality be enhanced in my employing organization if it were to provide a child-care facility for the dependent children of employees?'
(5) Each team will make a survey (if participants come from the same organization each team could survey a different department and pool the results). Preferably the survey should cover the whole research population, ie all employees. If this is not feasible, at least the teams should survey a representative sample of all employees who do *not* have dependent children and the whole population of those who do.

(6) All members of each team should collaborate in writing the questionnaire, though how they allocate their roles is up to them. The questionnaire will be written during the coming week and discussed at the next meeting.

Week 2

(1) Discussion of the questionnaire. These are some of the questions it should be designed to answer:
- What percentage of employees who do not have dependent children would support the proposal, on the grounds that provision of a child-care facility would increase productivity or otherwise add to the total quality of the organization's product or service?
- What arrangements are currently being made by parents to have their dependent children cared for while they are at work? In what ways, if at all, are these arrangements unsatisfactory (ie do they cause problems that adversely affect the quality of the parent's work)?
- What is the proportion, among the population of parents of dependent children, of sole supporting parents? What are the particular child-care problems for this group? How do these problems affect the quality of their work?

(2) Emphasize the need for collecting empirical evidence (ie facts and figures). TQM is not about people's opinions so much as statistical evidence of quality control.

(3) When you and the whole group are satisfied that each team has an appropriate questionnaire, act as a resource person while people discuss arrangements for administering it and analysing the results. Probably there will be several participants who have experience in using a data base and who will volunteer to organize the data.

Evaluation

Week 3

Ask each team in turn to report on the results of their survey.

Closing If the surveys indicated the organization would benefit from providing child-care facilities for employees' children, and if you want the exercise to continue during following weeks, here are some suggestions for follow-up research questions:

- How large would the facility be?
- Who would staff it?
- Where would it be located?
- What should be its hours of operation?

71 RELOCATION

Time required About 20 minutes.

Aims

- To encourage participants to start talking to each other and sharing ideas, as a preliminary to the course, seminar etc.
- To discuss briefly some of the personal problems that staff experience during an office relocation.

Group size Any number from about 3 to about 25; but you can run this activity with larger groups, and in environments that include a tiered lecture hall with fixed seating.

Environment Preferably a seminar room arranged café-style; but this is not essential. Prepare a copy of 'Where will I go?' for each participant. Provide writing materials for one person in five (approximately).

Procedure

(1) Distribute the copies of 'Where Will I Go?', one per person.
(2) Ask participants to turn to their neighbours (if they are in fixed seating); or to work with their group (if they are seated café-style) to discuss the handout; and to add any relevant comments that occur to them. Ask that their comments include suggestions as to how managers can remove or at least minimize the described stressors.
(3) Ask one member of each group to act as recorder, to write down people's suggestions and comments. Give each recorder a notebook and pencil, if they have no writing materials of their own.
(4) Allow about 10 minutes for this activity; then get everybody's attention and ask all recorders to read their notes aloud. Pick a random sample if there are many groups and you are running short of time. Post any comments that seem to you of key importance.

Evaluation What comments did people make about the survey responses? What did people see as their own most serious personal problems in relocation (or what do they think they would find most stressful if they had to relocate)? What suggestions did they have for managers, to alleviate these problems?

Closing Ask at random for any personal anecdote about relocation, that somebody might like to share with the class.

Where will I go?

The following is a selection of comments from a survey of office workers in a government institute in 1993 in Hawaii. They were shortly to be relocated from one department to another, in another part of the building, and they were asked: 'What are some of your major concerns about the relocation?' The replies included:

- Loss of control.
- Insecurity.
- Who will I have to report to?
- What will my new duties be?
- What will my new co-workers be like? We've been such a happy group here.
- Will my new environment be busy or quiet?
- Will my new office have a window?
- How far away will the photocopier be from my office?
- Where will the printer be for my PC?

© Elizabeth M. Christopher and Larry E. Smith, 1993. Published by Kogan Page.

72 WHO IS IT?

Time required About 20 minutes.

Aims

- To introduce the topic of cutting jobs.
- To encourage people to start talking and exchanging ideas.

Group size Any number from about 3 people. Large numbers can be divided into sub-groups.

Environment A seminar room, conference room, etc.

Procedure

(1) Announce the aims of the activity.
(2) Divide the group into sub-groups if necessary, of not more than 7 people in each discussion team.
(3) Ask everybody to imagine they are a group of office workers. They have heard on the grapevine, on good authority, that one person in the office is going to be 'moved' in the very near future – which is the company euphemism for a job cut. Ask them to discuss:
  - the kind of comments they might make to each other;
  - any public and communal action they might take;
  - any action they might take privately.
(4) Give everybody about 10 minutes for team discussion, then get everybody's attention and ask for general comments.

Evaluation

- What kind of comments?
- What kind of public action, if any?
- What kind of private action might people take in such a situation?

Closing Broaden the discussion to the subject of job-cutting in general. Call on people's experiences.

Index of activities

Bibliography

Belbin, R Meredith (1981) *Management Teams; Why they Succeed or Fail*, London: Heinemann.

Cameron, Kim S and David A Whetton (1984) 'A Model for Teaching Management Skills'; in D A Whetton and K S Cameron *Developing Management Skills*, Glenview, Ill: Scott, Foresman and Co.

Campbell, Donald T and Julian C Stanley (1963) *Experimental and Quasi-Experimental Designs for Research*, Chicago: Rand McNally.

Dewey, John (1974) *John Dewey on Education: Selected Writings*, Chicago: University of Chicago Press.

Duke, Richard (1975) *Gaming: the Future's Language*, San Francisco: Sage Publications.

Fiedler, Fred F and Martin M Chemers (1974) *Leadership and Effective Management*, Glenview, Ill: Scott, Foresman and Co.

Goffman, Irving (1975) *The Presentation of Self in Everyday Life*, New Jersey: Prentice-Hall.

Guthrie, Sir Tyrone (1971) *Tyrone Guthrie on Acting*, London: Studio Vista.

Hersey, Paul (1984) *The Situational Leader*, La Jolla, CA: Center for Leadership Studies.

Hersey, Paul and Kenneth H Blanchard (1977) *Management of Organizational Behavior: Utilizing Human Resources*, 3rd edn, New York: Prentice-Hall.

Hope, Joanne (1986) *Games Nurses Play*, Sydney: Pergamon.

Knowles, Malcolm S (1977) *The Modern Practice of Adult Education: Andragogy versus Pedagogy*, New York: Association Press.

Kolb, David A, Irwin M Rubin and James M MacIntyre (1984) *Organizational Psychology: an Experiential Approach to Organizational Behavior*, New Jersey: Prentice-Hall.

Laver, Michael (1979) *Playing Politics*, Harmondsworth: Penguin.

Lineham, Thomas E and Barbara Ellis Long (1970) *The Road Game*, New York: Herder and Herder.

Livingston, S and C S Stoll (1973) *Simulation Games, an Introduction for the Social Studies Teacher*, New York: Free Press.

Moore, Barry (1978) *Australian Management Games*, Sydney: University of New South Wales Press.

Moore, Peter (1987) *Let's Have Moore Drama*, Sydney: Methuen.

Parsons, Talcott (1962) 'The School Class as a Social System', in A H Halsey, J Floud and C A Anderson (eds) *Education, Economy and Society*, New York: Glencoe Free Press.

Pfeiffer, J William and John E Jones (1975) *A Handbook of Structured Experiences for Human Relations Training*, La Jolla, CA: University Associates.

Reddin, W J (1971) *Effective Management by Objectives: the 3-D Method of MBO*, New York: McGraw Hill.

Rogers, Carl R (1969) *Freedom to Learn*, Columbus, Ohio: Merrill.

Stanislavsky, Constantine (1962 [1937]) *An Actor Prepares* (translated by ERH), London: Geoffrey Bles.

Stone, Elizabeth (1981) 'A Game for APACE'; *APACE*, 13, December 1981 (PO Box 81, Wentworth Building, Sydney University, Australia 2006).

Via, Richard A and Larry E Smith (1983) *Talk and Listen: English as an International Language via Drama Techniques*, Oxford: Pergamon.

Walford, Rex (1979) *Simulation Games in the Classroom*, London: Longford

Index

3